A Many-Windowed House

Collected Essays

on American Writers

and American Writing

By Malcolm Cowley

Edited, with an Introduction

by Henry Dan Piper

Southern Illinois University Press
Carbondale and Edwardsville

Feffer & Simons, Inc., *London and Amsterdam*

Copyright © 1944, 1945, 1947, 1948, 1957, 1961, 1962, 1970 by Malcolm Cowley.
COPYRIGHT © *1970 by Southern Illinois University Press*
All rights reserved
Printed in the United States of America
Designed by Andor Braun
ISBN 0–8093–0444–9
Library of Congress Catalog Card Number 74–112384

To Kenneth Burke

CONTENTS

MALCOLM COWLEY IS KNOWN best for his perceptive criticism of the writers of his own generation—the generation born during the late 1890's. One thinks of *Exile's Return,* his memoir of American expatriate life in the 1920's, then of his "portable" anthologies of Faulkner and Hemingway and his editions of Scott Fitzgerald's short stories and of the "final" version of *Tender is the Night*—all of which did so much to awaken serious interest in these writers in the years after the last war.

One of the notable things about the present collection of essays is that they are concerned with writers from an earlier period of American history. They begin with Hawthorne and Whitman and end with essays on Dreiser, Frost, O'Neill, and Pound—these last having been Cowley's predecessors in that they came of age well before World War I. This volume reminds us how widely his range as a critic has extended beyond the contemporary scene, and how firmly his judgments of his own generation have been grounded in an informed knowledge of the native literary past.

Another significant point about these essays is that they all date from after World War II. They are, in other words, the fruits of a long career in the service of American letters—one that began some fifty years ago when Mr. Cowley's first professional essay in criticism was published in the February 1920 issue of the *Dial.*

One forgets that Cowley began as a critic of French literature. When his undergraduate studies at Harvard were interrupted by World War I, he volunteered for noncombatant duty and ended up driving a truck for the French military transport service. In 1921, after he had belatedly completed his studies and received his university degree, he was awarded an American Field Service Fellowship for the study of French literature at the University of Montpellier; and this was renewed the following year for further study in Paris. There he helped several other Americans launch the avant-garde magazine *Secession.* And in 1923, after he had settled in Greenwich Village, he helped edit another little magazine, *Broom,* for which he had also written in Europe. At that time his aim in life was to become a man of letters in the great French tradition—not an easy aim since he was married and enjoyed no private means of support. In 1929 his first volume of poems appeared: *Blue Juniata.* As a critic, his most impressive accomplishment during these early years was a series of essays on contemporary French literature that were published in the *Bookman* between 1922 and 1926. They included a report on recent French poetry as well as assessments of Proust, Barbusse, Duhamel, MacOrlan, and Vildrac. He also published translations from the works of Soupault and Vildrac, other translations of French novels, including MacOrlan's *On Board the Morning Star* and Radiguet's *The Count's Ball,* and he translated a volume of Paul Valéry's essays, *Variety.*

In 1929, at the suggestion of his friend Edmund Wilson, Cowley joined the editorial staff of the *New Republic,* and the next stage of his education as a man of letters began. Two weeks later the stock market collapsed and the twenties plunged to their violent end. This is hardly the place to recount in detail the story of Cowley's turbulent career on the *New Republic,* where he succeeded Wilson in the influential post of literary editor in 1930. Nor is there room to describe his involvement with Communist and other Popular Front groups in the protest movements of the thirties. The important point is that Cowley, never a party-liner, climbed down from his ivory tower and involved himself in the action in the streets. He did so without compromising his integrity as a responsible editor and critic. In the process the Jazz Age esthete developed his social as well as his artistic conscience.

Between 1929 and the end of World War II, Cowley's criticism was published almost exclusively in the *New Republic*, usually in the form of twelve-hundred-word essays and book reviews. Then, in 1944, he was asked by the Viking Press to undertake the first of his trail-blazing Viking "portable" anthologies, in this case a selection from the writings of Hemingway. This was followed two years later by his *Portable Faulkner*—a volume that, as Robert Penn Warren has said, "marked the great turning point in Faulkner's reputation in the United States." In 1947, as the result of an invitation from the Program in American Civilization at Princeton University, Cowley was able to devote considerable time to studying and writing about the history of Naturalism in American literature. The following year, 1948, he edited a volume of selections from the works of Hawthorne and a collected Whitman.

Thus, it has only been since the end of World War II that Cowley has been free to undertake in a large, leisurely way, the critical assessments of major nineteenth- and early twentieth-century American writers that have been gathered together for the first time in the present volume. Until now they were buried in journals and magazines, or in the particular volumes where they appeared as introductions or separate chapters. As a result, neither their importance nor Cowley's importance as one of our leading critics has been adequately appreciated. A good example of such oversight is Stanley Edgar Hyman's *The Armed Vision*, first published in 1948 and still the best assessment we have had of recent American literary criticism. Although Hyman acknowledged Cowley's importance as a critic, he omitted an extended discussion of his work on the ground that most of his important critical essays had not yet been collected in book form. The present volume is a partial attempt to correct that deficiency—partial because a

second volume will also appear. Mr. Cowley himself is engaged in assembling a book on his own generation that will
incorporate a great many of the previously uncollected essays
he has written about its leading writers—Faulkner, Fitzgerald,
Hemingway, Hart Crane, Thomas Wolfe, and others, many
of whom were his friends.

Looking back over the past fifty years, we can see now that
one of the most important developments of recent times has
been the creation in this country of an impressive body of
critical opinion. The same forces that, after World War I,
produced a flowering in our fiction, poetry, and drama, stimu-
lated an aggressive, competitive, and highly articulate literary
criticism as well. Standards in American critical writing were
much higher by 1945 than they had been in 1920. For this
Malcolm Cowley, both as critic and editor, deserves more
credit than has been hitherto appreciated. He is unique in that
he has been intimately associated with, and respected by, the
leaders of successive trends and fashions in literary opinion,
and yet throughout has managed to go his own way and
remain his own man.

As a young man he learned from his French masters, as
well as from his own accomplished experiments in poetry, the
cardinal virtues of economy, simplicity, and clarity. He had
gone to high school in Pittsburgh with Kenneth Burke, and
they have remained lifelong friends. But Cowley has seen
more clearly than most that Burke has been rather less a
literary critic than a philosopher of criticism; that is his real
and great importance. After Burke, R. P. Blackmur has probably been the most influential critic of Cowley's generation. It is
significant that Blackmur, in an important essay discussing
Eliot's *After Strange Gods* and Cowley's *Exile's Return*, after
acknowledging his great intellectual debts to Eliot, lined himself up with Cowley as a human being. Cowley has deservedly
won the thanks of Robert Penn Warren and other Faulkneri-

ans for his important contributions to Faulkner criticism. And it is worth noting that Allen Tate, in a recent essay on Poe, describes Poe as "the first committed and perhaps still the greatest American literary journalist on the high French model: a critical tradition represented today by Edmund Wilson and Malcolm Cowley."

It is not surprising to find Tate linking Cowley and Wilson. Both began their apprenticeships as students of French literature. They worked together on the *New Republic* and for a time held similar social as well as esthetic points of view. But in spite of these similarities, there are important differences between them that the present volume helps to emphasize. First of all, Wilson's career as a serious literary critic had pretty much ended before most of the essays in this book had been written. Wilson's major literary studies, *Axel's Castle* (1931), *The Triple Thinkers* (1938), *The Wound and the Bow* (1941), and *The Boys in the Back Room* (1941), all date from before the end of World War II. Then, too, as Leonard Kriegel recently said in *The Nation*, "Cowley . . . , if he did not possess Wilson's broad scholarship, did have an extraordinarily sensitive mind—far more sensitive to the nuances of poetry, for instance, than Wilson's was." Finally, except for his early essays on James and Hemingway, Wilson has been more concerned with British and European than American literature. The closest parallels to the present volume are F. O. Matthiessen's *American Renaissance*, Lionel Trilling's *The Liberal Imagination*, and Alfred Kazin's *On Native Grounds*. It deserves a place on that narrow shelf of books about the American literary past that also represent standards of what criticism should be.

Looking back over his own career, it has seemed to Cowley that the most important influence has been the example of Paul Valéry. He met and talked with Valéry as a young man in Paris, and came to think of him as the man of letters par excellence. Valéry was not only an accomplished critic and the most admired poet of the time; he also possessed a remarkable sense of detachment from his métier. His ideal was Leonardo da Vinci, the truly universal man. For Valéry, as Cowley wrote in the introduction to his 1927 volume of translations of Valéry's essays, the pursuit of literature was not an end in itself but rather "a form of mental exercise because it was difficult. His primary object was a defense of the conscious mind."

In 1927, Cowley's essay went on to say, the prevailing assumptions and ideologies that seemed most likely to threaten objective criticism in the United States were Dadaism (a movement in which Cowley himself had participated earlier in Paris), Freudianism, Behaviorism, the Irrationalism represented by D. H. Lawrence and Sherwood Anderson, and the enervated, genteel Humanism of the American academy. Later, during the 1930's, when Cowley's sympathies were aroused by economic and social suffering, Valéry's example would shield him from the temptations of orthodox Marxism —Stalinist or Trotskyite. Not that he always escaped them, of course. The point is rather that he survived so much more gracefully and independently of fashions than the other Popular Front critics of the Depression era. Bernard Smith (with whom Cowley collaborated in 1937 in editing *Books That Changed Our Minds*), Mike Gold, the Granville Hicks of the 1930's, Joseph Freeman—who reads them now?

If Cowley has followed any general rule it has been chiefly that criticism is a form of literature and therefore, above all, must be well written. So far as his critical method is concerned, the best statement I have seen is his 1961 essay, "Criticism: A Many-Windowed House," which has been included as the last essay in this volume:

> I always start and end with the text itself, and I am willing to
> accept the notion of the textual or categorical critic that the

principal value of a work lies in the complexity or unity of its internal relations. But I also try to start with a sort of innocence, that is, with a lack of preconceptions about what I might or might not discover. To preserve the innocence I try not to read the so-called secondary or critical sources until my own discoveries, if any, have been made. . . . It is a mistake to approach a work of art as if it were an absolutely separate production, a unique artifact, the last and only relic of a buried civilization. Why not approach it as the author does? It seems to me that any author of magnitude has his eye on something larger than the individual story or poem or novel. He wants each of these to be as good as possible, and self-subsistent, but he also wants it to serve as a chapter or aspect of the larger work that is his lifetime production, his *oeuvre*. This larger work is also a part of the critic's subject matter.

The *oeuvre*, "the larger work"—it is Cowley's consistent concern with this aspect of the writer's art that serves as one of the important unifying themes of this volume. In his view, every work of art has a continuing reciprocal relation with the artist's other separate works as well as with the totality of his writings, and the nature of these relations is a legitimate subject for criticism.

These relations, of course, may also interest the biographer or the literary historian. Thus there is always the potential danger that the critic may be lost in the byways of literary history and biography. But that is simply one of the possible risks he runs. The writer's *oeuvre* itself possesses a history; therefore the critic may legitimately follow that history to any sources outside the works themselves that may help him to come to terms with the works in their various literary relations. He may, in other words, turn fruitfully to letters, reminiscences, interviews and other data that help to illuminate that history. Literary criticism is an art, not a science with immutable laws. The value of the critic's judgments depends ultimately on his own intelligence, sensibility, and eloquence.

In these essays Cowley confronts the American writer's work as a whole. The question he seems to ask most insistently is, What was it that transformed a writer of talent into an author of genius? And, looking at these writers as a group, he inquires further if there is any recurring pattern in the separate answers to this question that tells us something in a general way about the situation of the writer in this country during the past hundred years or so.

In Cowley's view, the American writer begins as an alienated youth who learns his lonely craft in social and often actual physical isolation. The moment when he is capable of realizing his creative powers in the production of a major work of art comes only after he has first been wrenched out of his accustomed isolation by some profoundly moving experience involving other human beings. "There is a period or phase in the lives of many great writers," Cowley says in his essay on Whitman, "that might be described as their descent into the underworld."

> At some moment, perhaps very early, they are crippled or stricken by disease (how many epileptics and syphilitics!), or they are made conscious of their social or sexual inferiority, or they become involved in a scandal or go to prison—there are scores, hundreds of paths by which they may descend; but descend they do, until they see their world from beneath and until they feel, as Dostoevsky did in his youth when he was led to execution, a double sense, of their isolation first and then of their brotherhood or identity with all the outcast and diseased and rejected of the earth. Later they emerge into sunlight, but for a long time they walk the streets as if in disguise and continue to feel that they belong with the secret people of the caves —among whom they number, as time goes on, more and more of humanity.
>
> It would be better, surely, if this sense of human brotherhood might come from above and not from below—not from wounds or vices or disfigurements, not from physical or spiritual clubfeet or humpbacks, but from an overflowing measure of health and wisdom; from fulfilled love and happy marriages; from the perception that human beings, even the best, are foolish and sinful and tragic in their common destiny. Sometimes the vision does come from above. There is Emerson cool on a hilltop, but in American literature there are not many others like him; most of the respectables are men whose visions

lie behind them, as Whitman's vision lay when he was safely moored in Mickle Street, Camden, after a stormy life.

It is this *saison en enfer* that reveals to so many American writers their hitherto unrecognized connection with society. The discovery that he is trapped in a tragic predicament, that it is his fate as a human being to have his freedom as an individual in unceasing conflict with his instincts as a social animal, not only defines the writer's humanity but releases hitherto untapped reserves of creative energy. His subsequent attempts to reconcile imaginatively this otherwise irreconcilable paradox are the source of his most lasting art.

It seems to me that this is not only the primary unifying theme of all these essays, but that it underlies Cowley's unconscious assumptions about the nature of art as well as many of his most helpful judgments. And it opens up fresh avenues of speculation about American literature as well as the relationship of the American writer to his society. It also serves Cowley as a means of coming to terms with much poor writing in such uneven writers as Hawthorne and Whitman. It helps him to explain why Dreiser's *Sister Carrie* and the naturalistic plays of Eugene O'Neill are the most important consequences of the school of American naturalism.

In this volume Cowley emerges more clearly than ever as essentially a humanist critic—not the genteel milk-and-water Humanism of the academy, but in the tradition of Poe and Valéry. His criticism is directed at the connection between the work of art and the writer's humanity. He judges the work not only for its own sake but also in the light of the writer's total achievement. What he finds is that man's ceaseless struggle to preserve his integrity as an individual yet to fulfill his nature as a member of society has been the source of the most important American literature, as indeed it has been of all literature.

Both the selection and editing of these essays have been my

responsibility. But I am greatly indebted to Mr. Cowley for many courtesies as well as his continued interest and advice. Several of the essays, notably "Hawthorne in Solitude" and "Myths in American Writing," have never before been printed integrally. To restore the full text, Mr. Cowley has provided me with the original manuscripts. Wherever the text that appears here differs substantially from its previously published form, this fact has been recorded in an appropriate footnote.

I also want to acknowledge my gratitude to the Office of Research and Projects, The Graduate School, Southern Illinois University, for financial assistance in preparing the text of this book, and to my colleagues, Robert P. Griffin, Harry T. Moore, Sidney Moss, and Earle Stibitz, for helpful suggestions.

Henry Dan Piper

Carbondale, Illinois
31 October 1969

A Many-Windowed House

Hawthorne in Solitude

AFTER FOUR moderately happy, moderately social years at Bowdoin College, Hawthorne came back to Salem in 1825 and disappeared like a stone dropped into a well. He used to say that he doubted whether twenty persons in the community so much as knew of his existence. He had thought that while writing his first books he might support himself by working for his uncles, who were prosperous stagecoach proprietors; then later he might travel into distant countries. But the books didn't come out—except for a poor little romance called *Fanshawe* that was printed at his own expense—and meanwhile the place in his uncles' counting house was deferred from month to month, the travels from year to year. Day after day he spent in his room; it was an owl's nest, he said, from which he emerged only at dusk.

If he had lived in Boston he might have found others who shared his ambitions or at least understood them. Boston in 1825 had the beginnings of a literary society, but Salem was a little desert where it seemed impossible for any writer to flourish. Salem was shipping and politics; it was the waterfront, the new Irish slums, and the big houses on Chestnut Street where people asked, "Who are the Hawthornes?" Any young man of Salem who tried to enter literature as others entered business or the law was condemned to solitude; and Hawthorne was doubly condemned, by his character as well as by his interests. He was intensely shy and proud—shy *because* he was proud, with a high sense of personal merit, a respect for his ancestors, and a fear of being rebuffed if he went into society. The fear grew stronger as his clothes grew shabbier and his manners more reserved. "I sat down by the wayside of life," he said, "like a man under enchantment, and a shrubbery sprung up around me, and the bushes grew to be saplings, and the saplings became trees, until no exit appeared possible, through the tangling depths of my obscurity."

Portions of this essay were published as "Hawthorne in Solitude," *New Republic*, 119, August 2, 1948, 29–33, and "Hawthorne in the Looking Glass," *Sewanee Review*, 56, Autumn 1948, 545–53. It is now published in its entirety for the first time.

As the years passed he fell into a daily routine that seldom varied during autumn and winter. Each morning he wrote or read until it was time for the midday dinner; each afternoon he read or wrote or dreamed or merely stared at a sunbeam boring in through a hole in the blind and very slowly moving across the opposite wall. At sunset he went for a long walk, from which he returned late in the evening to eat a bowl of chocolate crumbed thick with bread and then talk about books or politics with his two adoring sisters, Elizabeth and Louisa, both of whom were already marked for spinsterhood; these were almost the only household meetings. The younger Hawthornes were orphans; their father was a sea captain who had died of yellow fever at Surinam when Nathaniel was four years old. Madame Hawthorne, as his mother was called, had fallen into the widow's habit of eating in her room, and Elizabeth often missed dinner because of her daylong solitary rambles. There was an old aunt dressed in black who wandered through the house or, in summer, worked among the flowers like the ghost of a gardener.

In summer Hawthorne's routine was more varied; he went for an early-morning swim among the rocks and often spent the day wandering alone by the shore, so idly that he amused himself by standing on a cliff and throwing stones at his shadow. Once, apparently, he stationed himself on the long toll-bridge north of Salem and watched the procession of travelers from morning to night. He never went to church, but on Sunday mornings he liked to stand behind the curtain of his open window and watch the congregation assemble. At times he thought that the most desirable mode of existence "might be that of a spiritualized Paul Pry, hovering invisible round man and woman, witnessing their deeds, searching into their hearts, borrowing brightness from their felicity and shade from their sorrow, and retaining no emotion peculiar to himself." At other times—and oftener with the passing years—he was seized by an impulse to throw himself into the midst of life. He came to feel there was no fate so horrible as that of the mere spectator, condemned to live in the world without any share in its joys or sorrows.

No man is a mere spectator, and even Hawthorne had a somewhat larger share in worldly events than he was afterwards willing to remember. Each summer he took a fairly long trip through New England, riding in his uncles' coaches, and once he traveled westward to Niagara and Detroit. During the trips he talked—or rather, listened—to everyone he met in coach or tavern, and "enjoyed as much of life," he said, "as other people do in the whole year's round." Even at home he was less of a hermit than he later portrayed himself as being; sometimes there was company in the evening and sometimes he paid visits to his three Salem friends. One of these, William B. Pike, was a carpenter and a small Democratic politician, in that Whig stronghold. Hawthorne shared his political opinions and must have discussed with him the questions of party patronage that would play an important part in both their lives. He could sometimes be seen at a bookstore that stocked the latest novels and, as time went on, he began writing for the Salem *Gazette*. But there were not enough of these contacts with the world to destroy his picture of himself as a man completely alone. He began to be obsessed by the notion of solitude, both as an emotional necessity for a person like himself and also as a ghostly punishment to which he was self-condemned. "By some witchcraft or other," he said in 1837 when he was trying to escape from his owl's nest and had started to correspond with his Bowdoin classmate, Longfellow, ". . . I have been carried apart from the main current of life, and find it impossible to get back again. Since we last met, which you remember was in Sawtell's room, where you read a farewell poem to the relics of the class,—ever since that time I have secluded myself from society; and yet I never meant any such thing, nor dreamed what sort of life I was going to lead. I have made a captive of myself, and put me into a dungeon, and now I cannot find the key to let myself out,—and if the door were open, I should be almost afraid to come out."

Those years of self-imprisonment in Salem were the central fact in Hawthorne's training as a writer. They served as his apprenticeship and his early travels, corresponding to the years that other American writers of his time spent wandering in Europe or making an overland expedition to Oregon or sailing round Cape Horn on a whaler. In recent terms they were his postgraduate work, his year in Paris or Rome, his military service, everything that prepared him for his career. He worked or idled under his own supervision, traveled into himself, and studied the inner landscape. It was the Salem years that deepened and individualized his talent.

Talent cannot be acquired, cannot be explained, and in Hawthorne's case we have to start with the fact that he possessed it from boyhood. Moreover, it was a sturdier sort of talent than has usually been attributed to him, at least by critics with the habit of regarding him as a delicate plant that was incapable of bearing much fruit and would have withered in the sun. His Concord neighbors had a different picture of him. Emerson, for example, was convinced that he had greater resources than he ever displayed in his works, and Margaret Fuller said of him in the Brook Farm days, "We have had but a drop or two from that ocean." We never had more than a trickle and perhaps the inner ocean was not so vast as she believed; yet Hawthorne's hundred-odd stories were only a few of those foreshadowed in his notebooks. Besides his four published novels he once had five others fully outlined in his head. The wonder is not that he never wrote them, but rather that some of his projects were finished with careful workmanship at a time when circumstances were unfavorable to Hawthorne's type of richly meditated fiction. His talent had to be robust in order to survive and had to be exceptionally fertile in order to produce, against obstacles, the few books he succeeded in writing.

We can merely wonder at the talent in itself, but we can try to understand some of the factors that contributed to its development. When Hawthorne was nine years old he injured one foot in a game of bat-and-ball and the doctors judged that he might be permanently lame. The lameness disappeared after two years, but meanwhile it had kept him home from school and left him to follow his own bent. It was at this time that he formed the habit of reading for hour after hour as he lay stretched out on the parlor carpet. *Pilgrim's Progress* was his favorite book—later it was to be the only one that he often mentioned in his stories—but he also liked Shakespeare and *The Faery Queen* and the crimes described in *The Newgate Calendar*; in fact the boy would read anything, no matter how difficult, so long as it told a story. He raced through the Waverley novels one after another, almost as fast as they reached Salem.

When he wasn't reading or building castles with blocks for a series of kitten-princesses, he listened to the stories that could be heard in a New England household. There were family traditions; many of them dealt with Colonel John Hathorne, as the name used to be spelled, who had been a judge in the Salem witchcraft trials and who had been cursed, with all his descendants, by one of the women he condemned to death. Other traditions dealt with a vast tract of land in Cumberland County, Maine, which rightfully belonged to the family although the title-deeds had been lost; and still others clustered round Daniel Hathorne, the Revolutionary privateer, known as the sternest man who ever walked a quarterdeck. The voyage of his brig, the *Fair American*, had been the subject of a ballad:

> Bold Hathorne was commander, a man of real worth,
> Old England's cruel tyranny induced him to go forth.

The little boy liked stories of the Revolution and he also liked to hear about the superstitions that survived in the New England countryside. Much later Hawthorne was to speak of an old woman who "made it her serious business and sole amusement," he said, "to tell me stories at any time from morning till night, in a mumbling, toothless voice, as I sat on a log of wood, grasping her check-apron in both my hands. . . . There are a thousand of her traditions lurking in the corners and by-places of my mind."

Besides listening to stories, the boy invented long and fanciful stories of his own, which he told to his two admiring sisters. Usually they were about the wonderful adventures he would have when he was grown up, and they always ended with the words, ". . . and I'm never coming back again." He had picked a career for himself long before he went away to college: he was going to write books, a whole shelf of them, with "Hawthorne's Works" printed on the back. The books were going to deal with his native land; that requirement was clear in his mind from the beginning. Later his purpose became a little more specific. He was going to write romances in which he would retell the history and preserve the vanishing myths of New England; and he would thus make its soil "fertile with poetry," in the same way that Scotland—"cold, cloudy, barren, insignificant little bit of earth," as he later called it—had been transformed by Sir Walter Scott into a motherland of legends known everywhere in the world.

When Nathaniel was fourteen years old he spent a year in Maine, on the shore of Sebago Lake. He used to go skating alone till midnight, before the great snows fell; and in summer he fished for trout or wandered through the woods with his gun. Those nights and days became his image of remembered happiness. "I lived in Maine like a bird of the air," he said not long before his death, "so perfect was the freedom I enjoyed. But it was there I first got my cursed habits of solitude." One such habit was that of talking silently to himself. In his boyhood he started an inner monologue that lasted for most of his waking hours and went on, apparently, from youth to age. It was his principal solace in Salem, during the lonely years that followed his graduation from college. Even after he had emerged from his "owl's nest," it continued to be his substitute for spoken conversation; and he once observed in his notebook that he doubted whether he had ever really talked with half a dozen persons in his life, either men or women.

But the inner monologue also served another purpose, as time went on; it was the workshop where he forged his plots and tempered his style. Before writing his stories he told them to himself, while walking by the sea or under the pines; he liked a solitary place where there was nothing to distract his attention. In Rome, much later, he preferred the Pope's garden on the Quirinal: "It would suit me to have my daily walk along such straight paths," he said in his notebook, "for I think them favorable to thought, which is apt to be disturbed by variety and unexpectedness." When he was living at The Wayside, in Concord, he tramped through the sweetfern and huckleberry bushes on the hilltop until his feet had made a path that was visible for thirty years after his death. He said in a letter to his friend and publisher, James T. Fields, "In compliance with your exhortations, I have begun to think seriously of that story, not, as yet, with a pen in my hand, but trudging to and fro on my hilltop." He trudged out and, in his silent fashion, talked out all his stories before he tried to set them down.

There is more to be said about this inner monologue which played an essential part in his life and work. In one sense it was a dialogue, since Hawthorne seems to have divided himself into two personalities while working on his stories: one was the storyteller and the other his audience. The storyteller uttered his stream of silent words; the audience listened and applauded by a sort of inner glow, or criticized by means of an invisible frown that seemed to say, "But I don't understand." —"Let me go over it again," the storyteller would answer, still soundlessly; and then he would repeat his tale in clearer language, with more details; perhaps he would go over the doubtful passages again and again, until he was sure that the listener would understand. This doubleness in Hawthorne, this division of himself into two persons conversing in solitude, explains one of the paradoxes in his literary character: that he was one of the loneliest authors who ever wrote, even in this country of lost souls, while at the same time his style was that of a social man eager to make himself clear and intensely conscious of his audience. For him the audience was always present, because it was part of his own mind.

Another paradox is also connected with his solitude and self-absorption. Hawthorne was reserved to the point of being secretive about his private life, and yet he spoke more about himself, with greater honesty, than any other American of his generation. Not only did he write prefaces to all his books, in which he explained his intentions and described his faults more accurately than any of his critics; not only did he keep journals in which he recorded his daily activities; but also most of his stories and even, in great part, his four novels are full of anguished confessions. One can set side by side two quotations from his work. In the preface to his *Mosses* he said, "So far as I am a man of really individual attributes I veil my face; nor am I, nor have I ever been, one of those supremely hospitable people who serve up their own hearts, delicately fried, with brain sauce, as a tidbit for their beloved public." But he also said at the end of *The Scarlet Letter*, when drawing a moral from Mr. Dimmesdale's tragic life, "Be true! Be true! Show

freely to the world, if not your worst, yet some trait whereby
the worst may be inferred." Divided between his two impulses,
toward secrecy and toward complete self-revelation, he
achieved a sort of compromise: he revealed himself, but
usually under a veil of allegory and symbol.

No other writer in this country or abroad ever filled his stories
with such a shimmering wealth of mirrors. Poe detested mirrors; when he wrote an essay on interior decoration he admitted one of them—only one—to his ideally furnished apartment,
but on condition that it be very small and "hung so," he said,
"that a reflection of the person can be obtained from it in none
of the ordinary sitting places of the room." Hawthorne went to
the other extreme by adorning his imagined rooms and landscapes with mirrors of every description—not only looking-
glasses but burnished shields and breastplates, copper pots,
fountains, lakes, pools, anything that could reflect the human
form. And the mirrors in his stories have supernatural functions as well: sometimes they are tombs from which can be
summoned the shapes of the past (as in "Old Esther Dudley"); sometimes they prophesy the future (like Maule's
Well, in *The House of the Seven Gables*); often they reveal
the truth behind a delusion (as in "Feathertop," where the
scarecrow impresses people as a fine gentleman until they look
at his image in a mirror); and always they serve as "a kind of
window or doorway into the spiritual world."—"I am half
convinced that the reflection is indeed the reality—the real
thing which Nature imperfectly images to our grosser sense,"
Hawthorne said in his notebook after describing a scene mirrored in the little Assabet River. He even wrote a story,
"Monsieur du Miroir," in which the hero is simply his own
reflected image.
    "From my childhood I have loved to gaze into a spring,"
says the narrator of another Hawthorne story, "The Vision of
the Fountain." One day the young man sees his own eyes
staring back at him, as usual; but then he looks again— "And
lo!" he says, "another face deeper in the fountain than my own
image, more distinct in all the features, yet faint as thought.
The vision had the aspect of a fair young girl with locks of

paly gold." This substitution of a girl's face for that of the youth bending over the spring makes one think of Narcissus in love with his twin sister—according to one version of the Greek myth—and gazing into a pool because he fancies that his own mirrored features are hers.

In Hawthorne's life as well as in his stories there are curious suggestions of the Narcissus legend. He had been a beautiful boy, petted by his relatives and admired by strangers; I think it was one of his aunts who said of him that he had "eyelashes a mile long and curled up at the end." Always he loved to wander by the edge of little streams. One characteristic he showed from the beginning was an abhorrence for ugliness in women. "Take her away!" the little boy said to one woman who tried to be kind to him. "She is ugly and fat and has a loud voice." Forty years later he would be roused to homicidal anger by looking at English dowagers. "The grim, red-faced monsters!" he said in his usually even-tempered notebook. "Surely a man would be justified in murdering them —in taking a sharp knife and cutting away their mountainous flesh, until he had brought them into reasonable shape." At times he was like Thomas Bullfrog in one of his own stories. "So painfully acute was my sense of female imperfection," Mr. Bullfrog says, "and such varied excellence did I require in the woman whom I could love, that there was an awful risk of my getting no wife at all, or of being driven to perpetrate matrimony with my own image in the looking-glass."

Mr. Bullfrog's predicament was like the one in which Hawthorne involved himself during the Salem years when he had no other companions: in a sense he did marry his own image. Many of his tales read like confessions of a self-love that was physical as well as moral. It is true that he continued to elaborate the New England legend, but after 1834 another note appeared in his stories: more and more of them were allegories that dealt with self-absorption, self-delusion, self-condemnation, a whole series of reflexive emotions. They also expressed feelings of guilt, as one can see from the development of Hawthorne's mirror images. Thus, Roderick Elliston, the hero of "The Bosom Serpent," is tormented by a snake that lives in his own breast. The snake has come from an innocent-looking fountain (another mirror), where it had lurked since the time of the first settlers. Elliston spends "whole miserable days before a looking-glass with his mouth wide open, watching, in hope and horror, to catch a glimpse of the snake's head far down within his throat." "The Bosom Serpent" was published in 1843, when Hawthorne was happily married and living in Concord, at the Old Manse. By that time he was able to look back almost tranquilly on his old dilemma and even to give the story a happy ending—for Elliston is freed from the snake by his wife's love. But some of the stories that Hawthorne wrote in his Salem days—I am thinking especially of "Young Goodman Brown" and "The Minister's Black Veil"—so testify to his sense of being judged and condemned that they might have been cries from the pit.

There are of course other secret sins than the one to which Hawthorne may have yielded. What we know, as distinguished from mere probabilities, is that he came to regard his separation from normal society as something sinful in itself, a crime that was also a punishment. He began to think of himself as a man not only self-judged and condemned, but self-confined in a prison that had no visible bars. The key was in the lock; at any moment he might have stepped over the threshold and lived among his neighbors. What kept him in his solitary chamber was the feeling that year by year the world was becoming more unreal for him and, even worse, that he was becoming less real than the world; he was a shadow effectively walled in by shadows. As time went on he came to resemble one of his own characters, Gervayse Hastings of "The Christmas Banquet," who considered himself the unhappiest of men. "You will not understand it," Hastings tells his rivals in misery. "None have understood it—not even those who experience the like. It is a chilliness—a want of earnestness—a feeling as if what should be my heart were a thing of vapor—a haunting perception of unreality! . . . Mine—mine is the wretchedness! This cold heart. . . ."

Sometimes Hawthorne pictured himself as caught in a whirlpool or drifting helplessly towards a cataract; one of his despondent letters to his classmate Horatio Bridge closed with the words, "I'm a doomed man and over I must go." The fact was that he had already been carried down into a sort of private hell, exactly the size of the room in which he brooded out his days. Ice, not fire, was the torment he suffered there. The images that recur in his work are those of coldness and torpor from coldness; among his favorite adjectives are "cold," "icy," "chill," "benumbed," "torpid," "sluggish," "feeble," "languid," "dull," "depressed." He spoke of having "ice in the blood" and sometimes thought of the heart as being congealed or turned to stone. He also expressed a longing, not for mere warmth, but for an all-consuming fire to melt the ice and calcify the stone. It is curious to note how he fell into the habit of burning his letters to the family as soon as he returned home, how he burned all the available copies of his first novel, and how he burned a whole group of his early stories, which, from the reports of those who read them, were somber and fanciful works that the world would be glad to possess; it was as if he were trying to immolate himself. One of his few amusements in Salem was going to fires—but only after sending his sister Elizabeth to the top of the house to report whether they were big enough to be worth watching. "Come, deadly element of Fire,—henceforth my familiar friend!" is a last prayer uttered by one of his solitary heroes, Ethan Brand. With a burst of laughter Brand leaps into the lime kiln, as into hell. When the fire in the kiln burns down, there is the outline of a skeleton on top of the lime; and within the ribs is the shape of a human heart, like calcified marble.

But these metaphors of ice and fire were not all that Hawthorne learned from his years of self-absorption. He also learned—or at least he learned to suspect—that he was not alone in his nether world; others might be as bad as himself. Some of his stories began to express the notion of companionship in evil doing; for example, the good Mr. Hooper explains on his deathbed why he had insisted for years on hiding his face. "When the friend," he says, "shows his inmost heart to his friend; the lover to his best beloved; when man does not vainly shrink from the eye of his Creator, loathsomely treasuring up the secret of his sin; then deem me a monster, for the symbol beneath which I have lived, and die! I look around me, and lo! on every visage a Black Veil!" The same idea is expressed in "Young Goodman Brown." When the young man goes at nightfall into a forest that might be his own subconscious mind, he finds himself, not alone, but in the midst of a multitude assembled for a witch's sabbath. Among those pledged to Satan he recognizes everyone he had most admired in Salem village: the pious minister, the senior deacon, and even old Goody Cloyse, who had taught him his catechism. At last he stands before an unholy altar with Faith, his wife, while Satan addresses them both. "Evil is the nature of mankind. Evil must be your only happiness," Satan says. "Welcome again, my children, to the communion of your race."

For Hawthorne, too, evil was a sort of communion. He loathed it and struggled against it, most of all when he found it in his own heart; but nevertheless he recognized that it humbled his pride and bound him to other sinners. He might have said of himself what he later said of Mr. Dimmesdale, in *The Scarlet Letter*: "His intellectual gifts, his moral perceptions, his power of experiencing and communicating emotion, were kept in a state of preternatural activity by the prick and anguish of his daily life. . . . This very burden it was that gave him sympathies so intimate with the sinful brotherhood of mankind, so that his heart vibrated in unison with theirs, and received their pain into itself, and sent its own throb of pain through a thousand other hearts, in gushes of sad, persuasive eloquence."

It is characteristic of Hawthorne that he should have drawn a social lesson from a solitary experience. He was more of an individualist than Emerson, to judge by his life as a whole, and yet he did not preach the virtue of self-reliance; instead his moral in story after story was that every person must submit to the common fate. "The truly wise," he said in one of his early sketches—and often said again in different words—"after all their speculations, will be led into the common path, and, in homage to the human nature that pervades them, will gather gold, and till the earth, and set out trees, and build a house." Hawthorne, too, wished to gather gold and build a house; on one side of his nature he was a sturdy and harshly practical New Englander like the magistrates and sea captains from whom he was descended. "Let them scorn me as they will," he said of his ancestors, "strong traits of their nature have intertwined themselves with mine"; but he also had strong traits of the Byronic rebel. Everywhere in his character one finds a sort of doubleness: thus, he was proud

and humble, cold and sensuous, sluggish and active, conservative and radical, realistic and romantic; he was a recluse who
became involved in party politics and a visionary with a touch
of cynicism and a hard sense of money values. These contradic-
tions, these inner tensions, lend force to his stories and make
their author an endless study.

Out of his struggles with his conscience and his sense of
guilt, Hawthorne evolved a sort of theology that was peculiar
to himself, but was also profoundly Christian and on most
points orthodox. He believed in original sin, which consisted—
so I think he would have said—in the pride and self-centeredness of every individual. He believed that evil existed in all
hearts, including his own, and he therefore had no patience
with the modernists of his time who explained that evil was
merely accident or illusion. He believed in the brotherhood of
men, based on their common sinfulness and their weakness
before God. He believed in predestination, as his Calvinist
ancestors had done; but at the same time he had an instinctive
faith in the value of confession and absolution that sometimes
brought him close to Roman Catholicism. He never went to
church after leaving college and apparently he seldom prayed.
One might say that he was both too proud and too humble for
prayer: too proud to ask for help and too humble to plead his
own desires against the divine wisdom: "Men's accidents are
God's purposes" was the motto he scratched with a diamond
ring on a window of the Old Manse. He trustingly submitted
himself to Providence, and he believed in a future life where
each guilty person would be punished, if only as he himself
had been, by self-knowledge of his sins. On the whole his faith
was close to that of the Puritan fathers, but it was not derived
from their teaching; it was a practical Puritanism based on his
own experience. It was expressed in story after story, not
philosophically—for he did not think in abstractions—but in
terms of symbols as powerfully simple as those in *Pilgrim's
Progress*, and so much closer to the modern mind that in some
respects he seems nearer to Kafka than to John Bunyan.

In his plots he laid more emphasis on sin and retribution
than on redemption through divine grace; yet one can hardly
say that he regarded all sinners as hopelessly damned. Some, it
is true, might be led by gradual steps into what he regarded as

the Unpardonable Sin; it was an intellectual pride and selfishness that permitted them to manipulate human souls in order to satisfy their cold curiosity and lust for power; such men deserved the fate of Ethan Brand. Others, however, might be taught human brotherhood by their very crimes and, if they publicly confessed, might be taken back into the community. Still others might be redeemed simply by their love for one human being, and that was Hawthorne's salvation. When he fell in love with Sophia Peabody, it seemed to him that he had been drawn from the shadows and made real, together with the world about him, by the intensity of his passion. "Indeed, we are but shadows," he said in one of those letters to Sophia in which he poured out his feelings for the first time; "we are not endowed with real life, all that seems most real about us is but the thinnest substance of a dream,—till the heart be touched. That touch creates us,—then we begin to be."

It was Sophia's older sister, Elizabeth, who first brought the lovers together. Miss E. P. Peabody, as she called herself, was the friend of all the Boston cranks and reformers, a transcendental spirit who fluttered from enthusiasm to enthusiasm like an iron-willed butterfly. She had been excited by "The Gentle Boy" and other stories that appeared anonymously in the giftbooks and magazines; she suspected that they were all the work of the same author and hoped to discover a genius. When *Twice-Told Tales* appeared in 1837, she learned that the genius was a neighbor in Salem—indeed, one of her childhood playmates—and at once she laid siege to the Hawthorne household. It was a matter of patient months before she had charmed Louisa, the lively sister, who she said disappointedly was "just like other poeple," and Elizabeth, the intellectual sister, whom she admired as "the hermitess." Nathaniel was harder to entice from his solitude; but at last her evening of triumph came when the whole family paid her a visit. Miss Peabody excused herself and rushed upstairs to the room where Sophia was recovering from one of her daily headaches. "Oh, Sophia," she said, "you must get up and dress and come down! The Hawthornes are here, and you never saw anything so splendid as he is,—he is handsomer than Lord Byron!"

Sophia didn't feel strong enough to meet him. "If he has called once, he'll call again," she said.

Hawthorne did call again, in the afternoon, and this time Sophia came down in her simple white wrapper and sat on the sofa. When Miss Peabody said, "My sister Sophia," he rose and looked at her so intently that both women were frightened. Many years later Sophia told her children that she felt a magnetic power in his eyes and instinctively drew back. Then, as the weeks passed by and Hawthorne became a daily visitor, she began to realize that they had loved each other at first sight.

"Poor children," one thinks while reading the story of their courtship; for they both were children in their knowledge of the world. But again one thinks, "Lucky children," after picturing the fates that both of them escaped, in a provincial society full of old maids and cranky bachelors. Sophia was twenty-seven years old when they met; she suffered from violent headaches that had defied treatment by all the doctors and half the quacks in Boston. Often she had told her older sister that nothing would tempt her to marry and inflict on a husband the care of an invalid. Hawthorne was thirty-four and was trying to venture out from his solitary life, which had led him to fears of suicide or madness; but he seemed too shy and aloof ever to risk a proposal of marriage, and his sisters, moreover, were determined to keep him a bachelor. Somehow he groped his way to Sophia and she to him, both surmounting their inner obstacles, both cutting through a little maze of family intrigues; and they clung together as if they furnished, each to each, the only present refuge or hope of future salvation. Soon they were secretly engaged and were even addressing each other in their letters as husband and wife; but the marriage ceremony couldn't take place until Hawthorne was able to support a family.

In 1839 he obtained the first of his political appointments, as weigher and gauger in the Boston Custom House. He had a salary now, even if it was only $1,500 a year, but other obstacles delayed the wedding. Sophia decided that it would have to wait until she had recovered from her twenty-years' illness. "If God intends us to marry, He will let me be cured," she said; "if not, it will be a sign that it is not best." Hawthorne's sisters warned him against marrying an invalid; they said that his mother would die of the shock. Miss E. P. Peabody seems to have hoped that Hawthorne would recognize her own superior merits—that is one inference to be drawn from the family correspondence—but nevertheless she provided a meeting place for the lovers and helped them to exchange letters. She also encouraged Hawthorne's next step, which was to join the utopian community at Brook Farm in the hope that it would provide a home for himself and Sophia. For a time he shared the ideals of the other Brook Farmers and outdid them in physical labor; indeed, he worked so hard in the fields and the cow stable that he had no energy left for dreaming. "A man's soul," he said in a letter to Sophia, "may be buried and perish under a dung-heap or in the furrow of a field, just as well as under a pile of money." He left Brook Farm in the autumn and later resigned his post as chairman of the finance committee. His literary prospects looked brighter and at last he determined to tell his mother about the approaching marriage. "I already knew about it," Madame Hawthorne said, ". . . almost as long as you knew it yourself, and Sophia Peabody is the wife of all others I would have chosen for you." The sisters now declared that they were delighted with his choice. Sophia's headaches miraculously disappeared. After an engagement that had lasted for nearly four years, the wedding took place on July 9, 1842, and the lovers went to live in Concord, where they had rented the Old Manse. "I have married the Spring!" Hawthorne exclaimed in a letter. "I am husband to the month of May!"

Springlike as she was, Sophia had her faults, some of which were regarded as virtues by the Bostonians. She was painfully high-minded, even priggish; and when Hawthorne admiringly painted her portrait (as Hilda, in *The Marble Faun*), he presented a character that seems to us heartless and almost monstrous in its ideality. She tried to see nothing but the beautiful, the good, and the true. Unconsciously she acted as a censor of her husband's work, by admiring it for the wrong qualities; and she also played the conscious censor when she edited the notebooks for publication after his death. The fact remains that her love for him was earthly as well as ethereal.

She made him an admirable wife, devoted, uncomplaining in their early hardships, respectful of his need for solitude, and always regarding him as the sun around which her life revolved. In practical ways she also helped: she protected him from intrusions on his time and demanded little for herself; after he lost his second political post, in the Salem Custom House, it was her savings from her household allowance that enabled him to start writing *The Scarlet Letter*. Hawthorne made her an admirable husband, too; besides playing the father to her, and the dutiful son, he was also her passionate lover—at least until their younger daughter, Rose, was born in 1851; afterwards they decided to have no more children and their passion seems to have subsided into a steady and lifelong affection. Without this domestic security, his public career as a writer would have been impossible. All his novels and many of his stories were written for and because of Sophia.

After the popular success of the first three novels, there was a further change in Hawthorne: he became more conservative and directed more of his attention towards the external world. Brook Farm had been his farthest venture into radicalism and it had frightened him, especially when his associates began talking about sexual liberty. Now, forsaking the reformers who had been his first friends when he emerged from solitude, he began to see more of "the merchants, the politicians, the Cambridge men, and all those respectable old blockheads, who still, in this intangibility and mistiness of affairs, kept a death-grip on one or two ideas which had not come into vogue since yesterday morning." He tried to forget his earlier dilemmas and even came to dislike the stories in which he had expressed his sense of guilt. The change is implicit in one of his letters to James T. Fields, the junior partner of the publishing house that had taken over his work and, in 1854, was bringing out a revised edition of *Mosses from an Old Manse*. "When I wrote these dreamy sketches," Hawthorne said, "I little thought that I should ever preface an edition for the press amidst the bustling life of a Liverpool consulate. Upon my honor, I am not quite sure that I entirely comprehend my own meaning, in some of these blasted allegories; but I remember that I always had a meaning, or at least thought I had. I am a good deal changed since those times; and, to tell you the truth, my past self is not very much to my taste, as I see myself in this book."

Thanks chiefly to his marriage he had become a success by public standards; not only a famous romancer but a highly respected citizen like his Salem ancestors, a government official and the head of a family. He had even lived out his fable of the Great Stone Face: orphaned and seeking year after year for a father image, he had at last discovered in himself the benignant parent. Only one side of his double character was now revealed to the world and his own children. His son Julian, who didn't read the romances until after Hawthorne's death, found himself continually bewildered by them and "unable to comprehend," he said, "how a man such as I knew my father to be could have written such books. He did not talk in that way; his moods had not seemed to be of that color." The fact was that the books continued to mirror his earlier self; even the last unfinished novels, for all their details copied from life, were still based on his discoveries in that inner world where he had lived in desperate isolation. Now he had roofed over the entrance to the abyss and had built another life above it. He was honored, he was financially secure, and, after 1860, he found it impossible to write the novels that he started one after another—partly because he was tired and in ill health, partly because he kept setting higher standards for himself, but chiefly because he had blocked off the source of his inspiration.

"The best things come, as a general thing, from talents that are members of a group," says Henry James in his little book on Hawthorne; "every man works best when he has companions working in the same line, and yielding the stimulus of suggestion, comparison, emulation." Hawthorne never had such a stimulus, and for a long time after his work began to be printed he even lacked the feeling that it was being read; he wrote like a prisoner talking aloud in his cell. When he did find admirers, after 1837, they usually agreed with Sophia in praising him for the wrong reasons: most of them were Emersonian and idealistic, whereas Hawthorne's bent was towards psychological realism even when he was writing allegories. Fortunately he resisted their efforts to change him, and justified his own description of himself as "a most unmalleable man." Working alone, he had to look in himself for the answer to each of his literary problems. He often made elaborate mistakes, as might have been expected; the wonder is that so many of the answers he found were usable. Not in his life, but in his work, he foreshadowed the ideals that later American writers would try to realize and fixed the patterns that many of them would instinctively follow.

During his years of solitude Hawthorne learned more than others did in the marketplace. He learned, for example, that he had to respect his own limitations. "Four precepts," he wrote in his notebook for 1835: "To break off customs; to shake off spirits ill-disposed; to meditate on youth; to do nothing against one's genius." He learned—and this was a lesson he never forgot—that the best things he wrote were uttered by a voice deep within himself, whose speech he was unable to control. He surrendered himself to a power that was, so he said, "higher and wiser than himself, making him its instrument." The crowning effect that he hoped to achieve was "a happiness which God, out of His pure grace, mixes up with only the simple-hearted best efforts of men." Yet this inner voice, which he sometimes regarded as divine, more often seemed to him infernal; thus, he spoke of *The Scarlet Letter* as being "baked in hell-fire."—"When I get home, I will try to write a more genial book," he said when he was working on *The Marble Faun*; "but the Devil himself always seems to get into my inkstand, and I can only exorcise him by pensful at a time." There were months and years, however, when the Devil stayed out of his inkstand, and that was worse; at such periods Hawthorne felt that his work was contrived and inconsequential. "I have an instinct that I had better keep quiet," he said in one of his last letters to James T. Fields. "Perhaps I shall have a new spirit of vigor if I wait quietly for it; perhaps not."

He learned a wise patience that he sometimes explained as indolence. It was really watchfulness; he was crouching in wait for his own thoughts like a duck-shooter hidden in the reeds. There was, however, another side of the picture and he also learned to be active in pursuit of his thoughts. He collected impressions and stored them away in his notebook, so that a background would be ready for the inspiration when it came at last; and he learned to wrestle with it and force it from its obscurity. "This forenoon," he said in a diary for 1843, "I began to write, and caught an idea by the tail, which I intend to hold fast, though it struggles to get free. As it was not ready to be put on paper, however, I took up the *Dial*, and finished the article on Mr. Alcott." The *Dial*, organ of the Concord intellectuals, was one of his trusted tools, but it served a different purpose from that intended by its editors; Hawthorne read it when he was tired and it usually put him to sleep.

Catnaps over the *Dial* were part of his routine, for he had learned a system of working, resting, exercising, and returning to work with a fresh mind. In the summer—I am speaking of the first years after his marriage—he made entries in his notebook and hoed the garden, trying, as he said, to be "happy as a squash, and in much the same mode."—"I am never good for anything in the literary way," he wrote to Fields, "till after the first autumnal frost, which has somewhat the same effect on my imagination that it does on the foliage here about me,—multiplying and brightening its hues." All his four novels were finished during the winter, when he made a practice of writing from two to four hours each day—seldom longer than that, except when he was working excitedly on *The Scarlet Letter*, for he had found that the mood on which he depended was likely to vanish when he became weary. One respects him for insisting on leisure when he hadn't money to pay for it. He was willing to live on the cheapest foodstuffs available in Concord—his Christmas dinner in 1843 consisted of "preserved quince and apple, dates, and bread and cheese, and milk"; but, poor as he was, he refused to hurry along a story that needed time to ripen.

He wrote much more than one would infer from his easy schedule or from merely looking at the little shelf of books with "Hawthorne's Works" on the back. Besides the early stories he burned in his fireplace—there were many of them and once, he said, they set the chimney on fire—he did a quantity of hackwork when trying to break away from Salem and later when he was earning a living for himself and Sophia. In 1836, for a promised salary of five-hundred dollars a year (of which he received twenty dollars in all), he not only edited but wrote almost the entire contents of the *American Magazine of Useful and Entertaining Knowledge*. After the magazine went bankrupt, through no fault of the editor's, he wrote for a fee of one-hundred dollars (this time actually paid) a history of the world that went through scores of editions and eventually had a sale of more than a million copies. In England, during the four years when he was consul at Liverpool, he wrote nothing for publication except a preface to Delia Bacon's crazy book on Shakespeare; but he kept a journal that ran to 300,000 words, and it was more carefully expressed than most published novels. One might say that he taught himself to write by writing a great deal.

He also learned to write by constant reading. Having acquired the habit at the age of nine, he never relinquished it; in his last years he went through the Waverley novels a second time, reading them aloud to his family. We have a record of the books he borrowed from the Salem Athenaeum during most of his solitary period. His average was a hundred titles each year: biography, travel, New England history, encyclopedias (which he seems to have read from beginning to end), and bound volumes of English magazines; the record shows that he had a thirst for general information. He also read the latest novels, which he rented from a circulating library. In some respects his choice of books seems curious and impractical for a Romantic writer trying to keep abreast of the movement to which he belonged. Thus, he studied the French classics, especially Racine and Voltaire, but nowhere in his notebooks does he mention Balzac, Stendhal, Hugo, or any other French rebel of his own time. He was closer in spirit to the German Romantics, but not because he read them; once, with a German phrase book open beside him, he puzzled through a story by Johann Ludwig Tieck, but he never repeated the experiment. Some of his favorite English authors, besides Scott and Bunyan, were Pope, Swift, Addison, and Dr. Johnson—all of whom represented the classical standards against which his fellow Romantics had risen in revolt.

It was from these and other Augustan writers that he

seems to have learned the style of his early work. The style was old-fashioned, balanced, formal, one might almost say white-silk-stockinged and periwigged; it was a curious manner of writing for an author bent on penetrating the shadowy places of the heart. It was full of personified abstractions. "Sometimes," he said in describing one of his early heroines, "she stole forth by moonlight and visited the graves of venerable Integrity, and wedded Love, and virgin Innocence, and every spot where the ashes of a kind and faithful heart were mouldering." The sentiment is Romantic, while the language is that of an eighteenth-century drawing-room poet. But Hawthorne's style changed gradually as he grew older, until he was writing better and easier prose than any other American of his time. One reason for the change was his habit of walking out his stories, repeating them to himself as he wandered along the seashore or under the pines. The result was that his rather provincial drawing-room English developed into a natural, a *walked* style, with a phrase for every step and a comma after every phrase like a footprint in the sand. Sometimes the phrases hurry, sometimes they loiter, sometimes they march to drums. Although Hawthorne had no ear for music and couldn't tell one melody from another, his sense of rhythm was extraordinary.

Since he could never express himself in company—except sometimes in his later years over a bottle of wine—writing became his principal means of communication with the world; and he therefore tried to make each statement clear. He learned to use what he called "the humblest medium of familiar words and images."—"Every sentence," he said in the introduction to *Twice-Told Tales*, "so far as it embodies thought or sensibility, may be understood and felt by anybody who will give himself the trouble to read it, and will take up the book in the proper mood." He liked children and was proud of his ability to write for them without condescension: "I never did anything else so well as these old baby stories," he said when working on *Tanglewood Tales*.

Apparently he agreed with Poe in thinking that the writer's principal problem was how to produce "effects," which might be defined as states of feeling induced in his readers. Writing to his classmate Horatio Bridge, who had become a naval officer and was planning to keep a journal of his cruise to Africa, Hawthorne mentioned some of the methods by which effects might be achieved. "Begin to write always before the impression of novelty has worn off from your mind," he said, "else you will be apt to think that the peculiarities which at first attracted you are not worth recording; yet those slight peculiarities are the very things that make the most vivid impression upon the reader. Think nothing too trifling to write down, so it be in the smallest degree characteristic. You will be surprised to find on re-perusing your journal what an importance and graphic power these little particulars assume." In the course of time Hawthorne had trained himself to observe "little particulars"; he insisted on being a good reporter as well as an artist. He was a good journalist or magazinist, too; and one reads his articles on occasional subjects with wonder at the many original methods he found for presenting his rather tame material. Everything he published had the charm of solid craftsmanship. He was perhaps the first American writer with a professional attitude towards all his work.

One problem that obsessed him all his life was the relation between the inner and the outer world. Hawthorne tried different means of solving it, one after the other, but none of them proved satisfactory.

The inner world of dreams and moral compulsions had been the real subject of almost all his stories. Of course they had an outward setting, too, but it often lacked substance, being a mere projection or symbol of the landscapes inside his mind. Most of his plots were based on an inner event; it was usually some transgression, vaguely stated, that led to its own punishment without the intervention of policemen or magistrates; and there was always a moral implicit in the story.

As the plots were jotted down in his early notebooks, they were quite brief; often they consisted of a few phrases. "To trace out the influence of a frightful and disgraceful crime," he would say, "in debasing and destroying a character naturally high and noble—the guilty person alone being conscious of the crime." Again he would say: "A person to be in the possession of something as perfect as mortal man has a right to demand;

he tries to make it better, and ruins it entirely." The first of these plots was never used, while the second, after lying in Hawthorne's mind for six years, developed into one of his better stories, "The Birthmark." When they were first noted down, however, one seemed as promising or unpromising as the other; both were inner dramas and both carried an implicit moral: the first, that crime is self-punished; the second, that striving for perfection in this imperfect world is an act of sinful pride.

Before any of his plots became a narrative, Hawthorne had to find characters, invent actions for them that would reveal the inner conflict, and describe an outward setting that would symbolize the inner truth. The characters, the actions, and the setting would all have to be woven out of his mind, like a spider extruding its web. In the beginning, at least, Hawthorne couldn't copy from other lives than his own, because his experience, though deep, was too narrow. "I have another great difficulty in the lack of materials," he said in an early letter to Longfellow; "for I have seen so little of the world that I have nothing but thin air to concoct my stories of, and it is not easy to give a lifelike semblance to such shadowy stuff."

Having diagnosed his weakness, Hawthorne tried to cure it. The best remedy, he thought, would be more observation of the world; and so he began taking notes on every new scene or person he encountered in his summer wanderings. He practiced writing descriptions like a painter doing watercolor sketches; once, for example, he sat alone in the woods near Concord with his notebook in his lap and made a record of everything that came under his eyes. He filled eight pages with his small handwriting, then made a final comment: "How narrow, scanty, and meagre is this record of observation, compared with the immensity that was to be observed, within the bounds which I prescribed to myself. . . . When we see how little we can express, it is a wonder that any man ever takes up a pen a second time." Yet Hawthorne kept trying to express more and more of what he saw and more of what he heard and thought (his ears were always less keen than his eyes). Without being a naturalist like Thoreau, he learned to catch the changing moods of nature; and he developed his naturally keen sense of character. Said Lawyer Haynes, the one-armed drunken soapmaker he met in North Adams, "My study is man." Then, looking straight at Hawthorne, he added, "I do not know your name, but there is something of the hawk-eye about you too."

His notebooks came to play a curious part in his creative process: they were a hoard of objects and persons; they were the outer world reduced to words and made usable in his fiction. Instead of concocting his backgrounds out of thin air, he began to take them from his notebooks, as if he had requisitioned them from a warehouse, where they might have been stored for a decade or more. "Ethan Brand," published in 1851, is an example of this new method; it combines an inner drama over which he had brooded for several years with a collection of notes he had made during his visit to North Adams in 1838. One of the most effective chapters in *The Blithedale Romance* (1852) is the one describing the search for Zenobia's drowned body. Hawthorne had fished for the body of a suicide in 1845, when he was living at the Old Manse, and now he merely revised the notes he had taken on that occasion. More than two-thirds of *The Marble Faun* (1860) consists of descriptive passages transcribed from the Italian notebooks. The novel combines his two worlds, but without fusing them; inner drama and outer setting tend to separate like oil and water. Hawthorne kept looking for another answer to his problem.

He often thought of completely shifting his approach. Instead of starting with a drama from his inner world and surrounding it with objects copied from nature, might it not be better to start with the external world and brood over its meaning until he forced it to reveal its inner drama? That had been the "wiser effort" suggested in his introduction to *The Scarlet Letter*, where, as usual, he insisted on disparaging the work he had actually performed. "It was a folly," he said, "with the materiality of this daily life pressing so intrusively upon me"—he had been describing his three years in the custom house—"to attempt to fling myself back into another age; or to insist on creating the semblance of a world out of airy matter, when, at every moment, the impalpable beauty of my soap-bubble was broken by the rude contact of some actual circumstance. The wiser effort would have been to diffuse thought and imagination through the opaque substance of to-day, and thus to make it a bright transparency." Hawthorne greatly admired the seventeenth-century Dutch painters, especially Gerhard Douw, for their treatment of natural objects. "These painters," he said in his notebook, "accomplish all they aim at—a praise, methinks, which can be given to no other men since the world began. They must have laid down their brushes with perfect satisfaction, knowing that each one of their million touches had been necessary to the effect, and that there was not one too little or too much. And it is strange how spiritual, and suggestive the commonest household article—an earthen pitcher, for example—becomes when represented with entire accuracy. These Dutchmen get at the soul of common things, and so make them types and interpreters of the spiritual world." At times Hawthorne tried to copy their method. "Many passages of this book," he said when writing *The House of the Seven Gables*, "ought to be finished with the minuteness of a Dutch picture, in order to give them their proper effect."

There was no violent change in Hawthorne's theories when he tried to work inward from the surface of things instead of outward from the heart. All his life he believed that a sort of correspondence existed between the two worlds of nature and spirit; one might start with either and, with sufficient effort, one might end by expressing the same truths. In some respects his notion of correspondences brought him close to the Puritan divines like Cotton Mather, who also found a double meaning in everything. Mather was ready to explain even the humblest events—like a cow's going dry or finding her way home from the forest—as tokens of God's providence or Satan's wiles. Hawthorne had a similar faith in tokens that often made him sound old-fashioned; but he was an explorer, too, and some of his work looked forward to the still undiscovered fields of psychiatry and psychosomatic medicine. Here are a few entries from his notebooks that have a prophetic ring:

(1836). An article on fire, on smoke. Diseases of the mind and soul,—even more common than bodily diseases.

(1841). To symbolize moral or spiritual disease by disease of the body;—thus, when a person committed any sin, it might cause a sore to appear on the body;—this to be wrought out.

(1842). Imaginary diseases to be cured by impossible remedies—as, a dose of the Grand Elixir, in the yolk of a Phoenix's egg. The diseases may be either moral or physical.

(1842). A physician for the cure of moral diseases.

In working with these notions about moral diseases—which we have learned to call psychoses—and about the operation of the spirit on the body, Hawthorne was far in advance of his time and he was a little frightened by his boldness. Often his speculations played a part in his stories; a famous example of psychophysical parallelism is the scarlet A that appears on Mr. Dimmesdale's flesh after he has brooded for years over his guilt. In describing such incidents, however, Hawthorne always protects himself from the skeptics by saying "perhaps," or "it was the general belief," or "if all the stories were true." This ambiguity is carried to great length in his account of Mr. Dimmesdale's confession. Most of the spectators testify to having seen a scarlet letter imprinted on the minister's flesh, but they give three different explanations of its presence, and there are some who flatly deny that it could be seen, or indeed that Mr. Dimmesdale had confessed to anything improper. Hawthorne reports the controversy without taking sides, and yet he makes his attitude fairly clear in spite of all the conflicting statements: he believed that there was really a scarlet A on Mr. Dimmesdale's breast, and he believed that it was "the effect of the ever-active tooth of remorse, gnawing from the inmost heart outwardly." What happened in the heart became manifest in the flesh; and, conversely, one could arrive at inner truths by scrutinizing appearances.

Towards the end of his life, Hawthorne became more and more impatient with the books in which he embodied his misty theories. "My own individual taste," he complained in a letter to Fields, "is for quite another class of works than those which I myself am able to write. If I were to meet with such books as mine, by another writer, I don't believe I should be able to get through them. Have you ever read the novels of Anthony

Trollope? They precisely suit my taste; solid and substantial, written on the strength of beef and through the inspiration of ale, and just as real as if some giant had hewn a great lump out of the earth and put it under a glass case, with all its inhabitants going about their daily business, and not suspecting that they were made a show of." That was the sort of novel he admired, and it was even a sort of novel he had prepared himself to write—or so one judges after reading his English notebooks, with their solid grasp of character and their substantial pictures of persons and places. It was not, however, a sort of novel that he judged to lie within the limits of his genius. "I wish God had given me the faculty of writing a sunshiny book," he said; but he bowed to fate or Providence in this respect as in others; he wrote or tried to write the books that he had within him.

He was working towards a conception of the novel—or of the romance, as he preferred to call it—that was completely different from the notions prevailing at his time. "In writing a romance," he had said in a letter to Fields, "a man is always, or always ought to be, careering on the utmost verge of a precipitous absurdity, and the skill lies in coming as close as possible, without actually tumbling over." The last books he planned would have been a mixture of fantasy and realism; they would have been realistic in their method, with all the details copied from life, and realistic in their reading of human nature; but they would have been based on plots that were flatly impossible. Thus, in *The Dolliver Romance*, the book with which he struggled during the last year of his life, he would have told us how Grandsir Dolliver grew younger year by year and finally became a child again. Each step towards that impossible goal would have been as carefully visualized as any of the real scenes described in Hawthorne's notebooks. The book as a whole would have had the circumstantiality of a dream, while at the same time it would have been a vehicle for Hawthorne's broodings over mortality. If he had been able to finish *The Dolliver Romance*, it might have served as the bridge for which he had always been seeking, between the inner and the outer world.

Hawthorne was always dissatisfied with his own work and at the end he became obsessed with a sense of failure. One day when Emerson found him on the path that his feet had made among the sweetfern and the huckleberry bushes, Hawthorne said to him, "This path is the only remembrance of me that will remain." Yet he was a failure only when his achievements are measured against the inordinately high standards he set for himself. Measured by the easier standards of his time, the same achievements seem almost Himalayan. He advanced the art of fiction. Even before Poe, he was the first American—and possibly the first in any country—to write short stories in the modern sense of the term: not sketches or episodes, but stories built around a single effect and having the unity of a lyric poem. Moreover, he carried his prose experiments farther than Poe, for he was also the first American to write novels that were as tightly constructed as short stories.

There is more to be said about his conception of the novel. One can see by internal evidence that he was faced with difficulties in the longer form; his training as a story writer made it hard for him to keep the action continually moving forward; but he solved this problem by dividing his novels into scenes or tableaus, each strikingly visualized and balanced one against another; it was the dramatic method that Henry James would rediscover in his final period. Within the limitations of his technique and personality, each of his novels was different from all the others, not only in subject but in mood and treatment. One principle he followed instinctively was that every work of art must be right by its own laws, which are never quite the same as those governing any other work of art. Another principle was that each novel should be a painting complete within its frame. Besides being a series of balanced tableaus, the action of his novels consists of *interactions* among a few characters—usually four—with voices from the crowd as a sort of dramatic chorus; and the result is that each book becomes a system of relationships, a field of force as clearly defined and symmetrical as a magnetic field. He was the first American writer to develop this architectural conception of the novel; and even in France *Madame Bovary* wasn't published until seven years after *The Scarlet Letter* had appeared in Boston.

Flaubert and Hawthorne had not a little in common; their work revealed the same search for perfection (though Flaubert carried it farther), the same mixture of realism and romanticism, the same feeling that each new novel was a totally new problem in mood and organization. Hawthorne's work has a New England sparseness and accuracy of detail that is almost like Flaubert's Norman economy. Frederic Moreau, of *Sentimental Education*, was said to be a self-portrait of Flaubert; and one cannot fail to note his resemblance to Miles Coverdale, of *The Blithedale Romance*, who was said to be a self-portrait of Hawthorne. The striking difference between the two authors was that Flaubert regarded himself as living and working at the center of the civilized world, on an eminence from which life could be judged without moral preconceptions, whereas Hawthorne remained the complete provincial even when living in Europe. He was provincial in both the good and the bad sense of the word: in the good sense because he knew his province, accepted his part in it, and tested everything else in the world by New England standards (so that he carried the Puritan conscience to Rome, in *The Marble Faun*, and transferred the Greek legends to the Berkshires, in *The Wonder-Book*, after purifying them, as he said, of all moral stains); and provincial in the bad sense because his localism made him blind to other values than those accepted in Boston.

Sometimes his work had a sort of New England stuffiness, as if it were meant to be read in an unaired parlor. At his worst he wrote and acted less like Flaubert than like the late George Apley—as when he quailed at the notion of meeting George Eliot, who was living with a man she couldn't marry, and when he refused to admit that any sculptor was a genius unless he was able to portray heroism in frock coat and breeches. "I do not altogether see the necessity of ever sculpturing another nakedness," he said in his notebook for 1858. "Man is no longer a naked animal; his clothes are as natural to him as his skin, and sculptors have no more right to undress him than to flay him." Hawthorne had always been interested in clothes as symbols that revealed a man's nature while concealing it, and now his interest had become an obsession. Having dressed his thoughts in trousers, he no longer moved with the freedom of the naked mind.

Yet he was, for all his decorum, a man of strong passions who liked to write about women of strong passions. Two of his four novels deal with adultery and a third, *The Blithedale Romance*, is about a woman trying to escape from an undesirable husband who has reduced her sister to moral slavery. The heroine of *The Scarlet Letter* justifies her life in terms that shocked some of Hawthorne's early critics: "What we did," she says to her lover, "had a consecration of its own." In the background of *The Marble Faun*, adultery is compounded with incest and fratricide. Miriam is married to a near relative —one would guess her half-brother—who is a mixture of saint and devil. When the devilish side comes uppermost and he tries to resume their relationship, she encourages Donatello to kill him; and one assumes that she and Donatello became lovers that same night. I cannot imagine that Howells, for example, would have dared to tell such a story even discreetly and by implication, as Hawthorne told it; in most of the New England writers passion was not only censored in its expression but expunged from the heart. It is only the surface that is censored in Hawthorne and it is chiefly the surface that has aged; his underlying problems are as real to us today as when he first presented them.

Although he doubted that his work would be remembered, Hawthorne fixed a pattern for writers who came after him; and it was by no means the pattern that critics expected to find. It had been taken for granted that American literature would somehow correspond to the physical and social features of a new country: that it would be as broad as the continent, as hardy and uncouth as the pioneers, and as noisy as an election campaign. But the correspondence that really exists between literature and society can seldom be reduced to such parallels, because books are written by men of special training, from their special type of experience. Not many American writers have been frontiersmen or politicians or even businessmen; most of them have had the feeling of being more or less isolated from their neighbors. Whitman, a lonely man, tried to create a literature of democratic comradeship. After those first great poems in which he poured out his feelings, he made the mistake of conforming to a preconception of what he should write, and that is why much of his later work seems forced. Hawthorne in his solitude wrote what he had to write. Because he obeyed his instinct, which he personified as his genius or demon, he proved to be a better prophet than Whitman of the books that would be written after his death.

So far as there has been a continuous literary tradition in this country, it is the one that Hawthorne had a share in founding. So far as there has been a prevailing tone in our literature, it is not the one that critics tried to deduce from American geography or American politics. In one respect the critics proved to be right. Most of our writers have been democratic, for the simple reason that they were reared in a democratic society and that, in spite of their isolation, they shared its feelings. Hawthorne, who started in life as a Jacksonian Democrat, became more conservative as he grew older; but he retained an interest in ordinary persons—as persons, not as specimens—that set him apart from most of his European contemporaries. That faith runs through American literature; one finds it even in Henry James.

In other respects the best of our writing has taken a course that contradicts most of the prophecies made a century ago. To speak in general terms it has been, not broad and sweeping, but narrow and deep; not epical, but lyrical; not optimistic, but somber and self-questioning in its mood; not young, but middle-aged—one might almost say from the beginning; not realistic as a whole, but marvelously realistic in its grasp of details; not careless and uncouth, but often formalized and troubled by the search for perfection; not prevailingly social, but psychological, and interested from the first in what afterwards came to be known as depth psychology. On the whole it has been a literature of loneliness and one in which persons, however real in themselves, tend to dissolve into symbols and myths. Hawthorne's work continues to stand as one of its archetypes, at the beginning of a double line that runs through James to Eliot, with all his imitators, and through Stephen Crane to Faulkner and Hemingway.

Whitman: The Poet and the Mask

I HAVEN'T always been an admirer of Whitman's poetry. In the past when I tried to read *Leaves of Grass* from beginning to end, I always stopped in the middle, overcome by the dislike that most of us feel for inventories and orations. Even today, after reading all the book as Whitman wished it to be preserved and after being won over by what I think is the best of it—till I am willing, if not for the usual reasons, to join the consensus that regards him as our most rewarding poet—I still feel that *Leaves of Grass* is an extraordinary mixture of greatness, false greatness, and mediocrity. Whitman designed it as his monument, but he made the book too large and pieced it out with faulty materials, including versified newspaper editorials, lists of names from the back pages of a school geography, commencement-day prophecies, chamber-of-commerce speeches, and sentimental ballads that might have been written by the Sweet Singer of Michigan, except that she would have rhymed them. The fire bells ring in his poems, the eagle screams and screams again, the brawny pioneers march into the forest (décor by Currier & Ives), and the lovely Italian singer gives a concert for the convicts at Sing Sing, her operatic voice

Pouring in floods of melody in tones so pensive sweet and strong the like whereof was never heard.

In no other book of great poems does one find so much trash that the poet should have recognized as trash before he set the first line of it on paper. In no other book, great or small, does one find the same extremes of inspiration and bathos. It is as if Whitman the critic and editor of his own work had been so overawed by Whitman the poet that he preserved even the poet's maunderings as the authentic record

This essay originally was published as the introduction to *The Complete Poetry and Prose of Walt Whitman*, Pellegrini and Cudahy, New York, 1948, two volumes. Portions of it appeared earlier as "Walt Whitman: The Miracle," *New Republic*, 114, March 18, 1946, 385–88; "Walt Whitman: The Secret," *New Republic*, 114, April 8, 1946, 481–84; "Walt Whitman: The Philosopher," *New Republic*, 117, September 29, 1947, 29–31; "Whitman: The Poet," *New Republic*, 117, October 20, 1947, 27–30.

of genius. He did not succeed—though he worked on the problem all his life—in giving an organic form to the book as a whole. It doesn't grow like a tree or take wing like a bird or correspond in its various sections to the stages of the poet's life; instead it starts with a series of twenty-four "inscriptions," or doctrinal pronouncements, almost like twenty-four theses nailed to a church door. It reaches an early climax, with the "Song of Myself." It continues through celebrations of "woman-love," as Whitman called it a little coldly, and passionate friendship for men. Then, after a series of set-pieces—some of them magnificent, like the "Song of the Open Road"—after the Civil War sketches and the big symphonies of his Washington years, it dwindles away in occasional verses and old-age echoes.

The poems are grouped by their ostensible themes rather than by their underlying moods. Thus, a section or, as Whitman would say, a "cluster" of poems called "Sea-Drift" starts with the two great meditations he wrote during his period of dejection in 1859–60 ("Out of the Cradle Endlessly Rocking" and "As I Ebb'd with the Ocean of Life"), but it ends with a collection of minor and chiefly optimistic pieces that happen also to mention the sea. Another cluster called "Autumn Rivulets" consists in large part of late and occasional poems, like Whitman's bread-and-butter letter to the Seventeenth Regimental Band ("Italian Music in Dakota"), yet it also contains the marvelous "There Was a Child Went Forth" and other examples of his earlier and freshest work. In such an arrangement the man is lost, with his organic development; and the best poems are likely to be overshadowed, like young pines in a thicket of big-leaf poplars.

Almost all the American critics of Whitman's poetry have failed in their task of separating the pines from the poplars, the lasting values from what is trivial or sententious or weedy. It is true that Tennyson, Swinburne, and William Michael Rossetti were among his early English readers, that they were good critics as well as poets, and that, in general, they admired his work for its literary qualities instead of approaching it as a political or religious text. In this country, however, the poets of his time were hostile to Whitman; almost the only exception was Emerson in the very beginning. The hostility has vanished, but without giving way to enthusiasm. As a group the poet-critics of our time pay less attention to Whitman than to any other American author of the first magnitude. More and more Whitman studies are crowding the library shelves, but they are chiefly the work of two other groups: the liberal or nationalistic historians and the teachers or graduate students of American literature.

These latter groups are interested not so much in the poetry as in the historical or mythical figure of the poet. They *need* that figure; they need an author to represent in himself the vastness and newness of the country and the unity it achieved; they need someone in literature to play the same role as Daniel Boone in the forests or Davy Crockett in the canebrakes or Lincoln saving the Union. Whitman is there, dressed and bearded for the part, and they cannot fail to accept him as the literary archetype of the pioneer. But other readers, a little more familiar with the ways of authors, find something ambiguous in Whitman's portrait of himself. When he talks too much about loving every created person, they feel that he is indiscriminate in his affections, and that it is only a step from loving to hating everyone. When he talks too much about comradeship, they suspect him—not without reason—of being self-centered and lonely. When he celebrates the life of trappers and woodsmen or cries, "O pioneers!" they read his biography and are not surprised to learn that he was chiefly a stroller through city streets. And if they come to value his work far, far above that of the other nineteenth-century American poets, it is because of the poems in which he did not boast or posture, but spoke with marvelous candor about himself and his immediate world.

To find those poems in the mass of his work is like wandering without a guidebook from room to room of a French provincial museum and searching for pictures to admire. After looking at scores of stiff portraits and dozens of landscapes rightly rejected (or hung, it doesn't matter) by the French Academy, one suddenly finds a Corot, a Courbet with its clean lines, or a fifteenth-century Virgin with the colors still as tender as the day they were painted. Whitman's best poems— and most of them are early poems—have that permanent quality of being freshly painted, of not being dulled by the varnish of the years. Reading them almost a century after their publication, one feels the same shock and wonder and delight that Emerson felt when opening his presentation copy of the first edition. They carry us into a new world that Whitman discovered as if this very morning, after it had been created overnight. "Why, who makes much of a miracle?" the poet keeps exclaiming. "As to me I know of nothing else but miracles."

There is no other word but miracle to describe what happened to Whitman at the age of thirty-six. The local politician and printer, the hack writer who had trouble selling his pieces, the editor who couldn't keep a job, quite suddenly became a world poet. No long apprenticeship; no process of growth that we can trace from year to year in his published work; not even much early promise: the poet materializes like a shape from the depths. In 1848, when we almost lose sight of him, Whitman is an editorial writer on salary, repeating day after day the opinions held in common by the younger Jacksonian Democrats, praising the people and attacking the corporations (but always within reasonable limits); stroking the American eagle's feathers and pulling the lion's tail. Hardly a word he publishes gives the impression that only Whitman could have written it. In 1855 he reveals a new character that seems to be his own creation. He writes and prefaces and helps to print and distributes and, for good measure, anonymously reviews a first book of poems not only different from any others known at the time but also different from everything the poet himself had written in former years (and only faintly foreshadowed by three of his experiments in free verse that the New York *Tribune* had printed in 1850 because it liked their political sentiments). It is a short book, this first edition of *Leaves of Grass*; it contains only twelve poems, including the "Song of Myself"; but they summarize or suggest all his later achievements; and for other poets they are better than those achievements, because in his first book Whitman was a great explorer, whereas he later became a methodical exploiter and at worst an expounder by rote of his own discoveries.

At some point during the seven "lost years" Whitman had begun to utilize resources deep in himself that might have remained buried. He had mastered what Emerson calls "the secret which every intellectual man quickly learns"—but how few make use of it! —"that beyond the energy of his possessed and conscious intellect he is capable of a new energy (as of an intellect doubled on itself), by abandonment to the nature of things; that beside his privacy of power as an individual man, there is a great public power on which he can draw, by unlocking, at all risks, his human doors, and suffering the ethereal tides to roll and circulate through him; then he is caught up into the life of the Universe, his speech is thunder, his thought is law, and his words are universally intelligible as the plants and animals." Whitman himself found other words to describe what seems to have been essentially the same phenomenon. Long afterwards he told one of his disciples, Dr. Maurice Bucke: " 'Leaves of Grass' was there, though unformed, all the time, in whatever answers as the laboratory of the mind. . . . The *Democratic Review* essays and tales [those he published before 1848] came from the surface of the mind and had no connection with what lay below—a great deal of which, indeed, was below consciousness. At last the time came when the concealed growth had to come to light, and the first edition of 'Leaves of Grass' was published."

Whitman in those remarks was simplifying a phenomenon by which, it would seem, he continued to be puzzled and amazed till the end. The best efforts of his biographers will never fully explain it; and a critic can only point to certain events, or probable events, that must have contributed to his sudden discovery of his own resources. His trip to New Orleans in 1848 was certainly one of them. It lasted for only four months (and not for years, as Whitman later implied), but it was his first real glimpse of the American continent, and it gave him a stock of remembered sights and sounds and emotions over which his imagination would play for the rest of his life.

A second event was connected with his interest in the pseudoscience of phrenology. The originators of this doctrine believed that one's character is determined by the development of separate faculties (of which there were twenty-six according to Gall, thirty-five according to Spurzheim and forty-three according to the Fowler brothers in New York); that each of these faculties is localized in a definite portion of the brain;

and that the strength or weakness of each faculty can be read in the contours of the skull. Whitman had the bumps on his head charted by L. N. Fowler in July 1849, a year after his return from the South. In these phrenological readings of character, each of the faculties was rated on a numerical scale running from one to seven or eight. Five was good; six was the most desirable figure; seven and eight indicated that the quality was dangerously overdeveloped. Among the ratings that Whitman received for his mental faculties (and note their curious names, which reappeared in his poems) were Amativeness 6, Adhesiveness 6, Philoprogenitiveness 6, Inhabitiveness 6, Alimentiveness 6, Cautiousness 6, Self-esteem 6 to 7, Benevolence 6 to 7, Sublimity 6 to 7, Ideality 5 to 6, Individuality 6, and Intuitiveness 6. It was, on the whole, a highly flattering report, and Whitman needed flattery in those days, for he hadn't made a success of his new daily, the Brooklyn *Freeman*, and there was a question whether he could find another good newspaper job. Apparently the phrenological reading gave him some of the courage he needed to follow an untried course. Seven years later he had Fowler's chart of his skull reproduced in the second or 1856 edition of *Leaves of Grass*.

Another event that inspired him was the reading of Emerson's essays. Later Whitman tried to hide this indebtedness, asserting several times that he had seen nothing of Emerson's until after his own first edition had been published. But aside from the Emersonian ideas in the twelve early poems (especially the "Song of Myself") there is, as evidence in the case, Whitman's prose introduction to the first edition, which is written in a style that suggests Emerson's, with his characteristic rhythms, figures of speech, and turns of phrase. As for the ideas Whitman expressed in that style, they are largely developments of what Emerson had said in "The Poet" (first of the *Essays: Second Series*, published in 1844), combined with other notions from Emerson's "Compensation." In "The Poet" Emerson had said:

> I look in vain for the poet whom I describe. . . . We have yet had no genius in America, with tyrannous eye, which knew the value of our incomparable materials, and saw, in the barbarism and materialism of the times, another carnival of the same gods whose pictures he so much admires in Homer; then

in the Middle Ages; then in Calvinism. . . . Our log-rolling, our stumps and their politics, our fisheries, our Negroes and Indians, our boasts and our repudiations, the wrath of rogues and the pusillanimity of honest men, the northern trade, the southern planting, the western clearing, Oregon and Texas, are yet unsung. Yet America is a poem in our eyes; its ample geography dazzles the imagination, and it will not wait long for meters.

. . . Doubt not, O poet, but persist. Say "It is in me, and shall out." Stand there, balked and dumb, stuttering and stammering, hissed and hooted, stand and strive, until at last rage draws out of thee that *dream*-power which every night shows thee is thine own; a power transcending all limit and privacy, and by virtue of which a man is the conductor of the whole river of electricity.

Whitman, it is clear today, determined to be the poet whom Emerson pictured; he determined to be the genius in America who recognized the value of our incomparable materials, the Northern trade, the Southern planting, and the Western clearing. "The United States themselves are the greatest poem," he wrote, he echoed, in his 1855 introduction, conceived as if in answer to Emerson's summons. He abandoned himself to the nature of things. At first balked and dumb, then later hissed and hooted, he stood there until he had drawn from himself the power he felt in his dreams.

There was, however, still another event that seems to have given Whitman a new conception of his mission as a poet: it was his reading of two novels by George Sand, *The Countess of Rudolstadt* and *The Journeyman Joiner*. Both books were written during their author's socialistic period, before the revolution of 1848, and both were translated from the French by one of the New England Transcendentalists. *The Countess of Rudolstadt* was the sequel to *Consuelo*, which Whitman had described as "the noblest work left by George Sand—the noblest in many respects, on its own field, in all literature." Apparently he gave *Consuelo* and its sequel to his mother when they first appeared in this country, in 1847; and after her death he kept the tattered volumes on his bedside table. It was in the epilogue to *The Countess of Rudolstadt* that Whitman discovered the figure of a wandering musician who might have been taken for a Bohemian peasant except for his fine white hands;

who was not only a violinist but a bard and a prophet, expounding the new religion of Humanity; and who, falling into a trance, recited "the most magnificent poem that can be conceived," before traveling onward along the open road. *The Journeyman Joiner* was also listed by Whitman among his favorite books. It is the story—to quote from Esther Shephard, who wrote an interpretation of Whitman based on his debt to the two novels—"of a beautiful, Christlike young carpenter, a proletary philosopher, who dresses in a mechanic's costume but is scrupulously neat and clean. He works at carpentering with his father, but patiently takes time off whenever he wants to in order to read, or give advice on art, or share a friend's affection."

There is no doubt that both books helped to fix the direction of Whitman's thinking. They summarized the revolutionary current of ideas that prevailed in Europe before 1848, and his early poems would be part of that current. But the principal effect of the two novels was on Whitman's picture of himself. After reading them he slowly formed the project of becoming a wandering bard and prophet, like the musician in the epilogue to *The Countess of Rudolstadt*. He no longer planned to get ahead in the world by the means open to other young journalists: no more earning, saving, calculating, outshining. He stopped writing for the magazines and, according to his brother George, he refused some editorial positions that were offered him; instead he worked as a carpenter with his father, like the hero of *The Journeyman Joiner*.

About this time there is an apparent change or mutation in his personality. Whitman as a young editor had dressed correctly, even fastidiously; had trimmed his beard, had carried a light cane, had been rather retiring in his manners, had been on good but not at all intimate terms with his neighbors, and, whenever possible, had kept away from their children. Now suddenly he begins dressing like a Brooklyn mechanic, with his shirt open to reveal a red-flannel undershirt and part of a hairy chest, and with a big felt hat worn loosely over his tousled hair. He lets his beard grow shaggy, he makes his voice more assured, and, in his wanderings about the docks and ferries, he greets his friends with bear hugs and sometimes a kiss of comradeship. It is as if he has undertaken a double task: before creating his poems he has to create the hypothetical author of the poems. And the author bears a new name: not *Walter* Whitman, as he was always known to his family and till then had been called by his newspaper associates, but rather *Walt* Whitman,

> . . . *a kosmos, of Manhattan the son,*
> *Turbulent, fleshy, sensual, eating, drinking and breeding.*

The world is his stage and Whitman has assumed a role that he will continue to play for the rest of his life. Reading his letters we can sometimes see him as in a dressing room, arranging his features to make the role convincing. In 1868, for example, he sent his London publisher a long series of directions about how his portrait should be engraved from a favorite photograph (he was always having his picture taken). "If a faithful presentation of that photograph can be given," he said, "it will satisfy me well—of course it should be reproduced with all its shaggy, dappled, rough-skinned character, and not attempted to be smoothed and prettified . . . let the costume be kept very simple and broad, and rather kept down too, little as there is of it—preserve the effect of the sweeping lines making all that fine free angle below the chin. . . . It is perhaps worth your taking special pains about, both to achieve a successful picture and likeness, something characteristic, and as certain to be a marked help to your edition of the book." There is more in the same vein, and it makes us feel that Whitman was like an actor-manager, first having his portrait painted in costume, then hanging it in the lobby to sell more tickets.

He had more than a dash of the charlatanism that, according to Baudelaire, adds a spice to genius. But he had also his own sort of honesty, and he tried to live his part as well as acting it. The new character he assumed was more, far more, than a pose adopted to mislead the public. Partly it was a side of his nature that had always existed, but one that had been suppressed by social conventions, by life with a big family of brothers and sisters, and by the struggle to earn a living. Partly it represented a real change after 1850: the shy and self-centered young man was turning outwards, was trying to people his loneliness with living comrades. Partly it was an attempt to compensate for the absence in himself of qualities he admired in others; for Whitman had already revealed himself as anything but rough, virile, athletic, savage, or luxuriant, to quote a few of what were now his favorite adjectives. Partly his new personality was an ideal picture of himself that he tried to achieve in the flesh and came in time to approximate. You might call it a mask or, as Jung would say, a *persona* that soon had a life of its own, developing and changing with the years and almost superseding his other nature. At the end one could hardly say that a "real" Whitman existed beneath the public figure; the man had become confused with his myth.

We might find it easier to picture the complexities of his character if we imagined that there were at least three Whitmans existing as separate persons. There was Whitman I, the printer and small politician and editor, always described by his associates as indolent, timid (except when making public speeches), awkward, and rather conventional in his manners. He disappeared from public sight after 1850, yet he survived for thirty years or more in his intimate relations with his family. Then there was Whitman II, the *persona*, who characterized himself as "one of the roughs, large, proud, affectionate, eating, drinking and breeding, his costume manly and free, his face sunburnt and bearded, his posture strong and erect, his voice bringing hope and prophecy to the generous races of young and old." This second Whitman, ripening with age—and becoming much more discreet after he moved to Washington and went to work for the government—at last merged blandly into the figure of the Good Gray Poet. He wrote poems, too, as part of his role, but most of them were windy and uninspired.

The real poet was still another person; let us call him Whitman III. He never appeared in public life; he was hardly more than a voice from the depths of the subconscious; but the voice was new, candid, powerful; and it spoke in different words not only from Whitman the young editor but also from Whitman the gray bard of Democracy. Whitman III was boastful but often tender and secret where Whitman II was bluff and lusty. He was feminine and maternal rather than physically adventurous; but at the same time he was a revolutionist by instinct where Whitman I was liberal and Whitman II merely sententious. He appeared from nowhere to write the "Song of Myself" and the other poems published in 1855. He had little to say after 1860 and fell silent forever in 1874, whereas the *persona* lived after him till 1892; yet during his brief career he wrote—or dictated to the other Whitmans—all the poetry that gave *Leaves of Grass* its position in world literature.

But what explains the mystery of the poet's birth? There was an apparently quite ordinary fellow named Walter Whitman who wrote editorials and book reviews and moral doggerel; then there was an extraordinary showman named Walt Whitman who peddled his personality as if it were a patent medicine; but there was also for six years, and at intervals thereafter, a poet of genius known by the same name. How did he come to exist? Was it merely because Whitman the editor visited New Orleans, had a phrenological reading, was inspired by Emerson's doctrine of the representative individual, and tried to make himself over into a character by George Sand? Is there any other cause for what we must still regard as the Whitman miracle?

The only evidence that bears on this question consists of Whitman's early notebooks and of the poems themselves, which are of course a less trustworthy guide. Still, they return so often to one theme that its importance in his life seems fixed beyond dispute. Whitman had apparently been slow to develop emotionally as well as intellectually. The poems suggest that, at some moment during the seven shadowy years, he had his first fully satisfying sexual experience. It may have been as early as his trip to New Orleans in 1848, to judge from what he says in a frequently quoted poem, "Once I Pass'd through a Populous City," which, incidentally, has more biographical value in the early draft discovered by Emory Holloway than it has in the altered and expurgated version that Whitman published. Or the Louisiana episode, if real, may have been merely an introduction to his new life, and the decisive experience may have come later, during his carpenter years in Brooklyn.*

---

* It may also have come earlier, in 1847, the year when he started the first of the private notebooks preserved in the Library of Congress. The notebook hints at a change or revelation in his

Whenever it occurred, the experience was so intense that it became an almost religious ecstasy, a moment of vision that wholly transformed his world. Whitman describes such a moment in the marvelous fifth section of the "Song of Myself":

> *Swiftly arose and spread around me the peace and*
> *knowledge that pass all the argument of the earth,*
> *And I know that the hand of God is the promise of my*
> *own,*
> *And I know that the spirit of God is the brother of my*
> *own,*
> *And that all the men ever born are also my brothers,*
> *and the women my sisters and lovers,*
> *And that a kelson of the creation is love,*
> *And limitless are leaves stiff or drooping in the fields,*
> *And brown ants in the little wells beneath them,*
> *And mossy scabs of the worm fence, heap'd stones, elder,*
> *mullein and poke-weed.*

After this experience Whitman had to revise not only his general and philosophical picture of the world but also his private picture of himself. "I am not what you supposed," he would say in one of his 1860 poems, "but far different." The discovery of his sexual direction must have been a shock to him at first; but he soon determined to accept himself with all his vices and "smutch'd deeds," just as he accepted everything in the universe. He wrote: "I am myself just as much evil as good, and my nation is—and I say there is in fact no evil." All his nature being good, in the larger view, he felt that all of it should be voiced in the poems he was planning to write.

At first his revelations concerning one side of his nature were made obliquely, in language that could be easily under-

---

life. There may be a reference to this change in the fine but puzzling poem that is printed as the eleventh of the fifty-two chants in "Song of Myself." It begins:

> *Twenty-eight young men bathe by the shore,*
> *Twenty-eight young men and all so friendly;*
> *Twenty-eight years of womanly life and all so lonesome.*

Whitman was twenty-eight years old in 1847. Considering that the poem was included in "Song of Myself," one feels that he may have identified himself with the young woman, "handsome and richly drest," who watched the bathers lovingly from her hiding place "aft the blinds of the window."

stood only by others of his own type. By 1860, however, when he was preparing the third edition of his poems, the impulse to confess himself had become so strong that he was no longer willing to speak by indirection. "Come," he said, "I am determin'd to unbare this broad breast of mine, I have long enough stifled and choked." And in the first of his "Calamus" poems, written for that edition, he proclaimed his resolve "to sing no songs today but those of manly attachment":

> *I proceed for all who are or have been young men,*
> *To tell the secret of my nights and days,*
> *To celebrate the need of comrades.*

There has been a long argument about the meaning of the "Calamus" poems, but it is or should be clear enough from the title under which they were published. Whitman is sometimes vague and hard to follow in his metaphysical symbols, but his sexual symbols are as simply conceived as an African statue of Potency or Fertility. The calamus root is one of those symbols, even though Whitman disguised the fact when writing to William Michael Rossetti, his English editor, who had asked him for an explanation. " 'Calamus' is a common word here," Whitman replied, "it is a very large and aromatic grass, or root, spears three feet high—often called 'sweet flag'—grows all over the Northern and Middle States—(see Webster's Large Dictionary—Calamus—definition 2). The recherché or ethereal sense, as used in my book, probably arises from it, Calamus presenting the biggest and hardiest spears of grass, and from its fresh, aromatic, pungent bouquet." But if Rossetti had referred to Section 24 of the "Song of Myself," he would have discovered what the poet meant. In that section Whitman exults in his own body and describes the various parts of it in metaphors drawn from the animal and vegetable worlds. The calamus plays its proper part in the description:

> *Root of wash'd sweet flag! timorous pond snipe! nest of*
> *guarded duplicate eggs! it shall be you!*

The sweet flag or calamus root, the "growth by the margin of pond-waters," was simply Whitman's token or symbol of the male sexual organ. "This," he said in a poem, "O this shall henceforth be the token of comrades, this calamus-root shall."

The poems under this general title were poems of homosexual love, in its physical aspects and with its metaphysical lessons. They were "blades" or "spears" or "leaves" of the calamus, to use another of Whitman's favorite symbols; and, as he said in his letter to Rossetti, they were bigger and hardier than all the other leaves of grass.

Whitman during his early career as a poet was rash and prudent simultaneously. He insisted on making a full confession, but at the same time he hoped the confession would be misunderstood. "Aspirations. Keep the secret—keep it close," he wrote in one of his notebooks. He changed the gender of his pronouns (as notably in his revision of "Once I Pass'd through a Populous City") and invented a sort of common gender for nouns by adding "or woman" almost every time he used the word "man." Before printing the "Calamus" poems, he performed the same sort of operation on a larger scale, in accordance with a direction to himself that he jotted down in another notebook: "Theory of a Cluster of Poems the same *to the passion of Woman-Love* [the italics are his own] as the *Calamus-Leaves* are to adhesiveness, manly love." This cluster when written and assembled became the "Children of Adam" poems; most of them are cold, selfish, forced and therefore shocking to normal readers, where the "Calamus-Leaves" are tender, honest and have their own sort of dignity. "There is something in my nature *furtive* like an old hen!" Whitman said much later to his disciple Edward Carpenter; and he added, "I think there are truths which it is necessary to envelop or wrap up." During his old age in Camden, it seemed on one occasion that too much of the truth might be laid bare. His English biographer John Addington Symonds wrote him in some perplexity about the "Calamus" poems, by which Symonds confessed that he had been led astray in his youth; now he wanted to know their real meaning. Whitman seems to have conferred with his friends; then he sent Symonds a letter of which only two passages have so far been published:

> About the questions on Calamus etc., they quite daze me. Leaves of Grass is only rightly to be construed by and within its own atmosphere and essential character—all its pages and

pieces so coming strictly under. That the Calamus part has ever allowed the possibility of such construction as mentioned is terrible. I am fain to hope that the pages themselves are not to be even mentioned for such gratuitous and quite at the time undreamed and unwished possibility of morbid inference— which are disavowed by me and seem damnable.

. . . My life, young manhood, mid-age, times South, etc., have been jolly bodily, and doubtless open to criticism. Though unmarried I have had six children—two are dead—one living Southern grandchild, fine boy, writes to me occasionally—circumstances (connected with their fortune and benefit) have separated me from intimate relations.

No certain trace of the six illegitimate children has ever been found (although there was a bit player in the silent movies who wore a beard like Whitman's and claimed to be his son). No letters from or about the children or their mothers were among the accumulation of papers that Whitman left at his death. He repeated the story on other occasions, but none of his oldest friends accepted it. Some of them said in a kindly way that Whitman was old and ill when he wrote the letter to Symonds, and probably believed his own fabrication, although they couldn't be sure. If he did come to believe that he had fathered six children, then the Whitman legend invented for the public had displaced and destroyed in his own mind the picture of the Whitman who lived.

After the concealments, evasions, and apologies of the poet himself and most of his critics, it is time to restore this living figure, so far as we can find him in the records. He was not "emotionally versatile" in the sense in which some of his recent biographers have used the phrase. They imply that he could turn his affections from one sex to the other, but the evidence fails to show that Whitman was ever sexually attracted by women. There was no romance in his life with a highborn Creole lady; nor was there any other romance (except with young men like Peter Doyle, the Washington horsecar conductor) that careful students have been able to trace. He was not "unconsciously" or "half-consciously" homosexual; after 1855, and perhaps as early as 1847, he was completely aware of his own nature. His abnormality was not an "unhealthy mood" that passed after 1860; it continued for the rest of his active life. And it was never something that could be overlooked by his critics as having a merely private or biographical interest; on the contrary, it was part of the impulse that set him to writing poetry; it served as theme for a whole section of *Leaves of Grass,* besides being a minor theme in other sections; and it became curiously interwoven with Whitman's notions about a future democracy, which would have to be based, he said, on manly comradeship or adhesiveness.

The meaning he attached to this last word is one of the clues to his thinking. "Adhesiveness" was a cant term of the phrenologists, who used it to denote the faculty for friendship, just as "amativeness" denoted, in their language, the faculty for loving the opposite sex, and "philoprogenitiveness" the faculty for loving one's children. But Whitman, after submitting himself to a phrenological reading and being given the highest rating for all three qualities, soon began to use the word "adhesiveness" in a sense that the phrenologists had not intended. Once he defined it for a Washington paper by which he was being interviewed: it was, so he said, "a personal attachment between men that is stronger than ordinary friendship. The 'Calamus' poems celebrate it." That sounds innocent enough, but some of his private notebooks are more specific, and more tortured. In one of them he wrote (1870):

> Depress the adhesive nature
> It is in excess—making life a torment
> All this diseased, feverish disproportionate adhesiveness

Feverish and disproportionate, it set him roving through the streets in search of young men, preferably rough and bearded, who might be interested in his type of affection. There is another notebook, preserved in the Library of Congress,* which hints at some of his adventures. One page of it, reproduced by Esther Shephard in her book, *Walt Whitman's Pose,* is a list of names, each followed by a few identifying remarks for Whitman's records. The names, with one exception, are those of the men whom Whitman accosted in New York omnibuses or beer cellars or on the Brooklyn ferry during four days of July 1862. The page reads:

---

* This notebook was later stolen, with some other Whitman papers, but the Library has a photocopy.

Henry Kelly, Madison avenue, about 24, born in Lawrence, Mass. father Irish, mother English, has worked about the Lawrence factories—had a brother and sister in Pemberton Mill when it fell.—has travel'd some time south and west with Dan Rice's show—florid face—manner fresh and direct—(I notice a few gray hairs)—seems to be inclined to join the army —rode all the way to Wall st. and back to Howard (July 10— talk about the mishaps &c of a showman's life south & north).

Morse

Charles Winthrop x x x x (45 5th av) July, '62—Yankee, says he has a farm and is workg to get money for it &c

James L. Metcalf is appointed in the 5th precinct. July 7th '62

Frank Sweeney, (July 8th, '62) 5th av. brown face, large features, black moustache (is the one I told the whole story to, about Ellen Eyre)—talks very little

— — — Pell, young man, American, introduced by Chas. Kingsley, at 6th st. lager beer house, night July 8th '62

Isaac Bennet, deck hand, ferry, square built young fellow, black moustache & imperial—July 10th, '62

It would seem from Whitman's notebook and letters that he was particularly attracted by young men in the transportation industry: by ferry deckhands, Broadway omnibus drivers, horsecar conductors and railway brakemen or firemen. It would also seem—although the evidence here is inconclusive— that from 1855 until his removal to Washington at the end of 1862 he formed part of a homosexual group that met in Pfaff's and other Broadway lager-beer cellars, while it remained distinct from the literary bohemians who also met in Pfaff's. Whitman formed part of the second group, too, but he was less interested in the writers than in those whom he called, in italics, "*the boys.*" In Washington he formed part of no group except that of his own literary admirers. Still, when he wrote to his "dear comrades" in New York, he kept assuring them that he was "no backslider."—"Tell Fred his letter was received," he said in 1863. "I appreciate it, received real pleasure from it—'twas a true friend's letter, characteristic, full of vivacity, off-hand, and below all a thorough base of genuine remembrance and good will—was not wanting in the *sentimental* either (so I take back all about the *apostate*, do you understand me, Freddy, my dear?)."

Reading his intimate letters, with the allusions so easy to

interpret, and the still more intimate diaries, one feels toward Whitman almost as Proust's narrator felt toward the Baron de Charlus, when he saw him crossing a courtyard where the Baron thought he was unobserved. "I could not help thinking how angry M. de Charlus would have been," the narrator says, "could he have known that he was being watched; for what was suggested to me by the sight of this man who was so insistent, who prided himself so upon his virility, to whom all other men seemed odiously effeminate, what he made me suddenly think of, so far he momentarily assumed her features, expression, smile, was a woman." And there is more that applies to Whitman in that first chapter of *Cities of the Plain* (in the second volume of the four-volume edition of *Remembrance of Things Past*). The narrator observes the Baron's meeting with Jupien the tailor, who is another of the same type; and this leads him into a whole series of reflections on the inhabitants of Sodom. He says, in the Scott Moncrieff translation:

> I now understand how, earlier in the day, when I had seen him coming away from Mme. de Villeparisis's, I had managed to arrive at the conclusion that M. de Charlus looked like a woman: he was one! He belonged to that race of beings, less paradoxical than they appear, whose ideal is manly simply because their temperament is feminine and who in their life resemble in appearance only the rest of men; there where each of us carries, inscribed on those eyes through which he beholds everything in the universe, a human outline engraved on the surface of the pupil, for them it is not that of a nymph but of a youth. Race upon which a curse weighs and which must live amid falsehood and perjury, because it knows the world to regard as punishable and scandalous, as an inadmissible thing, its desire, that which constitutes for every human creature the greatest happiness in life; which must deny its God, since even Christians, when at the bar of justice they appear and are arraigned, must before Christ and in His name defend themselves, as from a calumny, from the charge of what to them is life itself.

Whitman too, in his later years, was forced to defend himself, as from a calumny, from the charge of what to him was life itself. But there is another phrase that casts an even clearer light on his character: "Their ideal is manly simply because their temperament is feminine." Here in a few words Proust has stated the contradiction that many readers have felt in Whitman's work: it speaks always of daring, vigor, sweep, turbulence, all the qualities that Whitman regarded as peculiarly masculine; it praises America as the home of "the roughs and beards and space and ruggedness and nonchalance that the soul loves"; it calls on us to desert all settled things and to follow the open road wherever it leads; it sings the joy of the soldier, "To see men fall and die and not complain! To taste the savage taste of blood!"—yet it does all this in a style that is loose, even limp, ecstatic in a passive way, and lacking in hard contours; and it is written by a man who stayed close to home, who traveled by preference in the Broadway omnibus or the Navy Yard horsecar to the end of the line and back, and who, though able-bodied, served through the Civil War in the Washington hospitals visiting the wounded, enveloping them with his maternal solicitude, and boasting at the end that "Many a soldier's kiss dwells on these bearded lips." His motto was not, "I strive, I build," but rather, in his own words, "I suffer'd, I was there." When he praised male vigor and ruggedness he was like a devoted wife or like a lover celebrating the charms of his mistress—not as qualities he possessed in himself, but as those he sexually admired.

From the clinical point of view and without reference to moral or esthetic problems, Whitman's life after 1855 might be presented as the case history of a successful readjustment. He wrote his first great poems at a time when he seemed on the edge of becoming a sick personality. There are various technical names like narcissism, autoeroticism, and extreme introversion that apply to the condition from which he suffered. His early poems are those of a man engaged in a passionate love affair with his own person. "I have heard what the talkers were talking," he says; ". . . while they discuss I am silent, and go bathe and admire myself." I doubt whether any other poet has expressed self-love with so much ardor. "If I worship one thing more than another," he says, also in the "Song of

Myself," "it shall be the spread of my own body, or any part of it. . . . I dote on myself, there is that lot of me and all so luscious."

At the time he wrote those lines and for some years afterwards, he was in danger, as the psychologists would say, "of losing contact with reality." He formed impossible projects for himself. At one time he determined to become what he called a "wander speaker"—"perhaps launching at the President, leading persons, Congressmen, or Judges of the Supreme Court," he said in his notebook for 1857; ". . . the greatest champion America ever could know, yet holding no office or emolument whatever,—but first in the esteem of men and women." Having worked as a carpenter with his father, like Jesus, he was planning to found a new religion. It was an age of new religions in America, and Whitman sometimes regarded himself as a prophet rather than a poet, with *Leaves of Grass* as his testament, like the Book of Mormon. It should eventually consist, he believed, of 365 chants or chapters, one for each day in the year. There is one of his notes that reads, "The Great Construction of the New Bible. Not to be diverted from the principal object—the main life work—the three hundred and sixty-five.—It ought to be ready in 1859." While revolving these projects in his mind, he was living not so much in America as in his dreams of spiritual power.

He was saved from falling into delusions by a sort of proletarian toughness and practicality; and even more by the fact that his genius was finding a path for itself. His early poems might be regarded—still from the clinical standpoint—as a first step in his cure. Singing as he did "of physiology from top to toe" and hinting at his vices and "smutch'd deeds," he was making a public confession that left him with the feeling of having been absolved from guilt. As for Whitman's discovery of his homosexuality, it might be said to have had a mixed effect on him (if we continue to discuss his case from the medical point of view). Partly it aggravated his condition because it separated him from normal society. Partly it was another step in his recovery, because it made him less self-centered and gave his affections some other object than himself.

His sexuality was at first astonishingly generalized, so that he could describe a dip in the surf as if it were a passionate love affair, "The souse upon me of my lover the sea, as I lie willing and naked." He said of himself in writing an anonymous review of the first edition of *Leaves of Grass*, "If health were not his distinguishing attribute, this poet would be the very harlot of persons. Right and left he flings his arms, drawing men and women with undeniable love to his close embrace, loving the clasp of their hands, the touch of their necks and breasts, and the sound of their voice. All else seems to burn up under his fierce affection for persons." In reality his affection was *not* for persons; it was rather for anonymous handclasps, anonymous necks and breasts, anonymous voices—integers, flesh, crowds brushing against him, figures in crowds, even the winds and the waters; anything but individuals. Again he wrote of himself:

> *I am he that aches with amorous love;*
> *Does the earth gravitate? does not all matter, aching,*
> *   attract all matter?*
> *So the body of me to all I meet or know.*

"What can be more mechanical?" D. H. Lawrence said in passing judgment on those lines, printed by Whitman as a complete poem. "The difference between life and matter," Lawrence continued, "is that life, living things, living creatures, have the instinct of turning right away from *some* matter, and of blissfully ignoring the bulk of most matter, and of turning towards only some certain bits of specially selected matter. . . . No, Walt, you give yourself away. Matter *does* gravitate, helplessly. But men are tricky-tricksy, and they shy all sorts of ways. Matter gravitates because it *is* helpless and mechanical. And if you gravitate the same, if the body of you gravitates to all you meet or know, why, something must have gone seriously wrong with you." Something *had* gone seriously wrong with Whitman in the years after 1855. Some of his poems—especially those in the "Children of Adam" group—have the impersonal and self-generated frenzy of a steam engine in rut. Very soon, however, he found a personal object for his affection.

The only evidence we have regarding Whitman's love affair consists of the poems he wrote in 1859 and 1860. They are not the sort of evidence that law courts would accept, since the poetic "I" is often or always a fictitious character. Still, there is such an immediacy of feeling in several poems of the two years that it is reasonable to interpret them as based on his own experience. Whitman, if the poems speak truly, fell in love with a young man whose name we shall probably never know. He was happy for a time—so happy that he asked to be remembered by "recorders ages hence" as "the tenderest lover . . . Who was not proud of his songs, but of the measureless ocean of love within him, and freely pour'd it forth"; but soon the lovers were separated, either by death or by a quarrel. Whitman fell into the state of dejection that is recorded in "Out of the Cradle Endlessly Rocking" and a few of the "Calamus" poems. He thought of his career as at an end. In another poem written about the same time, "As I Ebb'd with the Ocean of Life," he described himself and his work as "loose windrows," like the rubbish left by the tide, and he apostrophized the unknown God:

> *You up there walking or sitting,*
> *Whoever you are, we too lie in drifts at your feet.*

Yet even at this moment when he seems to have contemplated suicide, he was closer to mental health than he had been a few years before. He had admitted the real existence of other individuals, instead of merely loving the crowd; and he was facing the sorrows imposed on him by living men.

I am not trying to write a biographical sketch of Whitman, but merely to mention some of the events that marked or hastened his readjustment. The Civil War was the greatest of those events, in the poet's life as it was in American history. It put an end to his period of dejection and gave him a shared purpose to which he could devote himself. At first he wrote newspaper articles and a long poem, "Beat! Beat! Drums!" which he hoped would encourage others to enlist; then he heard that his brother George was wounded and, in December 1862, he paid a visit to the Army of the Potomac. He found when he reached the front that George had recovered; but it was just after the slaughter at Fredericksburg and the hospital tents were crowded with other wounded soldiers lying on the frozen ground. Whitman did the little he could for them; "I cannot leave them," he wrote in his diary. Instead of going back to New York he decided to stay in Washington as a hospital visitor. He said of himself in the best of his Civil War poems, "The Wound-Dresser":

> *Arous'd and angry, I'd thought to beat the alarum, and*
> *   urge relentless war,*
> *But soon my fingers fail'd me, my face droop'd and I*
> *   resign'd myself*
> *To sit by the wounded and soothe them, or silently*
> *watch the dead.*

Afterwards Whitman liked to imply that he had served among the soldiers during the whole war and that, besides nursing the wounded in Washington hospitals, he had been for long periods at the front. His actual war work was briefer—perhaps two years in all—and less official; it consisted of writing letters for the wounded, making them lemonade in summer, giving them newspapers and small sums of money collected from benevolent persons, and sitting for hours beside the dying. Perhaps his greatest service was simply to be *there*, with his look of large health, at a time when most of the wounded had no visitors and no feeling that their life or death mattered to others. Whitman tried consciously to give them the will to live; and he may have been right in thinking that he had kept scores or hundreds of men from giving up the fight. If they were beyond saving, their last moments were rendered a little less painful by the presence of the red-faced, gray-bearded stranger who looked like the spirit of Fatherhood, but spoke to them as tenderly as their mothers.

Whitman had found a useful and socially recognized expression for the impulses that set him apart from other men; and he found more than that in Washington during the war. At times he saw Lincoln almost daily as the President rode in a little procession from his summer lodgings to the White House, and they often exchanged bows and glances; so that Whitman felt there was a wordless sympathy between them. "I love the President personally," he wrote in his diary. He had never loved his father in that fashion and had always felt half-orphaned; but now he had found a spiritual father. That was a step in his readjustment; and so too was his friendship with the young horsecar conductor Peter Doyle, whom he met every day after work; for years they lived on terms of calm affection. It was as if, after the unhappy love affair hinted at in some of the "Calamus" poems, Whitman had entered into a sensible marriage.

"I give here a glimpse of him in Washington on a Navy Yard horse car, toward the close of the war, one summer day at sundown," John Burroughs says in *Birds and Poets*. "The car is crowded and suffocatingly hot, with many passengers on the rear platform, and among them a bearded, florid-faced man, elderly but agile, resting against the dash, by the side of the young conductor, and evidently his intimate friend. The man wears a broad-brim white hat," and is Whitman, of course, while the young conductor is probably Peter Doyle. As for Burroughs, the spectator, he describes the scene as if he were taking snapshots with a candid camera:

Among the jam inside the door, a young Englishwoman, of the working class, with two children, has had trouble all the way with the youngest, a strong, fat, fretful, bright babe of fourteen or fifteen months, who bids fair to worry the mother completely out, besides becoming a howling nuisance to everybody. As the car tugs around Capitol Hill the young one is more demoniac than ever, and the flushed and perspiring mother is just ready to burst into tears with weariness and vexation. The car stops at the top of the Hill to let off most of the rear platform passengers, and the white-hatted man reaches inside and gently but firmly disengaging the babe from its stifling place in the mother's arms, takes it in his own, and out in the air. The astonished and excited child, partly in fear, partly in satisfaction at the change, stops its screaming, and as the man adjusts it more securely to his breast, plants its chubby hands against him, and pushing off as far as it can, gives a good long look squarely in his face—then as if satisfied snuggles down with its head on his neck, and in less than a minute is sound and peacefully asleep without another whimper, utterly fagged out. A square or so more and the conductor, who has had an unusually hard and uninterrupted day's work, gets off for the first meal and relief since morning. And now the white-hatted man, holding the slumbering babe also, acts as conductor the rest of the distance, keeping his eye on the passengers inside, who have by this time thinned out greatly. He makes a very good conductor, too, pulling the bell to stop or go as needed, and seems to enjoy the occupation. The babe meanwhile rests its fat cheeks close on his neck and gray beard, one of his arms vigilantly surrounding it, while the other signals, from time to time, with the strap; and the flushed mother inside has a good half hour to breathe, and cool, and recover herself.

That is Whitman seen as Proust's narrator saw the Baron de Charlus crossing the courtyard and momentarily assuming the features, expression, and smile of a woman. It is, however, one of the last intimate glimpses we obtain; for another event of his Washington years had made Whitman much more cautious about revealing himself. In January 1865 he had been appointed to a clerkship in the Indian Bureau of the Department of the Interior, a sort of political sinecure. In June of that year the Secretary of the Interior, a professional Methodist named James Harlan, read a copy of *Leaves of Grass* that he found in Whitman's desk, and discharged his clerk as the author of an indecent book. Whitman's friends not only wrote letters and published a pamphlet in his defense, but found him another clerkship, in the Attorney General's office, which he was to hold for the next eight years. Thus, he did not suffer financially from the scandal and it helped in a way to bring his work before the public; but Whitman was frightened, as many other government clerks and administrators have been when they were discharged for their outside activities. After 1865 the prudent side of his nature was uppermost, and he no longer felt, or no longer indulged, his passion for public confession. He became more discreet in his dress, his actions, his language, and even the ideas expressed in his poems. He couldn't ever be a conventional bureaucrat, but nobody seemed to feel any more that he was out of place in a government office.

The stroke of paralysis that he suffered in January 1873 was the end of his active career. His "inexpressibly beloved" mother died four months later, and Whitman in his grief relapsed into a complication of diseases from which he never fully recovered, although he lived on for nineteen years. They were bitter years at first, when he was still hoping to regain his physical strength and his imaginative powers; but then he resigned himself to old age and indolence. He reread his favorite books, he rearranged his poems and wrote new ones on occasional themes; chiefly he occupied himself with the defense of his literary reputation. Camden, where he now lived, had a ferry like Brooklyn and he liked to ride back and forth on it.

As his strength declined he assumed a new role, that of the seated Buddha, serene and large in the midst of his infirmities.

When we consider the fate of other poets like Poe, Baudelaire, Nerval, and Hölderlin who tried to explore the subconscious and dreamed immoderate dreams, Whitman in his last years seems amazingly well adjusted. He was now conscious at all times of the social limitations on human conduct. "Be radical, be radical, be not too damned radical," he said to his young friend Horace Traubel. He was shrewd about people, a little sharp in his financial dealings—like an old Long Island farmer—and strong in his family ties; he spent a great deal of time and other people's money in designing a tomb for all the Whitmans. And he enjoyed a sort of success: he lived on a mean street, but in a house he owned; he had money in the bank; his rich admirers sent him barrels of oysters in season and baskets of champagne (he was fond of both); and although his work was still not officially recognized in his own country, he was famous in Europe and had his American disciples to compare him with "a greater than Socrates." Speaking for the last time, I hope, from the clinical point of view, one can say that Whitman in his age had effected a cure of himself and had moved from his private world into a stable relation with society. He is a reassuring, even an inspiring figure: good and gray, but not so much a poet as the effigy on a poet's tomb.

Whitman's philosophy is a subject of enormous complexity and relatively minor importance.* Although he left school at the age of eleven or twelve, he was all his life a great reader of books and newspapers, a great clipper-out of magazine articles. Newton Arvin, in a chapter of his fine *Whitman*, has traced many of the poet's ideas to their sources—a difficult undertak-

*   If I were writing this essay in 1970, the passage that follows is one that would be completely recast. In 1947 I did not realize that the ideas implied by "Song of Myself" are consistently mystical, in the proper sense of the word, and that they bear a strong resemblance to various Indian philosophies or cosmologies. For a later and, I hope, a more accurate statement of Whitman's philosophy, see my introduction to *Leaves of Grass: The First* (*1855*) *Edition*.

ing, involving such questions as whether he acquired the ideas at first, second, or third hand, and at what period of his life, and whether he understood them as the original author intended, and how he changed them for his own purposes. At the end of the long chapter one is left with a feeling of respect for Whitman's mass of information, but also with a diminished sense of his individuality. He seems not so much as independent thinker as a repository for all the notions, consistent or inconsistent, that might be held by a liberal mid-nineteenth-century American reader. He said in the "Song of Myself":

> *Do I contradict myself?*
> *Very well then I contradict myself,*
> *(I am large, I contain multitudes.)*

—And he *did* contain multitudes; he contained, for example, moods or notions taken from the Hebrew prophets and psalmists; from the Ossianic chants of James Macpherson; from the Comte de Volney (author of *The Ruins*); from our own Tom Paine and Sir Walter Scott; from Elias Hicks (the great Quaker schismatic), Frances Wright (the apostle of feminism), Emerson, Carlyle, George Sand, Goethe (of the autobiography), Darwin, Hegel (his most admired philosopher), and from almost all the other famous or forgotten men and women who helped to form the mind of the nineteenth century. On the other hand he contained them, not as the sky contains stars, by fixed laws, and not as a tree has roots; but rather as a river in flood contains driftwood or an attic contains the family relics.

He never went over the relics, discarding those of no value and arranging the others systematically. He was indolent, as he often said, and opposed on principle to any form of intellectual discipline. His work is full of separate statements and hints and intuitions, some of great value and all making it richer as poetry—which in dealing with Whitman should be our chief concern; but they are dangerous as philosophical guides because they point in all directions. Nationalism and internationalism; socialism, fascism (including its racial doctrines), and private enterprise; naturalism and idealism; the love of life and the blind hunger for death: all these quarreling tendencies, and others, can be illustrated by quotations from his poems. As a philosopher he lights our way sometimes in lightning flashes, but sometimes with a wayward glow, like a jack-o'-lantern that might lead us into a swamp.

Almost his only exercise in consecutive thinking was *Democratic Vistas*, published in 1871. Here he was working on a theme close to his heart: not democracy in general, but the dependence of a democracy like ours on its outstanding individuals, and the role that a national literature should play in forming such individuals. "All else in the contribution of a nation or age, through its politics, materials, heroic personalities, military eclat, &c., remains crude," he said, ". . . until vitalized by national, original archetypes in literature. They only put the nation in form, finally tell anything—prove, complete anything—perpetuate anything." In reality he is writing an essay on national myths or archetypes and the poet's role in creating them—his own role, in other words; and the essay contains as many fresh and usable insights as the best of Emerson's.

There is only a footnote in *Democratic Vistas* that mentions his central idea about the basis of democracy. To find that idea expressed at length, we have to turn back to the "Calamus" poems and, after the symbolical interpretations offered by a hundred critics, we have to read them with the notion that Whitman meant in them exactly what he said. In the "Calamus" cluster we find him acting as prophet and proselytizer for his doctrine of fervent manly comradeship or adhesiveness. He says in the fourth of the poems, "For You O Democracy":

> *I will plant companionship thick as trees along all the*
> *rivers of America, and along all the shores of the great*
> *lakes, and all over the prairies,*
> *I will make inseparable cities with their arms about each*
> *other's necks,*
>> *By the love of comrades,*
>> *By the manly love of comrades.*

He then boasts of his intention to travel westward, preaching adhesiveness as he goes:

> *A promise to California,*
> *Or inland to the great pastoral Plains, and on to Puget*
> *Sound and Oregon;*

Sojourning east a while longer, soon I travel toward you,
to remain, to teach robust American love.

At this point we begin to see that Whitman is trying to
identify, or at least confuse, homosexuality with Americanism.
The intention becomes clearer in another passage:

I believe the main purport of these States is to found a
superb friendship, exalté, previously unknown,
Because I perceive it waits, and has always been waiting,
latent in all men.

And this strange confusion at last develops into a definite
political program, perhaps the only one of its sort since Plato.
The program is most clearly expressed in an untitled poem, an
address to the states, published in the third or 1860 edition of
Leaves of Grass, less than a year before the Civil War:

There shall from me be a new friendship—It shall be
called after my name,
It shall circulate through The States, indifferent of place,
It shall twist and intertwist them through and around
each other—Compact shall they be, showing new
signs,
Affection shall solve every one of the problems of free-
dom,
Those who love each other shall be invincible,
They shall finally make America completely victorious,
in my name.

As the best means of preventing war between the states, he
then suggests manly affection in all the houses, "countless
linked hands," north and south, and comrade kissing comrade
at parting in the streets. . . . It has become the fashion among
Whitman critics to hold that this doctrine was changed in later
years, sublimated, socialized, cleansed, so to speak, of its sexual
elements and somehow carried to a more spiritual plane, so
that it could be used as the philosophical basis for an ideal
democracy. The history of this address to the states does not
bear out their contention. When the Civil War was fought in
spite of Whitman's suggested remedy, the poem disappeared
from the "Calamus" cluster, but not from the book. Shortened,
expurgated, and given a title, "Over the Carnage Rose
Prophetic a Voice," it was printed in the fourth or 1867 edition

as one of Whitman's war poems. It was no longer so explicitly homosexual or brashly self-assertive—it no longer announced that the new and superb friendship was to be "called after my name"; but it continued to prophesy that "The most dauntless and rude shall touch face to face lightly," and continued to inform the divided states that their hope was in loving comrades: "These shall tie you and band you stronger than hoops of iron."

Once seized upon, this notion of the close relation between homosexuality and democracy seems to have been retained as a central point in Whitman's thinking. He hadn't surrendered it in 1871, when he published *Democratic Vistas*. There it appears only in a footnote, as I said, but Whitman states the notion clearly: he tells us that manly friendship, "fond and loving, pure and sweet, strong and life-long, carried to degrees hitherto unknown," will be found to have "the deepest relations to general politics. I say democracy infers such loving comradeship," he goes on, "as its most inevitable twin or counterpart, without which it will be incomplete, in vain, and incapable of perpetuating itself." To this notion he returned once again, when he discussed the "Calamus" poems in the preface he wrote for the Centennial Edition of his works, published in 1876. "Important as they are in my purpose as emotional expressions for humanity," he said,

> . . . the special meaning of the "Calamus" cluster of "Leaves of Grass," (and more or less running through the book, and cropping out in "Drum-Taps,") mainly resides in its political significance. In my opinion, it is by a fervent, accepted development of comradeship, the beautiful and sane affection of man for man, latent in all the young fellows, north and south, east and west—it is by this, I say, and by what goes directly and indirectly along with it, that the United States of the future, (I cannot too often repeat,) are to be most effectually welded together, intercalated, anneal'd into a living union.

Here the tone is vaguer, loftier, and more persuasive than in the "Calamus" poems to which he refers, but the change is chiefly in language; the meaning is essentially the same. Whitman lived for sixteen years after publishing the Centennial Edition and became increasingly disturbed by mention of his past indiscretions, which he tried to envelop or wrap up in the mists of legend; yet there is no sign that he abandoned his notion about the basis of democracy. It is, as he tells us often, his central notion as a philosopher, and it is simply irrelevant to American life. Apart from any moral considerations, it does not correspond to the usual experiences or the normal aspirations of young fellows north and south, east and west. Ask them at the nearest bar and grill if they think that democracy infers a fond and loving comradeship among men as its inevitable twin or counterpart. I know that I am carrying the question outside of literature, but Whitman at this point was talking, as he said, about general politics and he was talking nonsense.

The picture of Whitman as a democratic sage and prophet, the healthy, sane, and purely native embodiment of his own poems, has been convenient to historians and flattering to the national spirit, but it will have to be abandoned. It has led in the past to illusions, apologies, and a red-faced unwillingness to admit that he often lied about himself. It has led to serious misconceptions of American literature and whole bookstacks full of third-rate critical and creative writing. It has led to the notion that the ideal American poet or novelist is a rough-hewn aboriginal creature tallying in his works—as Whitman would say—the geographical features of the country: high as its mountains, broad as its prairies, tangled as its swamps. But American writers of stature have rarely been lettered savages or extroverts flinging their arms right and left to embrace multitudes; they have been, for the most part, hurt and lonely men—as Whitman was hurt and lonely when he wrote his first great poems; and they have been more concerned in their works with depth than with breadth of emotion; more interested in achieving psychological truth and honest craftsmanship than in reproducing the sweep of the continent as seen from a train window. "Great are the myths," I might say to those friends, chiefly in academic circles, who still believe in the legendary Whitman, "but they shouldn't be confused with history. This rugged and masculine poet who embodied the aspirations of American democracy, this father image of yours, was a fictional or dramatic creation that belongs in the same category as Rip Van Winkle and Leatherstocking and Huckleberry Finn. When the living Whitman dressed and acted the part, it was as if J. Fenimore Cooper, Esq., of the big house in

Cooperstown, had gone about in buckskin breeches carrying a long rifle. That wouldn't have made him a deerslayer; nor did Whitman's red-flannel undershirt make him the philosopher of the democratic masses.

"He created and dressed and acted a part," I would say, "and always when acting he was a bad poet who wrote chamber-of-commerce speeches and cried, 'O pioneers!' but invoked the pioneers in flat images and awkward rhythms, without the grace that comes from intimate belief. What we have to rediscover is the Whitman who wasn't acting, who spoke from the depths of his nature and wrote the greatest poems of his time. We have to rescue him from the pundits and politicians and give his work back to poetry."

The statement has to be made that Whitman, in his poetry, gained something at first from discovering his own abnormal tendencies. Later he would pay a heavy price for them, when they involved him in ambiguities and falseness and flat poems like sheets of paper torn from the top of his mind. He would suffer in his literary character, besides what he lost in his character as a man; but at first the discovery was part of the stimulus that set him working. Some extraordinary challenge was needed before this second-rate Brooklyn journalist could begin to write poems as candid and fresh as if no other poet had spoken before him. He had to become conscious of his *difference* from other human beings before he could feel what he called "this terrible, irrepressible yearning . . . this never-satisfied appetite for sympathy, and this boundless offering of sympathy," which drove him to write *Leaves of Grass*. In his loneliness—for at first he seems to have met few others of his kind—he began to express a new sense of brotherhood, not with the capitalized People, but with all the crippled, diseased, abnormal, and even criminal population of a great city. Already in the "Song of Myself" he proclaimed his identity with the wounded slave, the cholera patient at his last gasp, and the convicted felon. "Not a mutineer walks handcuff'd to jail," he said, "but I am handcuff'd to him and walk by his side. . . . Not a youngster is taken for larceny but I go up too, and am tried and sentenced." A little later he developed the same theme in one of the most powerful of his shorter poems, "You Felons on Trial in Courts":

Inside these breast-bones I lie smutch'd and choked,
Beneath this face that appears so impassive hell's tides
  continually run,
Lusts and wickedness are acceptable to me,
I walk with delinquents with passionate love,
I feel I am of them—I belong to those convicts and prostitutes
  myself,
And henceforth I will not deny them—for how can I
  deny myself?

There is a period or phase in the lives of many great writers that might be described as their descent into the underworld. At some moment, perhaps very early, they are crippled or stricken by disease (how many epileptics and syphilitics!), or they are made conscious of their social or sexual inferiority, or they become involved in a scandal or go to prison—there are scores, hundreds of paths by which they may descend; but descend they do, until they see their world from beneath and until they feel, as Dostoevsky did in his youth when he was led to execution, a double sense, of their isolation first and then of their brotherhood or identity with all the outcast and diseased and rejected of the earth. Later they emerge into sunlight, but for a long time they walk the streets as if in disguise and continue to feel that they belong with the secret people of the caves—among whom they number, as time goes on, more and more of humanity.

It would be better, surely, if this sense of human brotherhood might come from above and not from below—not from wounds or vices or disfigurements, not from physical or spiritual clubfeet or humpbacks, but from an overflowing measure of health and wisdom; from fulfilled love and happy marriages; from the perception that human beings, even the best, are foolish and sinful and tragic in their common destiny. Sometimes the vision does come from above. There is Emerson cool on a hilltop, but in American literature there are not many others like him; most of the respectables are men whose visions lie behind them, as Whitman's vision lay when he was safely moored in Mickle Street, Camden, after a stormy life. Then he was part, if a minor part, of the social order and respectful of its standards; but his great poems were written when he stood apart from society with the sense, at times, of belonging to a confraternity of the damned. He said in the "Song of Myself":

> *Through me many long dumb voices,*
> *Voices of the interminable generations of prisoners and*
> *   slaves,*
> *Voices of the diseas'd and despairing and of thieves and*
> *   dwarfs,*
> *Voices of cycles of preparation and accretion,*
> *And of the threads that connect the stars, and of wombs*
> *   and of the father-stuff,*
> *And of the rights of them the others are down upon,*
> *Of the deform'd, trivial flat, foolish, despised,*
> *Fog in the air, beetles rolling balls of dung.*

Dates are important in reading Whitman. There were three stages of his life and, I think, only three at which he wrote great poems.

The earliest stage, which lasted from 1855 to 1856, was the period of Whitman's miraculous flowering. It was the time when he wrote, or revised for publication, the twelve poems of the first edition and the twenty new poems that were added to his book the following year. Most of those in the first edition are among his best and all are examples of his boldest style, his freshest notations on the life he had always known. The "Song of Myself," which fills nearly half of this first volume, contains in germ almost everything he would ever write. It is one of the great visionary poems of modern times. I don't know what to compare it with, except possibly Rimbaud's *A Season in Hell*, though it also has qualities suggesting Blake in *The Marriage of Heaven and Hell* and others suggesting Nietzsche in *Thus Spake Zarathustra*. There is nothing in American literature that in any way resembles it, except as a weak copy.

Some of the pure intensity of emotion that produced the first edition was carried over into the twenty new poems of the second, in 1856; but by then Whitman was less visionary and more calculating in his methods. If these new poems have one quality in common, it is that whether good or bad they are all inflated. One feels in reading them that Whitman had some kinship with the manufacturers and promoters of his busy era.

Having created a new poetic personality—in the same way that a business man might acquire a new invention—he was determined to exploit it and, as we can see from his notebooks, to produce more and bigger poems each year, like a thriving factory. Some of the 1856 poems are masterpieces, notably "Crossing Brooklyn Ferry" and the "Song of the Open Road"; but all of them, even the best, are padded out with lists of things seen or done, things merely read about, anatomical details, and geographical names. Actually it wasn't until much later, but it might as well have been after reading this edition, that Emerson said between pauses to one of Whitman's friends, "Tell Walt I am not satisfied—not satisfied. I expect —him—to make—the songs of the Nation—but he seems—to be contented to—make the inventories."

There are few inventories in the great poems of his second period, which coincided with his emotional crisis of the years 1859–60. That was the time when Whitman wrote the "Calamus" poems, some of which are mere statements of belief, to be read as if they were prose. Not all of them are prose, however; for others are tender and secret and, in their twisted way, his only real love poems. The same years produced his two great despairing chants, "As I Ebb'd with the Ocean of Life" and "Out of the Cradle Endlessly Rocking." These, for Whitman, were the end of a long search. He had told us in the "Song of Myself" that he was looking for "a word unsaid" to express his world. Now at last he heard it, whispered by the sea, and it was not the word that such an expansive poet or his readers expected to hear—not "form" or "union" or "happiness" or "eternal life," but another word with a low and delicious music:

Whereto answering the sea,
Delaying not, hurrying not,
Whisper'd me through the night, and very plainly before
daybreak,
Lisp'd to me the low and delicious word death,
And again death, death, death, death.

At this ultimate point in exploring his mind, Whitman had found his two deepest longings, which were death and the womb of the mother-ocean; and he spoke of them in a tone of intense quiet, with a rightness that was lacking in his chants to democracy. The tone and the rightness were also lacking in the next poems he would publish. Like his first great period in 1855, this second period was followed by years in which his work was written more to a formula. "Drum-Taps," the section of this book that deals with the Civil War, has been overrated because of its subject matter. Most of the section is sentimental or bombastic, and it contains little of value except two or three vignettes of army life—good but inferior to his prose sketches in *Specimen Days*—and the fine "Wound-Dresser," in which, once again, he spoke candidly of himself.

The third period when he wrote great poems—but very few of them—was the years he spent in government service from 1865 to 1873. By then his style had become mannered and verbose and vague—Whitmanian in the worst sense—and he was losing his interest in daily scenes and occupations. He was trying to present, as he said, "no more the puzzling hour or day," but rather the lasting reality behind it: an experiment noble in purpose that has produced whole libraries of bad poetry. In Whitman's case it produced bad poems, too, full of scorn for the humble details that had given its rich texture to the "Song of Myself"; he now dismissed the details in a barbarous phrase as "the ostent evanescent"—in other words, as fleeting appearances. But in compensation for losing his sharp images and exact phrases, he had acquired another gift, for symphonic form. And his few great poems of the third period, from his dirge for Abraham Lincoln (1865) through "Proud Music of the Storm" and "A Passage to India" to "The Prayer of Columbus" (1874), which was his last ambitious work and the epilogue to his poetic career—all these are to be read for their interweaving of themes, for their orchestral effects, for their elevation of tone, but not by any means for richness of style or immediate, fresh visions of the poet's world.

It has become the convention among Whitman critics to describe the Lincoln dirge, "When Lilacs Last in the Door-yard Bloom'd," as the summit of his achievements and the one poem to be cast into bronze or chiseled into granite if all the rest of his work were to be destroyed. The judgment is based more, I think, on history and biography than it is on literature properly speaking. There was a national crisis and a national hero, who died at the moment of victory; and the lament for

his death by a national bard was a poem that *had* to be great,
by the logic of historical circumstances. Or again, there was a
foolish and boastful but enormously gifted poet who found
himself at last, by engaging in unselfish war work, and who
also found a spiritual father. When the father was killed, the
poet, then at the height of his powers, *had* to write his best
poem, by the logic of biography. But what if we read "When
Lilacs Last in the Dooryard Bloom'd" simply as a poem, as an
elegy that might have been sung for Charlemagne or the Cid or
any other hero of budding legend? What if it had been written
by a poet whose private life was unknown to us?

The Lincoln dirge is impressive when submitted to these
or any other tests. It sweeps us along on a wave of sustained
emotion; it rises to a climax in the "death carol," which occurs
at exactly the right place; and it shows symphonic power in its
choice and interweaving of three themes or symbols: the evening star, the lilac, and the hermit thrush. But for all the
orchestral richness of its form, the freedom combined with a
self-imposed discipline, there is something in the poem curiously generalized and conventional. Lincoln?—is he really
mourning Lincoln? The grief is personal, but it seems to have
no personal object. The three master symbols, however skill-
fully entwined, are rendered flat and toneless by the use in
presenting them of phrases that leave no echo: there is only,

> *The song, the wondrous chant of the gray-brown bird,*
> *And the tallying chant of the echo arous'd in my soul,*
> *With the lustrous and drooping star with the countenance*
> *   full of woe,*
> *With the lilac tall, and its blossoms of mastering odor.*

There is not one new or imaginative phrase, except perhaps
"lustrous and drooping" as applied to the evening star. Everything else is old and colorless; and we find the same shopworn
quality in passage after passage, including one in which the
poet tries to give us "pictures of growing spring and farms and
homes"—

> *With the fresh, sweet herbage under foot, and the pale*
> *   green leaves of the trees prolific,*
> *In the distance the flowing glaze, the breast of the river,*
> *   with a wind-dapple here and there,*

*With ranging hills on the banks, with many a line against
the sky, and shadows,
And the city at hand with dwellings so dense, and stacks
of chimneys,
And all the scenes of life and the workshops, and the
workmen homeward returning.*

In the "Song of Myself" a child had asked, "What is the grass?" holding out both hands full of it; and the poet had answered, "I guess it must be the flag of my disposition . . . or I guess it is the handkerchief of the Lord . . . bearing the owner's name someway in the corners. . . . And now it seems to me the beautiful uncut hair of graves." But here, in the Lincoln poem, the grass has become a formal symbol, a sort of ideogram; it is merely "the fresh, sweet herbage under foot." And it is so with all the other images (except "flowing glaze," which is good for the surface of the river): the leaves are "pale green," the trees are "prolific," the hills are "ranging," the city dwellings are "so dense," and the workmen are "homeward returning"—everything is formalized and conventionalized, as if described from a series of Currier & Ives prints instead of from the scenes before the poet's eyes. We cannot help turning pages and comparing this lifeless landscape with the poet's invocation to the "voluptuous cool-breath'd earth" in the twenty-first chant of the "Song of Myself":

*Earth of the slumbering and liquid trees!
Earth of departed sunset—earth of the mountains misty-
topt!
Earth of the vitreous pour of the full moon just tinged
with blue!
Earth of shine and dark mottling the tide of the river!
Earth of the limpid gray of clouds brighter and clearer
for my sake!
Far-swooping elbow'd earth—rich apple-blossom'd earth!
Smile, for your lover comes.*

In this earlier poem everything is copied from life, instead of from the lithographed copy of someone else's picture of life. More than that, everything has a life of its own. The trees are "slumbering and liquid," the full moon has a "vitreous pour," the river is mottled with "shine and dark," instead of light and darkness, and the earth—here he takes liberties with the language, but the right liberties—is addressed, is cajoled and courted, as "Far-swooping elbow'd earth—rich apple-blossom'd earth! Smile, for your lover comes." The last line would be intolerable in almost any other poet; but with Whitman, in that early mood, the rashness is permitted; for we feel that the earth *does* smile at him, that he *is* in reality her lover.

He loves everything, animate or inanimate, and proves his love by finding a phrase fresh from the heart to describe or invoke everything. It is in the early poems that we find his "splendid and savage old men," his "wing'd purposes," his "dumb, beautiful ministers," his prayer to the sea: "rock me in billowy drowse," his "night of the large few stars"—phrases each of which has been used or echoed hundreds of times since he discovered them, yet they keep their newness in Whitman's lines. Heaven comes down to earth in those early poems, and he shows us "letters from God dropt in the street," or lets us hear the sound of "Three scythes at harvest whizzing in a row from three lusty angels with shirts bagg'd out at their waists." Everything is heard, is seen, is touched, and finally embraced, as if it now existed for the first time. He calls us out of our houses: "Out of the dark confinement! out from behind the screen!" He takes us walking through the Manhattan streets; he says to us, "Listen!" and suddenly we hear,

> *The blab of the pave, tires of carts, sluff of boot-soles,*
> *   talk of the promenaders,*
> *The heavy omnibus, the driver with his interrogating*
> *   thumb, the clank of the shod horses on the granite*
> *   floor.*

He shows us people at their daily occupations and finds the words to fix them forever in our minds. Here are "Spar-makers in the spar-yard, the swarming row of well-grown apprentices . . ./The brisk short crackle of the steel driven slantingly into the pine,/The butter-color'd chips flying off in great flakes and slivers."—"The negro holds firmly the reins of his four horses, the block swags underneath on its tied-over chain,/The negro that drives the long dray of the stone-yard, steady and tall he stands pois'd on one leg on the string-piece." —"The carpenter dresses his plank, the tongue of his foreplane whistles its wild ascending lisp."—"The jour printer with gray head and gaunt jaws works at his case,/He turns his quid of tobacco while his eyes blur with the manuscript." In those early days of his career as a poet, Whitman's eyes never blurred; he wandered everywhere, as he said, "afoot with my vision." He showed and still shows us "The swimmer naked in the swimming-bath, seen as he swims through the transparent green-shine, or lies with his face up and rolls silently to and fro in the heave of the water." He carries us with him out of the city, along the sand-brown Long Island roads. He lets us join him,

> At he-festivals, with blackguard gibes, ironical license,
> bull-dances, drinking, laughter,
> At the cider-mill tasting the sweets of the brown mash,
> sucking the juice through a straw,
> At apple-peelings wanting kisses for all the red fruit I
> find.

He loves everybody and everything, identifies himself with everything, and makes it all distinct in his early poems, where everything has its own life down to the pismires building their nests and the leaves of sea lettuce that lie wilting in the windrows left by the tide. There is an experience that I think most of us have had, usually in late adolescence: for a moment or at most a day our eyes were opened by some extreme emotion, usually love or the fear of imminent death, and suddenly the homely objects around us took on new shapes, became filled with life and wonder; everything was intensely *itself*, yet we were part of it. With Whitman that momentary experience seems to have lasted for months or years, until he had written the finest long poem of his century. He also, for a wonder, wrote great poems in his late periods; but the "Song of Myself" is his miracle.

So many misconceptions about Whitman to be cleared away! The real but almost unknown poet was American, not by thesis or proclamation, but because he was born in America, absorbed it with his ears and eyes, and gave back honestly what he heard and saw. He was democratic, not by his vagrant philosophy, but by instinct, inheritance; and he was a democrat, as it were, from below, feeling his brotherhood with the crippled and despised, rather than with the healthy average persons he later celebrated in his poems. He looked for companionship, not because he was grandly expansive by nature, but because he was wounded and alone. He presented a showman's mask to the world. He was a great poet behind the mask —not because he was wise, but because, at first, he was rash and unworldly enough to reveal the depths of his nature; and not because he celebrated "the prairies, pastures, forests, vast cities, Kanada, the snows," but because he wrote of his own Manhattan and Long Island as no other poet has ever done; and not because he soared ecstatically to the heights where people become abstractions, but because in his early work the ecstasy that was real—whatever its source—cleared his eyes so that he could see the infinite wonder of little and homely things. "I know," he says in the magnificent fifth chant of the "Song of Myself," "that the hand of God is the promise of my own"; but then he adds, looking downward at the world he knows best,

> *And limitless are leaves stiff or drooping in the fields,*
> *And brown ants in the little wells beneath them,*
> *And mossy scabs of the worm fence, heap'd stones, elder,*
> *mullein and poke-weed.*

The Real Horatio Alger Story

THERE IS a myth embodied in the very name of Horatio Alger, Jr. It is of course the myth of the poor boy Struggling Upward from Rags to Riches by Luck and Pluck, goaded on by a boyish determination to Strive and Succeed. Anyone born in the slums who becomes a captain of industry or merchandising is sure to be labeled an Alger hero. But the myth embodied in Alger's name, the American dream of success, is not the myth we find in his books for boys—if we read them attentively—and it is certainly not embodied in the career of the author.

About that career we find surprisingly little that is known beyond question. The biography of Alger by Herbert R. Mayes (1928) was written when Mayes was a very young man and is full of errors at the few points where it can be compared with dependable information from other sources. Much of it is based on Alger's private diaries, which have vanished since Mayes used them. Nobody knows how many books Alger wrote. Mayes compiled a list of 119 titles, and there are later lists of 135 and 143.* But the only volume of *Who's Who in America* that appeared during Alger's lifetime tells a different story. Presumably Alger himself—or, if he was too ill at the time, his married sister, who was nursing him—had a chance to correct the entry that follows his name, and part of it reads:

> *Author:* Ragged Dick series, Tattered Tom series, Luck and Pluck series, Atlantic and Pacific series, etc., in all about 70 books, mostly juveniles, of which nearly 800,000 have been sold.

* The standard bibliography by Frank Gruber (The *Antiquarian Bookman*, November 13, 1948) lists 106 Alger books that Gruber thinks are his own work, plus eleven others presumably written by Edward Stratemeyer (although Stratemeyer once denied their authorship), and 17 books of which the authorship cannot be traced, although they were published under Alger's name—a grand total of 134.

"The Real Alger Story," *Horizon*, Vol. XII, No. 3, Summer 1970, 62–65. The essay incorporates material from two earlier pieces, "Holy Horatio," *Time*, August 13, 1945, 98, 100, 102; and "Alger Story," *New Republic*, 113, September 10, 1945, 319–320.

Alger died in 1899, the same year that the entry appeared, but dozens of books attributed to him were published afterward, in some cases as late as 1909. The explanation seems to be that a publisher bought the right to use Alger's name, then signed it to other juveniles that were actually the work of men he employed on a weekly salary. Nobody knows which, if any, of the later books are Alger's. Nobody knows how many copies were printed of the whole aggregation. "More than 100,000,000 copies sold!" exclaims the jacket of *Struggling Upward and Other Works*, a collection of four Alger novels that appeared in 1945. "They sold close to 200,000,000 copies, I am told," says Russel Crouse in his introduction to the same volume. Both figures are wildly implausible. It is true that Alger's books and those attributed to him were intensively merchandised after his death; they were priced as low as ten cents in paper and thirty-five cents in cloth; but it seems unlikely that their total sale was more than fifteen million, at a generous estimate.

No, Alger was not "the most widely read author of the ages," as his biographer insists on calling him, but he was faithfully read by a very wide audience. There must have been at least a million American boys who pictured themselves as Alger heroes. Over a period of forty years or more, boys collected Alger books and swapped them back and forth like tops or jackknives; his dreams had become a standard currency. Thousands of boys wrote to the author for advice, since they had come to regard him as a model of business acumen and avuncular wisdom. They would have been surprised to learn that Mr. Alger, in life, had been a most unhappy boy and that he had never grown up.

He was born in Revere, Massachusetts, on January 13, 1832 (to follow Mayes, who I suspect is right in this case; reference books give the year as 1834). He was the son of a Unitarian minister whose church was in neighboring Chelsea. "His name will be Horatio, after me," the father said, "not as a concession to any vanity of mine, but rather as a reminder to him that I shall expect him to continue the religious endeavors I have begun." Horatio Sr. tyrannized over the boy, made him read Plato and Josephus in translation at the age of eight (besides *Jack the Giant Killer*), and taught him Latin at nine.

When visitors came to the parsonage, the father would ask him, "What are you going to be, Horatio?" The boy would bring his heels together and recite, "I shall be a t-teacher of the ways of God, a p-preacher of His commandments, a wib-eral thinker, a woyal citizen." His schoolmates at Gates Academy called him Holy Horatio.

At Harvard he was the smallest man (five feet two) in the class of 1852, ranked tenth in his studies—he excelled in French and the classics—and wrote the class ode. He fell in love with a girl named Patience Stires, but Horatio Sr. persuaded her to break the engagement. During his senior year, Horatio Jr. noted in his diary, "Am reading *Moby Dick*," which had been published in November, "and find it exciting. What a thrilling life the literary must be! . . . Would it be possible for me to take up writing as a life work? The satisfaction resulting from a beautiful story must be inspiring—a story that rouses readers to a new sense of the fine things of life." From that moment Alger determined not to follow his father into the pulpit.

His first steps toward a literary career were teaching in boys' schools, writing pieces for the Boston papers, then helping to edit a new magazine that lasted only a few weeks. Left without resources, he surrendered to his father and entered the Harvard Divinity School. But he rebelled again on graduation day; having received a legacy from an eccentric old gentleman whom he had once befriended, he hurried off to Paris. There he became the lover of a cabaret singer named Elise Monselet, whom he had met while paying a tourist's visit to the Morgue. Elise had literary tastes: she worshiped the godlike Hugo and adored the author of *Scènes de la Vie de Bohême*. When Murger died at an early age—that was in January 1861—she and her lover sat in a café holding hands, the tears streaming down their cheeks.

Soon Alger sailed home, partly because his legacy was spent, but also to escape his second mistress, an English harpy who had snatched him away from Elise. On three occasions he tried to enlist in the Union army; twice he broke his arm before being enrolled, and the third time he nearly died of pneumonia. He was rescued by his father, who finally prevailed on him to be ordained. In December 1864, he became pastor of the little Unitarian church at Brewster, on Cape Cod, where his congregation regarded him as "gentle, solicitous of the welfare of others, and humble as it behooves one of the Lord's servants to be." But he hadn't forgotten literary ambitions, and he spent much of his time writing novels for boys— his Campaign Series—instead of sermons. After less than two years he resigned his pastorate and went to New York to dream of unfading laurels while leading the life of a needy hack.

His next novel for boys, *Ragged Dick*, deals with the rise to respectability of a homeless bootblack. There were thousands like him in New York after the Civil War, when drummer boys and war orphans ran wild in the city streets, much as the little *besprizorni* did in Moscow after the Russian Revolution. Alger's book attracted wide attention when it was serialized in a boys' magazine edited by the famous Oliver Optic. The superintendent of the Newsboys' Lodging House, Charles O'Connor, sought him out, gave him a room in the House, and became his closest friend for thirty years, besides providing him with what he regarded as his real home. A Boston publisher, A. K. Loring, offered him a contract for six books about Ragged Dick and his friends, all to be written in twenty months. After that, Alger thought, he would stop writing juveniles. "It will not be long," he told a Cambridge acquaintance in 1871, "before I get started on a novel that I hope will find a place in the company of fine writing." Ten years later he wrote to his Harvard classmate Addison Brown, "I must separate myself from juvenile fiction long enough to write a lasting work. As soon as a suitable theme appears, you may be certain I will seize it and permanently give up the line in which I have till now been engaged."

Meanwhile Alger was trying to live in the fashion of the romantic novelists he had seen from a distance in Paris. He sometimes disguised himself in a long cape and a tousled wig and wandered through the Manhattan streets—looking for material, he said. In his room with a thick carpet on the floor—not the room in the Newsboys' Lodging House—with reams of paper and dozens of sharp pencils on the desk, and a little bust of Shakespeare on the mantelpiece, he paced the floor in an artist's smock and waited for inspiration like Captain

Ahab on the lookout for the white whale. One spring evening
during his second visit to Paris, the inspiration came, and
Alger worked on his great novel most of the night. In the
morning he sent an urgent message to Una Garth, a married
woman with whom he had fallen in love. She wrote in her
diary, as transcribed by Mayes, "I spent the afternoon with
Horatio and read the opening paragraphs of his *Tomorrow*.
May the Lord spare the man from a knowledge of his own
incapacity!" Mrs. Garth did not completely spare him that
knowledge, and Alger put aside the great book while he wrote
another juvenile, *Struggling Upward*, which turned out to be
the dead mean and average of all his books for boys. Then,
tired of wrestling with the Muse and rejected by Mrs. Garth,
he temporarily lost his mind and was carried screaming to a
hospital.

When Alger recovered, he once again took refuge with
Charles O'Connor and continued writing books for boys. At the
Newsboys' Lodging House he acted as chaplain and also,
within his limited resources, as a general patron of the institu-
tion. He helped to set hundreds of homeless boys up in business by giving each of them a blacking box or a bundle of
newspapers. A very few of his novels were written with a social
purpose. Thus, *Phil the Fiddler*, one of the four reprinted in
1945, is a memorial to the crusade that Alger led against the
padrone system, by which hundreds of street musicians
brought to New York from southern Italy were kept as virtual
slaves. Their parents sold them to a *padrone*, who fed them
scantily, lodged them in cellars, beat them, and took their
earnings. The book helped to make the system illegal. *Jed, the
Poorhouse Boy*, also reprinted in 1945, was intended to call
attention to the plight of pauper children, and its early chapters bear a wraithlike resemblance to *Oliver Twist*. Jed himself
is something of a scapegrace and has a sharper tongue than
Alger's other heroes, besides an even greater talent for finding
rich protectors. Skeptical readers might call the book *A Fagot's
Progress*. But Phil and Jed are his boldest experiments in
character, and most of his other heroes are stamped from the
same metal with the same patented Alger die.

As the books tumbled out, they attracted wide attention;
letters for Alger poured into the Newsboys' Lodging House

from all parts of the country. But the books did not earn much money for their author, who, at the height of his reputation, still had to piece out his income by tutoring schoolboys in French and Latin. (A future justice of the Supreme Court, Benjamin N. Cardozo, was one of his pupils.) The trouble seems to have been that Alger never learned to be a business-man on the model of his heroes, and that he sold many of his books outright for modest sums instead of demanding royal-ties. Finally he made what might be called the ultimate sacri-fice for an author by selling the right to use his name. There is no record of the transaction, except the dozens of Alger books that appeared after his death, most of which are obviously the work of other imaginations. One would guess, however, that the sale took place during a period of ill health and despond-ency that followed the death of Charles O'Connor; perhaps in 1896, before Alger retired to Natick, Massachusetts, to be nursed by his married sister. Together with the use of his name, he was selling his dream of being inspired to produce a novel "that I hope will find a place in the company of fine writing."

What he left behind him was his bartered name—that and his own books for boys, which can be read with some interest even today. Boys of the new generation never ask for them, but like them well enough if they come across a stray copy. The style is formal to the point of burlesque, but correct except for a few Yankeeisms ("considerable" as an adverb, for exam-ple) and absolutely clear; it shows the results of Alger's classical training. The chapters are short and consist chiefly of dialogue, which is sometimes so innocent that it acquires a double meaning. ("I want to show you some engravings," says the rich Miss Davenport to the hero of *Tom Temple's Ca-reer*.) Still, the dialogue moves rapidly and is not without conscious humor of the sort one used to hear when boys were talking together outside a village store. Here is a fair sample from *Ragged Dick*:

> One of the boys, a rather supercilious-looking young gentle-man, genteelly dressed, and evidently having a very high opin-ion of his dress and himself, turned suddenly to Dick and remarked:
> "I've seen you before."

"Oh, have you?" said Dick, whirling around; "then p'r'aps you'd like to see me behind."

At this unexpected answer all the boys burst into a laugh with the exception of the questioner, who evidently considered that Dick had been disrespectful.

"I've seen you somewhere," he said in a surly tone, correcting himself.

"Most likely you have," said Dick. "That's where I generally keep myself."

Humor apart, the Alger books offer a curious picture of American culture after the Civil War. In the rather bleak world to which they introduce us, there is no art whatever, except that sometimes a young girl plays "Hearts and Flowers" on a square piano. There is no learning beyond the ability to read and cipher and, as all his heroes do, to write a flowing hand. There is no history: it is as if New York and the whole country from New England to the California diggings had been created overnight, with the excavations raw and the scaffolding still in place. Though Alger was an ordained clergyman, there is hardly a trace of religious feeling in his novels. Some of the heroes go to Sunday school, like Ragged Dick, but that is only because one of the teachers is a rich merchant who might help them to rise in the world. Here, from a book called *Hector's Inheritance*, is a sample of Alger's moral teaching:

"Have you any taste for any kind of liquor?"

"No, sir," answered Hector promptly.

"Even if you had, do you think you would have self-control enough to avoid entering saloons and gratifying your tastes?"

"Yes, sir."

"That is well. Do you play pool?"

"No sir," answered Hector, wondering whither all these questions tended.

"I ask because playing pool in public places paves the way for intemperance, as bars are generally connected with such establishments."

Playing pool is also a form of idleness, which leads to stealing, which sometimes leads to jail, but more often to poverty, the hell to which villains are assigned by his Yankee theology. His heaven is simply earning or being given a fortune (but always a modest one, for Alger himself had simple desires and a perfect ignorance of financial practices). Still, everything in his world has its cash value, and a boy who earns ten dollars a week rightly considers himself twice as good as a boy who earns five dollars a week. When the hero of *Tom Temple's Career* loses his inheritance of forty thousand dollars —Alger always gives an exact figure—he isn't in the least surprised that his guardian turns him out into the world or that his rich friends the Davenports ask him never to enter their house again. "Tom had always understood that they cared for him only because he was rich," the author explains, "and he was neither astonished nor disappointed at the change which had come over them." Elsewhere the author exclaims, "How gold reveals the virtues of those about us!" Even a beloved child has its price in gold. When Mr. Rockwell's only son falls overboard from the Brooklyn ferry (in *Ragged Dick*), he cries from the depths of his anguish, "My child! Who will save my child? A thousand—ten thousand dollars to anyone who will save him!" Dick plunges into the East River, thus achieving fame and what Alger regarded as a fortune.

The world of his novels is full of bullies, petty thieves, and confidence men. Even in the New England villages where most of his heroes are born, the leading citizen is likely to be a dishonest banker who steals the property of widows and orphans. Yet the same villages have their benevolent doctors, their self-sacrificing mothers; and the sturdy little hero, left homeless in the streets of New York, is certain to find a kind old merchant who buys him clothes and a watch. For all its bleakness, Alger's world is suffused with the optimism and faith in human nature of America in the Gilded Age. It is also suffused with a deep feeling of equality: family doesn't matter, trade or profession doesn't matter, national origin matters a little, but not a great deal; in the end nothing matters but money, and the honest newsboy has a better chance to earn it than a banker's idle son. Said A. K. Loring, his early publisher: "Alger is the dominating figure of the new era. In his books he has captured the spirit of reborn America. The turmoil of the city streets is in them. You can hear the rattle of pails on the farms. Above all you can hear the cry of triumph of the oppressed over the oppressor. . . . What Alger has done is to portray the soul—the ambitious soul—of the country."

Mayes, his biographer, has a different judgment. He explains Alger's success by saying, "He did not write down to boys. He never had to, for he was never above them."

It is true that Alger presents an obvious case of arrested development. During the Civil War he played at being a soldier and drilled a squad of Cambridge boys armed with broomsticks. Later, as if conscious of being only a boy in size, he preferred the company of bootblacks and match sellers to that of grown persons. At fifty he still liked to play with blocks, building one tower after another so high that it toppled over, and his other amusement was beating the big drum in the newsboys' band. The tower and the drum are obvious sexual symbols, but they would seem to suggest masturbation rather than the paedophilia one is always expecting to find in his life and work. He never married. Mayes tells us that he had in all three mistresses, but each of these in her own fashion was a figure of maternal authority. Thus, Elise first lured him to her door and then, as Alger hesitated, stamped her foot and gave him an order: "Don't stand here talking." Alger obeyed like a good-bad little boy.

In his novels the close personal relations are not sexual. They are sometimes fraternal—many of his heroes have beloved younger sisters—but more often they are parental and filial. The boldest approach to sexual passion is in the next-to-last chapter of *Sink or Swim*, which tells how Harry Raymond came back from the Australian gold fields with a fortune of $11,525—"which, for a boy of his age," Alger says, "was certainly a very comfortable capital." Little Maud Lindsay, "a bright, handsome girl of thirteen," was so glad to see him that she flung her arms around him. "Harry was rather embarrassed," Alger says, "at the unexpected warmth of his reception, but felt that it would be impolite not to kiss Maud in return, and accordingly did so." That is the only nonmaternal kiss in the twenty Alger books I have read and possibly in all the books he wrote (though not, I believe, in the posthumous books signed with his name).

No, Alger did not write down to boys. All the emotions in his novels are those proper to a preadolescent stage of development: rivalry with other boys, shame at wearing patched clothes, day dreams of running away (and of coming back to mother with a fortune), a possessive love for the mother, and rebellion against the wicked squire, who becomes a father symbol. Apparently these are Alger's emotions, obsessively relived instead of being merely remembered. The heroes are compensatory projections of the author, who dreamed of being as resolute as each of them, but who never disengaged himself from a painful family pattern—never, that is, except in the books he wrote for eternal boys like himself. "The cry of triumph of the oppressed over the oppressor" that A. K. Loring mentioned was, in reality, Horatio Jr.'s cry of triumph over a tyrannical father.

Every popular novel is also, on one level, a myth or a fairy tale, and most often a very old one. The myth or tale is especially clear in the Alger novel (which is of course one book with seventy or more different titles). But it is not the tale one expects it to be: not *Jack the Giant Killer*, which Alger read when he was eight years old and which presents the eternal fable of the poor boy who became immensely rich—as Andrew Carnegie did and John D. Rockefeller, Sr.—partly by luck but mostly by using his own sharp wits. Carnegie and the other robber barons were too grasping to be Alger boys—except in copydesk language—and the tale that Alger compulsively repeats is very different from theirs. Essentially it is the Greek myth of Telemachus, the supposed orphan who is forced to leave home and who sets out in search of a father. It is eventually the father's power, not his own, that restores him to his rightful place.*

* As an example of how the Alger story is almost universally misconceived by journalists and even scholars, one might take Kenneth S. Lynn's introduction to his book *The Dream of Success* (1955). The book is concerned with the mythology of success as it affected the work of five American novelists. Lynn says in his introduction, " . . . the Alger hero is the key to the meaning of the success mythology. Alone, unaided, the ragged boy is plunged into the maelstrom of city life, but by his own pluck and luck he capitalizes on one of the myriad opportunities available to him and rises to the top of the economic heap. Here, in a nutshell, is the plot of every novel Alger ever wrote; here, too, is the quintessence of the myth." Lynn seems to be confusing the Alger hero with Dick Whittington. Of course the Alger hero is not unaided; the oppor-

In Alger's version of the myth, the hero is always father-less and is always a boy of noble principles. Though he plays the part of a bootblack, a newsboy, or a fiddler, his open and prepossessing features betray his princely nature. Usually he comes from a New England village that takes the place of rocky Ithaca, and his widowed mother is besieged by a wicked squire who assumes the joint role of Penelope's suitors. Through the machinations of the squire, or of his idle and snobbish son, the hero is forced to run away. He somehow keeps alive in New York until the day when he meets and befriends a stranger, perhaps by rescuing his only child from drowning or from a runaway horse. The stranger, always a widower or a bachelor, turns out to be a rich and kindly merchant. He buys new clothes for the boy—dressing him, as it were, in princely robes—then sends him on a mission, a sort of knightly quest. On the boy's triumphant return, the merchant settles on him a little fortune, usually of ten or twelve thousand dollars, and adopts him as a son or nephew or ward. It is the moment in almost any Alger novel when the childless and truly fatherless author seems to be writing with a sob in his throat. "I am rich and lonely, and without near relatives," says the invalid Mr. Stoddard to the hero of *Tom Temple's Career*, "and I want you to come and live with me. Call me uncle. I shall be proud of such a spirited young nephew."

"All right, uncle," says Tom, smiling from an open heart.

Moralists used to complain at the turn of the century that the Alger hero did not earn his fortune by hard work, but had it drop into his lap. What they missed was the fairy-tale logic of the story. The hero is of course a prince in disguise, and he gains his little fortune by discovering the place and parentage that are his by right. Then he once again displays his princely character by rushing home to help his mother. Sometimes the adoptive father or uncle comes with him. "You need be under no anxiety about Luke and his prospects," the merchant says to the mother at the end of *Struggling Upward*. "I shall make

---

tunity he seizes is that of finding an adoptive father; and he never rises to more than a safe niche on the slope of "the economic heap." Though Lynn was writing a book about the effects in fiction of the Alger myth, it would seem that he never read an Alger novel with attention.

over to him $10,000 at once, constituting myself his guardian, and will see that he is well started in business." Sometimes— for example, in *Sink or Swim*—the hero arrives on the very morning of the day when his mother is to be married to the wicked squire, but then he takes out a roll of greenbacks and Squire Turner slinks away. As for the end of Alger's story—

> My readers [he says] may like to know how James Turner turned out in life. [James is the squire's idle and malicious son.] A year since, he obtained the situation of teller in a bank, his father standing surety for him. He soon developed expensive tastes, and finally disappeared, carrying away thirty thousand dollars of the funds of the bank. This loss his father had to make good, and in consequence he has become a comparatively poor man, and a very sour, morose man at that. . . . So the wheel of fortune has turned and those who were once at the top are now at the bottom.

Virtue has been rewarded, vice punished, and the whole operation has been pecuniary. In that preoccupation with exact sums in dollars, and in that alone, the Alger fable resembles the typical American success story as enacted in fiction or life. There is, however, a difference even here. The robber barons loved money for its own sake and each was determined to have more of it than anyone else. "I'm bound to be rich! *Bound to be rich!*" John D. Rockefeller, Sr. once exclaimed. The Alger hero will never be truly rich, since he has a generous spirit that makes him incapable of clawing and gouging his way into a palace on Fifth Avenue. Money in the Alger novel is chiefly a symbol of other things: emotional security, for example, and affection (as of the adoptive father for his ward, or of the hero for his mother), and manly power. Money is the bow of Ulysses that slays the wicked suitor—though instead of being slain, in the Alger version, the suitor loses his money and hence his virility. The real theme of the Alger novel is not pecuniary but filial and paternal. Alger is revenging himself on his own father three times: first he kills him before the story opens by making the hero an orphan; then he gives Horatio Sr.'s worst traits to the wicked squire; and finally he provides the hero with a father-by-choice to love and understand him.

Journalists have always misinterpreted the story he told, but it would seem that many of his young readers understood it instinctively. Among the thousands of letters written to Mr. Alger, one after another said in effect, "My father is like Squire Tarbox in your story. He never lets me have money to spend. He makes me . . ." and the letter would continue the list of the boy's real or fancied grievances. Often it would end with the question, "Should I run away?" How Alger answered such letters is not on record, but his books themselves are a sort of answer. "The father who mistreats you is not a real father," they say, "but a wicked impostor. Yes, run away if you must. Go to New York and earn your living as a bootblack or a newsboy, but never play pool in public places and always be kind to strangers. Some day one of the strangers will turn out to be a father in spirit, a real father, and he will give you a little fortune."

The real message of the Alger books had a deeper appeal to preadolescent boys than the mere prospect of becoming a money baron. What I cannot understand is how the author of the message—that timid bohemian, that failure by his father's standards and double failure by his own, since he neither wrote a great novel nor amassed even a modest fortune—should come to be regarded as the prophet of business enterprise; nor why the family melodrama that he wrote and rewrote for boys like himself should be confused with the American dream of success.

The Two Henry Jameses

THERE IS a rough justice in the fate of literary reputations, if we follow them through a period of years. Most—not
all—of the true ones survive, even when they have been buried
and must be exhumed from a mountain of trash. The false and
fabricated reputations are eventually winnowed out and blown
away; often without a single hot blast from the critics, they
crumble like very old newspapers. Do you remember the days
when *Jurgen* was regarded as a profound and devilishly clever
work, the lasting ornament of American letters? Or the days
when Dreiser *and* Joseph Hergesheimer were described in the
same breath as the two living masters of the novel? Or the
somewhat later days when Hemingway *and* Louis Bromfield
were coupled by the critics as the two giants of a new generation? A short time ago in the *New Yorker*, Edmund Wilson
wrote an essay ridiculing Bromfield, and most people wondered why he devoted so much space to proving what even the
little children and professors knew. Where are the debunking
biographers now, who won such easy triumphs over the
bearded New England worthies? Where are the proletarian
geniuses flung upward from the working class like Venus from
the waves, all garlanded with college degrees and Brooks
Brothers ties? Some of them were honest talents and have been
unjustly forgotten, but in that case they need not worry too
much; the world that neglected them may end by overwhelm-
ing them with praise.

Emerson's law of compensation seems to operate in such
matters. If an author is overvalued during his lifetime, he will
be blamed and overblamed after his death. If a great author
goes unread, like Blake or Melville, he will end by being
raised above his contemporaries. That was the fate of Donne,
who was seldom mentioned for two centuries after his death
and whose work was at one time unobtainable except in the big
libraries; by 1930 the wheel had turned and he was not only

This essay appeared in the *New Republic* in two parts: "The Return
of Henry James," 112, January 22, 1945, 121–122; and "The
Two Henry Jameses," 112, February 5, 1945, 177–180.

valued at his own great worth but exalted as a greater poet than Milton. Some reputations climb imperceptibly, reach what appears to be their proper level, and hold it through decades or even centuries. Others are thrown out of balance at the very beginning and never regain it; they come down through the years like a skier down a slope that frightens him, making wild sweeps from shadow into sun.

Henry James is the great example in our time of an author whose reputation fluctuated during his life, declined before his death, and has now reached a higher point than ever before. Out of all the books he wrote—and he was almost as prolific as Horatio Alger—there was only one short novel, *Daisy Miller*, that became what we should now call a best seller. Only two of his novels—*The Portrait of a Lady* in 1881 and *The Ambassadors* in 1903—were greeted, in publishers' cant, "with a chorus of critical approval." These two dates twenty years apart marked the high points of his career. James thought it had reached its lowest point in 1895, when he was hissed and hooted from the stage after the first performance of *Guy Domville*. He wrote to his old friend Howells: "I *have* felt, for a long time past, that I have fallen upon evil days—every sign or symbol of one's being in the least *wanted*, anywhere or by anyone having so utterly failed." But a worse blow was to strike him twelve years later, with the publication of the New York Edition of his novels and tales, for which he had revised the style of his earlier work and had written a preface to each novel or volume of stories. The whole was intended to serve as "a sort of comprehensive manual or *vade-mecum*" for students of fiction, besides preserving his work in lasting form, and it didn't quite go unnoticed. The *Nation* and the *New York Times Book Review* faithfully and briefly mentioned each successive volume; but there was, says Richard Nicholas Foley, who has written a thesis on the treatment of James's work by American periodicals, little or no serious discussion of the edition as a whole. It might as well have been buried in a vault in Kentucky, like the American stock of gold.

Today the New York Edition is out of print and practically unobtainable; when a book dealer manages to find a set, he can put almost any price on it that he has the courage to ask.* All of James's books in their original editions are collectors' items, even the critical works and the travel sketches. His work is more widely discussed and has more admirers than during his lifetime. It has become a commonplace remark to call him the greatest or even the only American novelist.

Of course there are other reasons for this posthumous glory besides the quality of his work and besides the law of literary compensation. The return of Henry James is also the almost mathematical result of two tendencies among American readers. The first is a literary nationalism that has been growing from year to year; one sign of it is the new courses in American literature that were being offered, before the war, in all our universities. After a century and a half of living in the future, we suddenly faced about and began the search for a "usable past"; and very soon we discovered that James, in spite of being an expatriate, was the most usable of all the dead American novelists. He was the only novelist (except for Cooper and Simms and Howells, all far beneath him in talent) who planned and executed his life work on the scale of the masters; he was the only one to achieve a continuous, unified, organic career.

The second tendency that contributes to James's reputation today is the general reaction against political or social standards in literature. It began simply as a reaction against proletarian novels and Marxian criticism, but by now it has developed much further, into a reaction against historical or genetic criticism of any type. Nothing satisfies its leaders except absolute, permanent, unchanging moral and esthetic values. Works of art are being judged in and for themselves, as if independent of any social background; and the works most likely to be praised are those most widely removed from any social movement and least contaminated with ideas. There seems to be no taint of them in James's novels. He never mentions social forces, although they figure in his work indirectly and almost secretly. He is the great example in his country of the "pure" novelist.

His working notebooks, as quoted by F. O. Matthiessen,

* Much later the New York edition was reissued by Scribner's, the original publisher.

abound in expressions of priestly or soldierly devotion to his craft. "A *mighty will*," he wrote for his own eyes while working on *The Bostonians*, "there is nothing but that! The integrity of one's will, purpose, faith!"—"Oh art, art," he wrote a few years later, "what difficulties are like thine; and, at the same time, what consolation and encouragements, also, are like thine? Without this, for me, the world would be, indeed a howling desert."—"But courage, courage, and forward, forward," he wrote before starting *The Tragic Muse*. "If one must generalize, that is the only generalization. There is an immensity to be done, and, without being presumptuous, I shall at the worst do part of it. But all one's manhood must be at one's side. " His two younger brothers had served in the Civil War, and Henry apparently had felt a sense of inadequacy or even guilt at being physically unable to join them. It was in the act of writing that he discovered a moral equivalent for the hardships and dangers of the military life. And a new generation of brave but quite unwarlike soldiers has come to admire him as a hero of art.

ii

Nevertheless a debate continues among James's readers and critics, with those who admire or at least concede the virtues of his early stories, but hold that his later work shows a rootlessness, a snobbishness, an unreality that might well be explained by his divorce from American life, standing against the others who believe that the three long novels he wrote when he was turning sixty are the high and frosty summits of American fiction. The debate goes back to the first publication of *The Wings of the Dove* (1902), *The Ambassadors* (1903), and *The Golden Bowl* (1904). William Dean Howells tried hard to end it in 1903, when he wrote his dialogue on "Mr. Henry James's Later work"; he spoke of course for the devoted Jacobites. In 1905 William Crary Brownell answered Howells in a longer essay that expressed his adverse moral judgments and his distinguished lack of comprehension. Van Wyck Brooks succeeded Brownell as leader of the anti-Jacobite faction, the Whig gentry. The simple thesis he advanced in *The Pilgrimage of Henry James* (1925) and still more forcefully in

New England: *Indian Summer* was that the later novels could not be so good as the early ones because James had lived too long in England. That was for some time the accepted opinion, in the years when James wasn't being read, although it was combated by Matthew Josephson in his *Portrait of the Artist as American* (1930) and was roundly denied by Stephen Spender, who seemed to be saying in *The Destructive Element* (1936) that James was the central writer of our time.

Henry James, the Major Phase, by F. O. Matthiessen, might be approached as merely another episode in these Jacobite wars, but it has one great advantage over the earlier forays and incursions. It is better armed; it is equipped with new evidence. Recently James's working notebooks from 1878 to 1914, in which he recorded his intimate thoughts and the slow growth of his novels, were presented by his nephew and namesake to the Houghton Library at Harvard. Mr. Matthiessen, with Kenneth B. Murdock, is now preparing them for publication.* He quotes from them extensively in the present volume; and they show that James regarded his later work as more ambitious than anything attempted in the past.

They also show that the year 1895 was the turning point in his career. Feeling that his novels would never be popular, he had been writing a succession of plays—to make money, as he flatly said, but also in the effort to overcome a sense of solitude. He seems to have resembled one of his characters—Mortimer Marshal in "The Papers"—to the extent of nursing a secret: "that to be inspired, to work with effect, he had to feel he was appreciated, to have it all somehow come back to him." Not much came back of the effort James put into his plays. One of them, a dramatized version of his early novel *The American,* had been indifferently received in London after a mild success in the English provinces. Four others had been printed with-

---

* This volume, *The Notebooks of Henry James,* was published in New York, 1947, by the Oxford University Press, which had published *Henry James, the Major Phase* in 1944. Later the most extreme of the anti-Jacobite statements was to be Maxwell Geismar's *Henry James and the Jacobites* (Boston, 1963), which most critics condemned as intemperate. From the other side, the most persuasive defense of James is of course Leon Edel's many-volumed life of the Master.

out being produced. A sixth, *Guy Domville*, closed in London after thirty-one performances that earned eleven hundred dollars for the author, as he wrote to his brother William; there had been many worse failures on the stage. But the first night of the play—January 5, 1895—had been worse than a failure; it was an international scandal. Some of the well-dressed people in the stalls approved of the play and cried, "Author, author!" The crowd in the pit hated it and bore a grudge against the producer on this and older counts. When the author appeared before the curtain, they greeted him with hoots and jeers and roars—James wrote to his brother—"like those of a cage of beasts at some infernal 'zoo.'" Newspapers in London and New York carried the story of how the uproar continued for fifteen minutes while the author stood there cowering under the storm.

Deeply humiliated, so that he could never bear to be reminded of that night, James abandoned for all practical purposes his attempt to win a larger public. It is true that he would later publish several stories described by him as "shameless potboilers"—including one great story, "The Turn of the Screw," but also including others that were genteelly romantic in the tone of the popular magazines and almost as mechanical in plot as if they had been signed by O. Henry. For the most part, however, his next years would be devoted to the sort of work he regarded simply as "the best." He wrote in his notebook just after the great fiasco:

> I take up my *own* old pen again—the pen of all my old unforgettable efforts and sacred struggles. To myself—today— I need say no more. Large and full and high the future still opens. It is now indeed that I may do the work of my life. And I will.

A month passed and he felt more confident:

> I have my head, thank God, full of visions. One has never too many—one has never enough. Ah, just to let oneself go—at last; to surrender oneself to what through all the long years one has (quite heroically, I think) hoped for and waited for —the mere potential and relative increase of quantity in the material act—act of appreciation and production. One has prayed and hoped and waited, in a word, to be able to work *more*. And now, toward the end, it seems, within its limits,

to have come. That is all I ask. Nothing else in the world. I bow down to Fate, equally in submission and in gratitude.

That notebook entry of February 14, 1895, foreshadows James's later period, though there was still to be some fumbling before the major works of the period were under way. Of one thing James was already certain: those works would utilize "the divine principle of the Scenario" that he had learned from his costly experience in the theatre. They would follow the scenic method, in other words, and would be as tightly constructed as plays. As for the "potential and relative increase of quantity in the material act," it was not to be long delayed. During the first five years that James spent in the little town of Rye, from 1898 to 1903, he produced a volume of work that was unprecedented even in his own generally fruitful career. He wrote two short novels, *The Awkward Age* and *The Sacred Fount*; two collections of stories, *The Soft Side* and *The Better Sort*; and a two-volume life of the sculptor William Wetmore Story, besides his three most richly elaborated novels. Nobody should doubt after rereading them that they are his best novels too. Mr. Matthiessen has every right to describe that period in James's life as "the major phase."

In his critical essay, each of the three great novels receives a chapter of outline and analysis, in the light of James's working notes, and each is assigned its rank. Mr. Matthiessen has many reservations about *The Golden Bowl* and a few about *The Ambassadors*; he believes that *The Wings of the Dove* is James's masterpiece, "that single work where his characteristic emotional vibration seems deepest." *The Ivory Tower*, which also receives a chapter, might possibly have been as good, he says, if James had lived to finish it. There is an introductory chapter, extremely interesting, on "the art of reflection" that James applied to all his work; and there is a long appendix analyzing the changes James made in *The Portrait of a Lady* twenty-five years after its first appearance, when he was preparing the New York Edition of his collected works. Simple in structure and temperate in expression, *Henry James: The Major Phase* is almost a model of the critical monograph.

There is, however, one fault or omission to be noted that

does not greatly affect the quality of the book, but that does have a bearing on the debate about Henry James. Mr. Matthiessen has not so much answered the arguments of the anti-Jacobites as he has introduced totally different arguments. Almost everything he says about the later James is true, but it is not quite the whole story. A great deal that Van Wyck Brooks says about him is also essentially true, even though overstated at times and written in the style of a highly cultured prosecuting attorney. It is true, for example, that James's later novels are rather thin in subject matter, considering their length and enormous elaboration. It is true that they reveal an ignorance of America and, even more strikingly, an ignorance of European life outside the international set. And it is true that they are novels about adultery (or something close to it, in *The Wings of the Dove*) that show a curious want of passion, almost as if James had written *War and Peace* without the battle scenes.

James himself, in the little book on Hawthorne that he wrote in 1879, gave us a sort of license to prefer his early work. He praised *The Scarlet Letter* in terms that might be applied to the first version of *The Portrait of a Lady*. Coming first among Hawthorne's novels, he said, it was simpler and more complete than the others. "It achieves," he continued, "more perfectly what it attempts, and has about it that charm, very hard to express, which we find in an artist's work the first time he has touched his highest mark—a sort of straightness and naturalness of execution, an unconsciousness of his public, and freshness of interest in his theme." James also admired *The Scarlet Letter* for its style. "It is admirably written," he said. "Hawthorne afterwards polished his style to a still higher degree, but in his later productions—it is almost always the case in a writer's later productions—there is a touch of mannerism. In *The Scarlet Letter* there is a high degree of polish, and at the same time a charming freshness; his phrase is less conscious of itself."

James's phrase, in his later novels, is extremely conscious of itself, and that is by no means its only fault. With its endless sentences dotted thickly with commas, it gives the impression of being both long-winded and short-breathed, as if the author were panting while he climbed an interminable flight of steps.

He says in one of his prefaces, "This, amusingly enough, is what, on the evidence before us, I seem critically, as I say, to gather," and we feel that his words are uttered in little gasps. Most of them, in the sentence just quoted, add hardly a shade to the meaning he is trying to convey. Sometimes his famous density is little more than verbosity, and the reader feels himself to be fumbling for ideas, with sticky fingers, in a tub of very old hen-feathers.

Mr. Matthiessen believes that James's revisions in the New York Edition were generally an improvement over his early style; but after reading the discussion carefully I am not so sure that I agree with him. Some of his retouches made the characters more vivid and others introduced effective figures of speech. There were many changes, however, that merely complicated the style. When Madame Merle faces her former lover, in the first version of *The Portrait of a Lady*, she says to him, "How do bad people end? You have made me bad." In the revised version she says, "How do bad people end? — especially as to their *common* crimes. You have made me as bad as yourself." That is more definite, if a little harder to grasp; but it lacks the classical finality of the original statement. In his revisions, James was proud of the way he handled the "he said —she said" problem. But why should it be a problem at all? Why not, like Hemingway, write "he said" and "she said" whenever they are necessary for the sense, instead of looking for elegant variations? The later James was obsessed with finding elegant variations: "she returned," "he just hung fire," "she gaily engaged," and it reminds one of reading a play with too many stage directions.

But the worst feature of James's later style is the inversions that are most noticeable in very short phrases. "Will that so much matter?" he says, instead of, "Will that matter so much?" Very often he forces the verb to the end of the sentence, as in German. He writes: "Maud a little more dryly said"—"Had he had time a little more to try his case"—"What in the world's that but what I shall be just *not* doing?"—"But what are they either, poor things, to do?"—"I suppose that's what I horribly mean"—"I'll go to him then now"—"He wonderfully smiled." English is becoming more and more an uninflected language like Chinese, in which the function of words is shown chiefly by their position in the phrase. To change that position arbitrarily; to write, "He wonderfully smiled," instead of "smiled wonderfully" (and what does "wonderfully" mean in that connection: "for a wonder"? — "wonderingly"? — "in a wonderfully pleasant fashion"?) is to violate the spirit of the language as shaped by all the living and dead millions who speak or have spoken it. Not only is it a symbol of James's separation from the public; it directly expresses and, in a real sense, it *is* that separation.

The anti-Jacobites are right to say that James's later work shows the bad results of exile and expatriation; but they explain his problem in much too simple terms. James was not merely, as they believe, expatriated in the sense of making his home in England. He was self-exiled from England too, until the First World War; he spent most of his life in the world of creation. He wrote in his notebook: "To live *in* the world of creation—to get into it and stay in it—to frequent it and haunt it—to *think* intensely and fruitfully—to woo combinations and inspirations into being by a depth and continuity of attention and meditation—this is the only thing." It was the only thing that James really desired; and it explains the great virtues of his later novels as well as their vices. The virtues and the vices were interrelated and intermingled. In order to become a great novelist, he made himself purely a spectator of life; he denied himself the luxury of holding opinions "even on the Dreyfus case," as he said; and thereby he lost his sense of participation in life and the sort of understanding gained by those who act on their opinions. In the pursuit of combinations and inspirations, he divorced himself from the public, and the divorce made him feel, "well, blighted to the root." At the same time, however, the liberty gained through being unpopular helped him to create independent and self-sustaining works of art. In his "major phase," to follow Matthiessen, or in his decadent period, to rephrase Brooks, there are not two Henry Jameses, one of them a hero in the world of creation, the other a fussy old snob in a fawn-colored vest. There is one Henry James who must be accepted in his strength and weakness.

If we accept him so, the strength far outweighs the weakness. What we remember in his later novels is not their narrowness or their awkward style, but rather their rare quality of self-dependent life. James said in his preface to *Roderick Hudson* that the novelist's subject was like the painter's: it consisted in "the related state, to each other, of certain figures and things." His emphasis falls on the word "related"; and we note that everything in his later novels exists, develops, declines, is extinguished or transformed, *in relation* to something else in the book—not in relation to something outside, to the reader's supposed knowledge of historical incidents or social forces. Everything is bathed in the same consciousness as in some transparent medium; the characters move like swimmers seen from below in utterly clear water. The whole pattern they form, in its complexity, possesses and keeps an inner balance like that of a painting or a symphony; and that explains the permanence of his novels. Their subject matter is not only limited, but in many cases it is fatally out of fashion: for example we feel that Lambert Strether's late discovery of life in Paris, in *The Ambassadors*, was not so much tragic as pathetic. There is no longer the contrast that James described at such length, between the innocent American and the sophisticated European. In these days, however, when innocent and direct Europeans are likely to be confronted with cynical Americans; when the moral standards of New York are more lax than those of Paris; when the millionaire and the nobleman have lost the high position that James assigned to them in his novels—even now, the best of those novels have an inner life that illuminates the life about us and will continue to illuminate our children's lives.

Lafcadio Herun-san

IT WAS a surprising experience to reread Hearn's work volume after volume. Some of it seemed as mannered and frilled as the fashions of sixty years ago, and not always the best fashions; at times it might have been copied from Paris models by an earnest but awkward provincial dressmaker. Perhaps I was expecting all of it to have this end-of-the-century air, this charm of the faded and half-forgotten; what surprised me was that so much of it remained new and genuine. Unlike many authors with broader talents, he had the métier, the vocation for writing, the conscience that kept him working over each passage until it had the exact color of what he needed to say; and in most cases the colors have proved fast. Many books written by his famous contemporaries are becoming difficult to read. One can't help seeing that Howells followed the conventions of his day, that Frank Norris was full of romantic bad taste; but Lafcadio Hearn at his best was independent of fashion and was writing for our time as much as his own.

No American author of the nineteenth century had a stranger life. He was born in 1850 on the Ionian island of Santa Maura—the ancient Leucadia, which explains his given name—and in 1904 his ashes were buried after a Buddhist ceremony in Tokyo. His ancestry was Maltese on his mother's side and hence may be taken as a mixture of Phoenician, Arab, Norman, Spanish, and Italian; on his father's side it was Anglo-Irish with—Lafcadio liked to think—a touch of Romany. He learned to say his first prayers in Italian and demotic Greek. Adopted by a wealthy great-aunt, Sarah Brenane, he was educated by private tutors in Dublin and at Catholic schools in England and France. He was a British subject until he became a naturalized Japanese at the age of forty-six; but he always thought of himself as an American writer.

"Yes," he said in a letter to an English friend in Japan, "I have got out of touch with Europe altogether, and think of

Introduction to *The Selected Writings of Lafcadio Hearn*, ed. Henry Goodman, Citadel Press, New York, 1949. A somewhat shorter version of the essay was published as "Lafcadio Herun-san," *New Republic*, 120, April 18, 1949, 22–24.

America when I make comparisons. At nineteen years of age, after my people had been reduced from riches to poverty by an adventurer,—and before I had seen anything of the world except in a year of London among the common folk,—I was dropped moneyless on the pavement of an American city to begin life. Often slept in the street, etc.," and he might have added that the "etc." included doorways, packing boxes, a stable, and a rusty boiler in a vacant lot. "Worked as a servant, waiter, printer, proofreader, hack-writer, gradually pulled myself up. I never gave up my English citizenship. But I had eighteen years of American life,—and so got out of touch with Europe. For the same reason, I had to work at literature through American vehicles."

It is doubtful whether he could have survived as a writer, or survived at all, if he had started his career in another country. Besides being a very small man—five feet, three inches in height—and nearly blind, so that his life was in danger whenever he crossed a street, he was as shy as an African pygmy and as quick to take offense as the king's musketeers. He had the beginnings of a classical education and absolutely no knowledge of how to earn a living. In New York and Cincinnati he was often close to starvation, but he was always rescued in time; for that was during the Gilded Age, when American life had a sort of hurried and absentminded ease, with few organized charities, but with more acts of casual kindness than a waif like Lafcadio would encounter in our own day. People found jobs for him, and when he lost or left the jobs they sometimes fed him like a stray kitten. The warmest shelter open to him was the Cincinnati Public Library, where the librarian asked him questions and gave him work to do. A printer named Henry Watkin promised to teach him the trade and meanwhile let him sleep behind the shop, in a box full of paper shavings.

By 1872, three years after his arrival in this country, he was working as proofreader for a small publishing house—the other men in the office called him Old Semicolon—and at night he was writing articles which he hoped to publish in the Cincinnati newspapers. He had carried the first article to Colonel John A. Cockerill, the editor of the *Enquirer*. "Do you pay for contributions?" he asked in a voice that could scarcely be heard. Cockerill said that he did and invited the big-spectacled waif into his private office. Producing a manuscript from under his very long coat, Lafcadio laid it on the table with trembling hands, "and stole away," Cockerill said, "like a distorted brownie, leaving behind him an impression that was uncanny and indescribable." The manuscript was printed, as were most of the others that Lafcadio brought into the office; sometimes his contributions filled one-fourth of the Sunday edition. Soon he was a salaried member of the *Enquirer* staff.

American daily journalism gave Hearn a chance he would have found in no other field. He had come to this country at a time when many serious writers, after fleeing to Europe, were complaining from a distance that American books had to be written and American magazines edited for a genteel audience composed chiefly of women. They forgot the newspapers, which were written for men and therefore retained more freedom of speech, besides a touch of cynicism. The newspapers of the time discussed dangerous topics like prostitution, adultery, and miscegenation, which couldn't even be mentioned in the magazines. When describing crimes of violence, their reporters were advised to copy the methods of the French naturalists. Their reviewers were permitted to indulge in fine writing and a show of curious learning. Although newspapers overworked their staffs and paid them miserable wages—standard figures in the Middle West were ten dollars a week for cubs and thirty dollars for star reporters—still they paid those wages every Saturday and thus provided the only sure livelihood for writers in revolt against the genteel tradition. Bierce, Huneker, Harold Frederic, Stephen Crane, David Graham Phillips, and Dreiser—almost all the skeptics, the bohemians, and the Naturalists—started their careers as newspaper men.

Hearn was a bohemian by necessity and a distant ally of the French late-romantic and decadent writers. As a newspaper man he could publish translations from Gautier and Loti that were daring for the time, besides original sketches that the magazines would have rejected as being godless or indecent (or simply overwritten). He could also publish editorials and reviews that displayed as in a showcase the fruits of his esoteric reading. On the *Enquirer* and later on the New Orleans *Times-Democrat* he became a sort of provincial Remy de

Gourmont, divorced from life but pillaging the whole world of books and presenting his readers with folk tales from Arabia and India, voodoo chants, and extracts from the best that was being written in Europe.

He had a purple style in his youth and the newspapers encouraged it. Describing a visit to a New Orleans hospital during a yellow-fever epidemic, he would say, "The grizzled watcher of the inner gate extended his pallid palm for the eleemosynary contribution exacted from all visitors;—and it seemed to me that I beheld the gray Ferryman of Shadows himself, silently awaiting his obolus from me, also a Shadow." The *Times-Democrat* printed that without deleting an adjective or a semicolon and Hearn was inspired to use still loftier language. "The spider at last ceased to repair her web of elfin silk," he said; "years came and went with lentor inexpressible." He was proud of that last phrase, though afterwards he learned to regret it. "My first work was awfully florid," he said when he was living in Japan. "I should like now to go through many paragraphs written years ago and sober them down." But although he blamed the newspapers for encouraging the weaker side of his work, he could also thank them for printing every word of it and for teaching him habits of industry.

There was another service, too, for which he could thank the newspapers that employed him; to some extent they protected him in his conflicts with the proprieties. Hearn was so conscious of his physical handicaps that he never made love to any woman of his own race whom he regarded as his social equal; on the other hand, he felt at ease with those who were more unfortunate than himself. In Cincinnati he married a colored woman named Alethea Foley, the mother of an illegitimate child by another white man, and lived with her in a tumbledown house next door to the stables of the Adams Express Company. Soon the Hearn household was a citywide scandal, one that would have kept him from earning a living if he had been a clerk or a teacher; fortunately a reporter was not expected to observe the conventions. Although the *Enquirer* became worried and discharged him in 1875, a year after his marriage, he was soon rehired by another paper, which paid him a lower salary and thought it was getting a bargain.

Hearn separated from Alethea in 1877; no divorce was necessary because mixed marriages were not legally recognized in Ohio. That same year he went to New Orleans, where he lived for some months on the edge of starvation and nearly died of dengue, or breakbone fever. He looked like an undernourished scarecrow when he was at last hired by a struggling newspaper, the *Item*, at a cub's salary of ten dollars a week. That was enough to live on, in New Orleans, and four years later he became the translator and staff critic for a larger paper, the *Times-Democrat*, at a star reporter's salary of thirty dollars. There were scandals about him in New Orleans, too, probably without much basis, but kept alive by the rebellious and sensual tone of his writing. Once again his newspapers protected him and were proud to publish his work.

It was not until he went north, in 1887, and tried to live by writing for the magazines that he began to feel exposed to the full force of social condemnation. He sought refuge in Martinique, where he declared that nature itself was "nude, warm, savage and amorous," and where he felt at ease in a society of mixed races. In 1889 he spent an unhappy summer in Philadelphia and an unhappier winter in New York; then he fled across the world to Japan.

Hearn reached Tokyo in the year 1890: the 23d Meiji by the Japanese system of reckoning from the return to power of the Mikado and the introduction of Western ways. The kingdom, not yet really an empire, was in a state of violent transformation, military, industrial, and cultural. With schoolboys by the hundreds of thousands studying English, there was a lack of qualified instructors. Hearn had come to Japan with a vague commission from Harper and Brothers for books and magazine articles, but he always quarreled with publishers and soon he was left to live by his own resources. This time, instead of starving, he became professor of English at the government schools in Matsue, which was the capital of a backward province slowly emerging from the feudal age. His monthly salary of 100 yen, or about $45, made him one of the richer inhabitants of the little city on the Sea of Japan.

All his life till then Hearn had felt himself to be marked off from the rest of mankind by his small stature, his strange appearance, and especially by his uneven eyes, one blind, marbled, and sunken in his skull, the other myopic and protruding, so that it looked like the single eye of an octopus. He had felt even more isolated by the scandals that had followed him since his marriage. In one of his letters he explained that, small as he was, he had powerful enemies, including Society, the Church—all the churches—and the English and American Press. "I am pretty much in the position," he continued, "of a bookkeeper known to have once embezzled, or of a man who has been in prison, or of a prostitute who has been on the street. These are, none of them, you will confess, *important* persons. But what keeps them in their holes? Society, Church and public opinion—the Press." In Japan he seemed to have escaped from these real or imagined enemies. His small stature ceased to worry him there, since he was taller than most of his Japanese colleagues and since the whole country, with its small houses and dwarf trees in miniature gardens, was designed on his scale. Even his strange appearance provoked no special comments. All foreigners looked strange to the Japanese, Hearn scarcely more than the others.

His two years in Matsue were a long idyll. Hearn loved the old Japan, more of which had survived there than in the larger cities, and he found that he loved the people, too. In Matsue they returned his affection. At first they were kind to him out of curiosity and because he was the first foreigner to live among them; but there is evidence that students and professors came to have a special respect for Herun—or Hellum, or Fellun, as they called him in their different dialects. When the first winter proved unusually severe for southwestern Japan, a friend on the faculty suggested to Herun-san that marriage was the best means of keeping warm. He also produced a candidate bride, Setsu Koizumi, the only child of an impoverished family belonging to the warrior or samurai caste. After freezing for two more nights, Hearn paid a formal visit to her parents and the wedding took place with little delay. Setsu was a polite and conscientious little moon-faced woman who wasn't beautiful by Japanese or any other standards. As time went on she proved to be self-willed and given to fits of hysteria, but Hearn said to the end that he had the best wife in the world.

He supported the whole Koizumi family, including Setsu's mother, her father, and her grandfather by adoption, as well as a collection of relatives who came for monthlong or year-long visits. Although he had rescued them from poverty, his relations with the family were not one-sided; Hearn had more to give, but the Koizumis were loyal to him and gave whatever they could. Once when he had a serious attack of indigestion he learned that Setsu's father had sworn to starve himself for a year if the gods would let his son-in-law recover. It was, however, Setsu's mother who cured him by learning to cook European meals. In general the Koizumis guarded his working hours, taught him Japanese customs, and kept him from being cheated; and in 1896 they formally adopted him as a son so that he could become a Japanese citizen.

By that time Hearn himself was a father. He was to have three sons and a daughter, but it was the firstborn, Kazuo, whom he idolized. On the night when the child was expected, he had knelt at his wife's bedside and prayed in broken Japanese. "Come into the world with good eyes," he had murmured again and again; but then the two midwives arrived and Hearn retired to a garden house. It was one o'clock in the morning when the great-grandfather, an old samurai, came dancing into the garden with his hands clasped above his head and his kimono sleeves fallen to his shoulders. "Hellum, Hellum!" he shouted. "Great treasure child is born." Later the old man used to carry Kazuo around the house while he sang at the top of his voice:

> *Urashima Taro lived a hundred and six years;*
> *Takeuchi Sukuné lived three hundred years;*
> *Tōbōsaku lived nine thousand years;*
> *Koizumi Kazuo—a million and more millions.*

Their common love for the firstborn was another bond that held the family together. Hearn, the former outcast, was now Papa-san and the center of a small community. He felt relieved from the Western burden of separateness he had carried all his life till then. "There are nearly twelve here," he said in a letter, "to whom I am Life and Food and other things. However intolerable anything else is, at home I enter into my little smiling world of old ways and thoughts and courtesies; where all is soft and gentle as something seen in sleep. It is so soft, so intangibly gentle and lovable and artless, that sometimes it seems a dream only; and then a fear comes that it might vanish away. It has become Me. When I am pleased, it laughs; when I don't feel jolly, everything is silent. Thus light and vapoury as its force seems, it is a moral force, perpetually appealing to conscience."

It was a moral force that would keep Hearn in Japan until he died. Reading his letters, honest and eloquent, and the touching book, *Father and I*, that Kazuo wrote when his own children were growing up, one can't help feeling a warm personal regard for this waif who had found a home. He was brave, honorable, and loyal. When his burdens piled up imperceptibly, so that a stronger man might have been crushed by them, he carried them without complaint; he had become a good husband and father, a great teacher, and a faithful subject of the Mikado. After the Matsue idyll he lost his illusions about Japan. Life was sterner in Kumamoto and Kobe and Tokyo, the cities where he lived for the next twelve years. His university career was always being threatened by intrigues in the Ministry of Education, so that sometimes he hated the Japanese government and even the people. "You can't understand my feeling of reaction in the matter of Japanese psychology," he wrote to his friend Professor Chamberlain. "It seems as if everything had suddenly become clear to me, and utterly void of emotional interest. . . . There are no depths to stir, no race-profundities to explore: all is like a Japanese river-bed, through which the stones and rocks show up all the year round,—and is never filled but in times of cataclysm and destruction."

No matter how he felt about the Japanese as a nation—and he had other moods than disillusionment—he was always faithful to his family. The children came first and especially Kazuo, who had become the center of his life. "Every year," he wrote to his future biographer, Elizabeth Bisland, "there are born some millions of boys cleverer, stronger, handsomer than mine. I may be quite a fool in my estimate of him. I do not find him very clever, quick, or anything of that sort. Perhaps there will prove to be 'nothing in him.' I cannot tell. All that I am quite sure of is that he naturally likes what is delicate, clean, refined, and kindly,—and that he naturally shrinks from whatever is coarse or selfish. . . . I must do all I can to feed the tiny light, and give it a chance to prove what it is worth. It is ME, in another birth—with renewed forces given by a strange and charming blood from the Period of the Gods." Often Hearn felt there were invisible walls that separated him from everything in Japan and even kept him from touching his firstborn son. He longed to escape, if only for a few months; in the Japanese winter, shivering beside a charcoal brazier, he dreamed of being alone in Manila or some other tropical city. There was money enough for the trip, but Hearn was beginning to fear that he hadn't long to live and he wanted to provide for the family. A later plan was to take Kazuo with him for a visit to the United States, where Hearn would lecture at a university in order to pay for the boy's schooling. But Cornell, which had invited him, changed its mind about the lectures and he stayed in Tokyo to rewrite them into a book; it was *Japan: An Attempt at Interpretation*, the last and most ambitious of his works.

His attitude toward writing had changed since he became a father. In earlier years his life had formed a fairly simple pattern of frustration and aggression; he was always being hurt or offended and was always picking quarrels. He slept with a loaded revolver under his pillow and often carried it, too—although the only time he used it was on his trip from Cincinnati south, when he saw a man gouge out a kitten's eyes; he fired at the man four times and missed. Apparently he wrote to prove that, small as he was, he could outdo his enemies. He confessed something of the sort in a letter to Ellwood Hendrick, one of the few friends with whom he never fought. Hearn underlined the key statement: "*Unless somebody does or says something horribly mean to me, I can't do certain kinds of work,—* the tiresome kinds, that compel a great deal of thinking. The exact force of the hurt I can measure at the time of receiving it: 'This will be over in six months'; 'This I shall have to fight for two years'; 'This will be remembered longer.' When I begin to think about the matter afterwards, then I rush to

work. I write page after page of vagaries, metaphysical, emotional, romantic,—throw them aside. Then the next day I go to
work rewriting them. I rewrite and rewrite them till they
begin to define and arrange themselves into a whole. . . . Pain
is therefore to me of exceeding value betimes; and everybody
who does me a wrong indirectly does me a right."

The letter was written from Kobe in 1895 and described an
emotional pattern that was changing. Even though Hearn
continued to quarrel with his associates, there had come to be
something dogged and perfunctory in the process; he was
merely following a ritual, like an atheist kneeling in prayer. He
looked for grievances so they would make him go to work, as
before; but writing had now become an end in itself and the
means of providing an inheritance for Kazuo and the family.
He couldn't stop working even when the doctors warned him
that he was straining his heart. "Money, money, money," he
often murmured; "I don't want money for myself, I only want
it for my wife and children." He earned money by writing as
much as he could—a book a year in addition to his teaching;
but he was also trying to do his best work and the double effort
killed him. His last words were in Japanese, *"Ah, byōki no
tamé"*—Ah, on account of illness. After the funeral, which was
conducted by a Buddhist archbishop, the family shrine was
moved into Papa-san's study; and twice a day the children and
later the grandchildren recited prayers before his photograph.

Rereading his work after many years, one is impressed by its
limitations as well as by its workmanship and integrity. It is
narrow in scope, as if his smallness and shortsightedness had
been moral as well as physical qualities. Sometimes it deals
with general ideas, but in an apprentice fashion and with
continual nods of deference to Herbert Spencer, who was
Hearn's only schoolmaster in philosophy. It is full of moods,
colors, and misty outlines, but lacking in pictures of daily life.
Hearn complained in a letter that he knew nothing about the
smallest practical matters: "Nothing, for example, about a
boat, a horse, a farm, an orchard, a watch, a garden. Nothing
about what a man ought to do under any possible circumstances." In short, he knew very little about the experiences of

other human beings, and that is only one of his disabilities as an author. He was never able to invent a plot and often begged his friends to tell him stories so that he would have something to write about. He had little power of construction beyond the limits of a short essay or a folk tale. Of the sixteen books he published during his lifetime only one—*Japan: An Attempt at Interpretation*—is a book properly speaking. The others are either loose novelettes like *Chita* and *Youma*, in which the atmosphere is more important than the story; or else they are collections of shorter pieces that appeared or might have appeared in the magazines.

It seems to us now that Hearn started by misestimating and underestimating his own gifts. "Knowing that I have nothing resembling genius," he said in a letter to Whitman's disciple, William D. O'Connor, "and that any ordinary talent must be supplemented with some sort of curious study in order to place it above the mediocre line, I am striving to woo the Muse of the Odd, and hope to succeed in thus attracting some little attention." In another letter to O'Connor he spoke of pledging himself to the worship of the Odd, the Queer, the Strange, the Exotic, the Monstrous. "It quite suits my temperament," he added mistakenly. The great weakness of his early sketches is that they aren't sufficiently odd or monstrous or differentiated from one another. The best of them are folk tales adapted from various foreign literatures. The others keep reverting to the same situation, that of a vaguely pictured hero in love with a dead woman or with her ghost (just as Hearn was in love with the memory of his mother, who disappeared from his life when he was seven years old). They are obsessive rather than exotic; and they are written in a style that suggests the scrollwork on the ceiling of an old-fashioned theater.

After his death Hearn's reputation suffered from the collections that others made of his early newspaper work, most of which should have been allowed to sleep in the files of the Cincinnati and New Orleans press. Even the books he wrote in his later New Orleans years—*Stray Leaves from Strange Literatures, Some Chinese Ghosts*, and *Chita*—though they all contained fine things are not yet his mature writing. *Two Years in the French West Indies* (1890) is longer and richer and shows how Hearn could be carried out of himself by living among a people with whom he sympathized. Still, it was not until after his first years in Japan that he really mastered a subject and a style.

He wrote to Chamberlain in 1893, "After for years studying poetical prose, I am forced now to study simplicity. After attempting my utmost at ornamentation, I am converted by my own mistakes. The great point is to touch with simple words." That is exactly what he did in the best of his later writing. Instead of using important-sounding words to describe events that were not always important in themselves, he depended on the events to impress the reader and looked for words that would reveal them as through a clear glass. Here, for example, is a crucial paragraph from "The Story of Mimi-Nashi-Hōïchi," a Japanese legend retold in *Kwaidan*:

> At that instant Hōïchi felt his ears gripped by fingers of iron, and torn off! Great as the pain was, he gave no cry. The heavy footfalls receded along the verandah,—descended into the garden,—passed out to the roadway,—ceased. From either side of his head, the blind man felt a thick warm trickling; but he dared not lift his hands.

Today we don't like the exclamation point after the first sentence, or the commas followed by dashes in the third; but Hearn was following his own theories about punctuation as a guide to the reader's voice. Primarily he was writing for the ear, not the eye; and the passage in its context sounds exactly right when read aloud. He almost always found the right words, as notably at the end of his story about a hunter who saw a pair of *oshidori*, or mandarin ducks, and killed the drake. Later the hunter felt an inner summons to revisit the same place—

> . . . and there, when he came to the river-bank, he saw the female oshidori swimming alone. In the same moment the bird perceived Sonjo; but, instead of trying to escape, she swam straight towards him, looking at him the while in a strange fixed way. Then, with her own beak, she suddenly tore open her own body, and died before the hunter's eyes. . . .
> Sonjo shaved his head, and became a priest.

Hearn would work for hours changing and rearranging the words in a brief and utterly simple passage like this one. "For

me words have colour, form, character," he said in a letter to
Chamberlain; "they have faces, ports, manners, gesticulations;
they have moods, humours, eccentricities;—they have tints,
tones, personalities"—and they had all these qualities in addition and largely without reference to their meanings. He
thought that the letter A was blush-crimson and the letter E
sky-blue; that KH wore a beard and a turban; that initial X
was a mature Greek with wrinkles, and that "—no—" had an
innocent, lovable and childlike aspect. He was affected by "the
whispering of words, the rustling of the procession of letters
. . . the pouting of words, the frowning and fuming of words,
the weeping, the raging and racketing and rioting of words,
the noisomeness of words, the tenderness or hardness, the
dryness or juiciness of words,—the interchange of values in the
gold, the silver, the brass and the copper of words." Words
were his David's pebbles against Goliath; they were the magic
spells that protected him from a world of enemies. No labor
with words was too great for him if it led to the perfect
incantation.

He told a correspondent that he had worked for months on
a single page before it expressed his mood and meaning.
"When the best result comes, it ought to surprise you," he said
in the same letter, "for our best work is out of the Unconscious." Not being one of the fortunate authors who are able to
draw up and execute plans for their books as if they were
building houses, Hearn had to depend on his unconscious mind
for suggestions. His two problems were how to set that mind
in operation and how to revise the impressions it yielded step
by step. He wrote his first drafts hurriedly and set them aside;
then he rewrote them time and again, finding that what he
called his "latent feelings" took shape in the process of revision. "Of course," he said to Chamberlain, "it looks like big
labor to rewrite every page half a dozen times. But in reality it
is the least possible labor. To those with whom writing is an
almost automatic exertion, the absolute fatigue is no more than
that of writing a letter. The rest of the work *does itself*,
without your effort. It is like spiritualism. Just move the pen,
and the ghosts do the writing."

Hearn was innocently boasting when he wrote that letter;
elsewhere he admitted that the process of composition was

always painful for him. Perhaps it was most painful during the moments before he sat down at his desk. He used to pace up and down his study, sometimes groaning, sometimes shrieking as if he had been possessed, not by ghosts eager to do his writing, but by the spirits of women dead in childbirth. At such moments his wife and little Kazuo would rush up to him crying, "Papa, Papa!" until their voices had called him back from his nightmare. "*Gomen, gomen*"—I'm sorry, he would say, brushing his hand over his eyes. A short time later his scratchy pen would start to move rapidly over sheet after sheet of paper. Hearn wrote with his head bowed and twisted to the left and his one nearsighted eye six inches from the manuscript. He had an extraordinary faculty of absorption in his work; as long as the pen was moving he could see nothing else, hear nothing and feel nothing. He liked to write at night by an oil lamp; sometimes when the wick was turned too high, soot would cover everything in the room by midnight. Sometimes when Kazuo and his mother came into the room next morning they would find the floor under his desk covered with gorged mosquitoes, like little red beans. "It must have been very itchy," they would say; and Papa-san would answer, "I didn't feel them." His method of composition helped to confine him to small forms, essays and tales that he could finish before exhausting himself and losing contact with his subconscious; but it also gave him a sort of deep-lying honesty within his limitations. In his best work one never finds the fault of less scrupulous writers, who proclaim one emotion by the meaning of their words while suggesting another by the color and sound of their words. What they usually suggest is an absence of emotion and a disbelief in what they are saying. Hearn's writing was true not only on the surface but in depth; not only to his conscious thinking but also to the submerged feelings that gave their rhythms to his prose. It wears well because it is all of a piece.

Besides his sense of language and his patient integrity he had something else in his later years that larger talents have often lacked: a subject. Of course the subject was Japanese culture in the broad sense, and a question still being argued is whether his picture of it was true by factual standards or was dangerously romanticized. That question we can let the experts decide, but not before we have noted that each of them seems to have a different notion of the truth. To another question, whether Hearn knew Japan, there can be only one answer.

He knew Japan, not as an observer, but as a citizen, the adopted son of Japanese parents and the father of Japanese children. He knew the faults of his countrymen by adoption, although he preferred to emphasize their virtues when writing for Western magazines. He foresaw the conflict between Japan and the West. He knew what arguments would touch the Japanese mind and what explanations were necessary before English poems could be understood by Japanese students. It is not surprising to learn that the students worshiped him; when he lost his post at the Imperial University they spoke of banding together to defend him, like the forty-seven *ronin* of the Japanese legend who avenged their feudal lord and then committed suicide in front of his tomb. Some of the students took down his lectures word for word; and after his death a whole series of volumes—four in this country, five others in Japan—was compiled and published from their notes. The volumes do not prove that Hearn was a great critic or that he always preferred the best to the second-best. What they do prove is that he was a great interpreter who, belonging to English literature, could still explain it as if he formed part of a Japanese audience.

More important for us than the lectures, which have their place in the history of Japanese thought, are the eleven books in which he performed the opposite task of interpreting Japan to the West. He never claimed that the books presented a complete picture of his new country. He liked to confess that he knew very little about Japanese economics or politics and he always hated the new industrial society that was developing in the Meiji era. He liked old things, courtesy, kindness, devotion, ancestor worship; perhaps he exaggerated their importance in Japanese society. Apparently he could grope his way through the newspapers, but he couldn't read Japanese classical books or write anything more than short letters to his wife, who had no English, in the private language they called "Mr. Hearn dialect," *Herun-san kotoba*. On the other hand, he had a householder's knowledge of Japanese life, a scholar's knowledge of religious customs, and something more than that, an intimate and sympathetic grasp of Japanese legends.

He learned the legends from various sources; some of his students collected them and his wife helped more effectively, by reading old books for him and retelling the stories in their private language. Hearn put the best of them into English, with the freedom of a storyteller working from oral sources. He described his work as translation, but it was more than that, as became apparent when similar tales were merely translated by others. The result in their case was folklore for the laboratory, preserved in formaldehyde, whereas Hearn's version was literature. Long before coming to Japan he had shown an instinct for finding in legends the permanent archetypes of human experience—that is the secret of their power to move us—and he later proved that he knew which tales to choose and which details to emphasize, in exactly the right English. Now that so much of his work in many fields has been collected into one volume, I think it will be apparent that his folk tales are the most valuable part of it and that he is the writer in our language who can best be compared with Hans Christian Andersen and the brothers Grimm.

A Natural History of American Naturalism

NATURALISM APPEARED thirty years later in American literature than it did in Europe and it was never quite the same movement. Like European Naturalism it was inspired by Darwin's theory of evolution and kept repeating the doctrine that men, being part of the animal kingdom, were subject to natural laws. But theories and doctrines were not the heart of it. The American Naturalists turned to Europe; they read—or read about—Darwin, they studied Spencer and borrowed methods from Zola because they were rebelling against an intolerable situation at home. What bound them together into a school or movement was this native rebellion and not the nature of the help that, like rebels in all ages, they summoned from abroad.

They began writing during the 1890's, when American literature was under the timid but tyrannical rule of what afterwards came to be known as the genteel tradition. It was also called Puritanism by its enemies, but that was a mistake on the part of writers with only a stereotyped notion of American history. The original Puritans were not in the least genteel. They believed in the real existence of evil, which they denounced in terms that would have shocked William Dean Howells and the polite readers of the *Century Magazine*. The great New England writers, descendants of the Puritans, were moralists overburdened with scruples; but they were never mealymouthed in the fashion of their successors. Gentility—or "ideality" or "decency," to mention two favorite words of the genteel writers—was something that developed chiefly in New York and the Middle West and had its flowering after the Civil War.

Essentially it was an effort to abolish the various evils and vulgarities in American society by never speaking about them.

"Naturalism in American Literature," in Stow Persons, ed., *Evolutionary Thought in America*, New Haven, Yale University Press, 1950. Portions of the essay were published as "Not Men: A Natural History of American Naturalism," *Kenyon Review*, 60, Summer 1947, 414–35, and as "Naturalism's Terrible McTeague," *New Republic*, 116, May 5, 1947, 31–33.

It was a theory that divided the world into two parts, as Sunday was divided from the days of the week or the right side from the wrong side of the railroad tracks. On one side was religion; on the other, business. On one side was the divine in human beings; on the other, everything animal. On one side was art; on the other, life. On one side were women, clergymen, and university professors, all guardians of Art and the Ideal; on the other side were men in general, immersed in their practical affairs. On one side were the church and the school; on the other side were the saloon, the livery stable, and other low haunts where men gathered to talk politics, swap stories, and remember their wartime adventures with the yellow girls in New Orleans. In America during the late nineteenth century, culture was set against daily living, theory against practice, highbrow against lowbrow; and the same division could be found in the language itself—for one side spoke a sort of bloodless literary English, while the other had a speech that was not American but Amurrkn, ugly and businesslike, sometimes picturesque, but not yet a literary idiom.

The whole territory of literature was thought to lie on the right side of the railroad tracks, in the chiefly feminine realm of beauty, art, religion, culture, and the ideal. Novels had to be written with pure heroines and happy endings in order to flatter the self-esteem of female readers. Magazines were edited so as not to disturb the minds of young girls or call forth protests from angry mothers. Frank Norris said of American magazines in 1895: "They are safe as a graveyard, decorous as a church, as devoid of immorality as an epitaph. . . . They adorn the center table. They do not 'call a blush to the cheek of the young.' They can be placed—oh, crowning virtue, oh, supreme encomium—they can be 'safely' placed in the hands of any young girl the country over. . . . It is the 'young girl' and the family center table that determine the standard of the American short story." Meanwhile there were new men appearing year by year—Frank Norris was one of them—who would not write for the young girl or the center table and could not express themselves without breaking the rules of the genteel editors.

These new men, who would be the first American Naturalists, were all in some way disadvantaged when judged by the social and literary standards then prevailing. They were not of the Atlantic seaboard, or not of the old stock, or not educated in the right schools, or not members of the Protestant churches, or not sufficiently respectable in their persons or in their family backgrounds. They were in rebellion against the genteel tradition because, like writers from the beginning of time, they had an urgent need for telling the truth about themselves, and because there was no existing medium in which they were privileged to tell it.

Instinctively the new writers began a search for older allies. There were a few of these to be found in America, but not enough of them to serve as the basis of a new literary movement. For most of their support, the rebels had to look eastward across the Atlantic.

They were especially attracted by the English evolutionary scientists and pamphleteers. Most of the young writers read the works of this whole English group, beginning with Darwin, whose observations were too rigorously set forth to please their slipshod literary tastes. They could not find much to use in Darwin's books, except his picture of natural selection operating through the struggle for life; most of their Darwinism was acquired at second hand. Huxley they seem to have read with less veneration but more interest, chiefly because of his arguments against the Bible as revealed truth and because of his long war with the Protestant clergy. Young writers, feeling that the churches were part of a vast conspiracy to keep them silent, believed that Huxley was fighting their battle. It was Herbert Spencer, however, who deeply affected their thinking. Spencer's American popularity during the last half of the nineteenth century is something without parallel in the history of philosophic writing. From 1860 to 1903 his books had a sale of 368,755 copies in the authorized editions, not counting the many editions that appeared without his consent. In the memoirs of many famous Americans born in the 1860's and 1870's, one finds the reading of Spencer mentioned as an event that changed the course of their lives. Said John R. Commons, the labor historian, speaking of his father's cronies, "Every one of them in that eastern section of Indiana was a Republican living on the battle cries of the Civil War, and every one was a follower of Herbert Spencer. . . . I was brought up on Hoosierism, Republicanism, Presbyterianism and Spencerism."

What was a family inheritance for Commons was a personal discovery for most of the young writers who belonged to the same generation. Hamlin Garland, when he was starving in Boston on three or four dollars a week, managed to borrow Spencer's books from the public library. After a five-cent breakfast of coffee and two doughnuts, he went "with eager haste," so he says, to Spencer's Synthetic Philosophy. Edgar Lee Masters read Spencer in Illinois, at the age of nineteen. Jack London read him in the little room in Oakland, California, where he was teaching himself to write. He says of his autobiographical hero, Martin Eden, that he opened Spencer's *First Principles* in bed, hoping that the book would put him to sleep after algebra and physics and an attempt at a sonnet. "Morning found him still reading. It was impossible for him to sleep. Nor did he write that day. He lay on the bed till his body grew tired, when he tried the hard floor, reading on his back, the book held in the air above him, or changing from side to side. He slept that night, and did his writing next morning, and then the book tempted him and he fell reading all afternoon, oblivious to everything." Theodore Dreiser read Huxley and Spencer in Pittsburgh, when he was working as a young reporter on the *Dispatch*. He tells us in *Newspaper Days* "that the discovery of Spencer's *First Principles* quite blew me, intellectually, to bits"; and he goes on to say:

> Hitherto, until I had read Huxley, I had some lingering filaments of Catholicism trailing about me, faith in the existence of Christ, the soundness of his moral and sociologic deductions, the brotherhood of man. But on reading "Science and Hebrew Tradition" and "Science and Christian Tradition," and finding both the Old and New Testaments to be not compendiums of revealed truth but mere records of religious experiences, and very erroneous ones at that, and then taking up "First Principles" and discovering all I deemed substantial—man's place in nature, his importance in the universe, this too, too solid earth, man's very identity save as an infinitesimal speck of energy or a "suspended equation" drawn or blown here and there by larger forces in which he moved quite unconsciously as an atom—all questioned and dissolved into other and

less understandable things, I was completely thrown down in my conceptions or non-conceptions of life.

Not many of Spencer's readers were left with this impression of being confused and "completely thrown down." There were many more who valued him because he fitted together the pieces of a universal scheme that had been shattered by their earlier loss of faith in Christian dogmas. Garland, for example, found that "the universe took on order and harmony" as he considered Spencer's theory of the evolution of music or painting or sculpture. "It was thrilling, it was joyful," he says, "to perceive that everything moved from the simple to the complex—how the bow-string became the harp and the egg the chicken." Spencer's chief value, for the generation of writers who studied him, was that he gave them another unified world picture to replace the Christian synthesis. In that early age of specialization, he was the only great lay scholar with the courage to expound a synthetic philosophy. Many young men worshiped him not merely as a teacher but as a religious prophet. "To give up Spencer," said Jack London's autobiographical hero, "would be equivalent to a navigator throwing the compass and chronometer overboard." Later, when he heard a California judge disparaging Spencer, the hero burst into a rage. "To hear that great and noble man's name upon your lips," he shouted, "is like finding a dewdrop in a cesspool." In his quieter way, Edwin Arlington Robinson was almost as loyal to the synthetic philosopher. He said in a letter written in 1898 to one of his few Harvard friends:

> Professor James's book is entertaining and full of good things; but his attitude toward Spencer makes me think of a dream my father once had. He dreamed he met a dog. The dog annoyed him, so he struck him with a stick. Then the dog doubled in size and my father struck him again with the same result. So the thing went on till the universe was pretty much all dog. When my father awoke, he was, or rather had been, halfway down the dog's throat.

But Spencer, enormous as he seemed, was no guide to young writers in the specific problems of their craft; nor was he a model to which they could point as justification for their dealing frankly with the world around them. In fiction and poetry they had to find other allies and, once again, most of these were transatlantic.

There were, for example, the English eighteenth-century classics, which could always be cited in arguments for honest realism. *Roxana, or the Fortunate Mistress* was one of Howells' favorites. "Did you ever read Defoe's 'Roxana'?" he said in a letter to his friend Samuel Clemens. "If not, then read it, not merely for some of the deepest insights into the lying, suffering, sinning, well-meaning human soul, but the best and most natural English that a book was ever written in." Still, he was more than a little worried by the effect that novels like *Roxana* and even scenes from Shakespeare might have on public morals. "I hope the time will come," he said in an essay written not long after his letter to Clemens, "when the beast-man will be so far submerged and tamed in us that the memory of him in literature will be left to perish; that what is lewd and ribald in the great poets shall be kept out of such editions as are meant for public reading." But this was only a pious wish, and perhaps not wholly sincere. General readers could still buy Defoe and Fielding and Smollett in unexpurgated volumes printed in England.

They could also buy translations of living Continental writers, sometimes in paperbound reprints that sold for as little as ten cents. Turgenev and Tolstoy both had a following among literary people, and Tolstoy, because of his reputation for frankness, even had a popular sale. Ibsen was not often played, but he was widely discussed. There was a complete translation of Balzac, which stood on the shelves of the larger public libraries, and there were many editions of his separate novels. Zola also had a large public here and an extensive underground influence, in spite of the fact that he was seldom mentioned in the critical journals without being sweepingly condemned. "I read everything of Zola's that I can lay hands on," Howells confessed in a letter to John Hay. "But I have to hide the books from the children!" Theodore Dreiser tells us in his memoirs that when he was working as a reporter on the St. Louis *Republic*, in 1893, the city editor kept advising him "to imitate Zola's vivid description of the drab and the gross and the horrible, if I could—assuming that I had read him," Dreiser added, "which I had not, but I did not say so."

By that time, however, he had gained a fairly definite notion of Zola's methods at second hand. Two of his colleagues on the St. Louis *Globe-Democrat*, where he had worked the preceding year, had written a novel in the Zola manner. It was about a young and very beautiful actress named Theo, who was the mistress of a French newspaperman. Though deeply in love with her, the hero was unfaithful on at least one occasion; and this, Dreiser said when he retold the story in his memoirs, "brought about a Zolaesque scene in which she spanked another actress with a hairbrush. There was treacherous plotting on the part of somebody with regard to a local murder, which brought about the arrest and conviction of the newspaper man for something he knew nothing about. This entailed a great struggle on the part of Theo to save him, which resulted in her failure and his death on the guillotine. A priest figured in it in some way, grim, jesuitical."

This novel, which never found a publisher, must have been one of the earliest attempts to write in the manner of the French Naturalists. Dreiser read it in manuscript and was greatly impressed, though he also wondered why his friends found it necessary to deal with French, not American, life when they wished to write in terms of fact. He didn't read Zola till much later in his career, so he tells us; but he discovered Balzac in 1894, when he was a reporter in Pittsburgh. "It was for me," he says, "a literary revolution. Not only for the brilliant and incisive manner with which Balzac grasped life and invented themes whereby to present it, but for the fact that the types he handled with most enthusiasm and skill—the brooding, seeking, ambitious beginners in life's social, political, artistic and commercial affairs (Rastignac, Raphael, de Rubempré, Bianchon)—were, I thought, so much like myself." Doors had opened in his mind. "Coming out of the library this day," he says, "and day after day thereafter, the while I rendered as little reportorial service as was consistent with even a show of effort, I marveled at the physical similarity of the two cities"—Pittsburgh and Paris—"as I conceived it, at the chance for pictures here as well as there. American pictures here, as opposed to French pictures there."

This experience of Dreiser's brings to light a curious phenomenon connected with the whole stream of foreign influence.

Not only did the rebels of Dreiser's generation learn technical methods from the European Naturalists, and find examples of frankness that supported them in their struggle with the genteel tradition; they also were inspired by Europeans to write about American scenes. They had to read European books in order to discover their own natures, and travel in imagination through European cities before they gained courage to describe their own backgrounds. Hamlin Garland, who was the most dogmatically American of them all, and the most vehemently opposed to the imitation of foreign masters, was at the same time a disciple of Ibsen, Tolstoy, and the French Impressionist painters. "In my poor, blundering fashion," he said long afterwards, "I was standing for all forms of art which expressed, more or less adequately, the America I knew. . . . Ibsen's method, alien as his material actually appeared, pointed the way to a new and more authentic American drama. 'If we must imitate, let us imitate those who represent the truth and not those who uphold conventions,' was my argument."

Meanwhile there were a very few living American authors whose work seemed to represent the truth and could therefore serve as models to the new generation. There was Whitman, still living meanly in his little house in Camden and still saying over and over that American books should deal with American life. There were the local-color novelists, scores of them, each studying the folkways of his native or deliberately chosen territory. Garland thought that they represented a national movement, but the truth was that they dealt with a very few sections of the country: chiefly New England, the Southern Highlands, Louisiana, or California.

There were, however, three local writers from the Middle West who described their respective backgrounds with less sentiment and decorum than those from other sections. Edward Eggleston, of southern Indiana, had published *The Hoosier Schoolmaster* in 1871, at a time when there were no American models for that sort of homely writing; his inspiration for the book, he said, was a translation of Taine's lectures on *Art in the Netherlands*, in which he first encountered the thesis that an artist should work courageously with the materials he finds in his own environment. Edgar Watson Howe, of Kansas, had failed to find a publisher for his *Story of a Country Town* and had printed it at his own expense, in 1883. It was the first novel to suggest that there were narrowness, frustration, and sexual hypocrisy in Midwestern lives. Joseph Kirkland, of Illinois, had read *The Hoosier Schoolmaster* and had wondered whether a similar background couldn't be presented more honestly than in Eggleston's book; in 1885 he published *Zury, the Meanest Man in Spring County*. Later he said to Garland, who greatly admired his novel, "Why shouldn't our prairie country have its novelists as well as England or France or Norway? Our characters will not be peasants, but our fiction can be close to the soil." Kirkland recognized the imperfections of his pioneer work; "I began too late," he said.

All these early realists began too late in their lives, and with insufficient preparation. Eggleston, whose books were popular in Scandinavia, was the only one who became a professional man of letters, and that was only after he had abandoned fiction for lecturing on American history. Kirkland was a lawyer who wrote in his spare time. Ed Howe was a newspaper editor. "When I quit the newspaper," he wrote to Garland, "I will write my best book, but I am successful at newspaper work and afraid to give it up." He never quit the newspaper or wrote another book as good as *The Story of a Country Town*. Men like Howe had no assurance that they could earn a living merely by writing novels; no assurance that there was any large public for the sort of truth they had to tell. Their few honest books pointed toward a road that they were unable to follow. But meanwhile, as a model for young writers, there was also William Dean Howells, who, for all his timidity, was trying to present the American world that lay before his eyes. Howells was the real patron and precursor of Naturalism in America.

Frank Norris, in one of his magazine pieces, "A Lost Story," described the old schoolmaster as he appeared to the literary rebels of 1898. "He was," Norris said, speaking of an imaginary character named Trevor, but undoubtedly thinking of Howells, "a short, rotund man, rubicund as to face, bourgeois as to clothes and surroundings, jovial in manner, indulging even in slang. One might easily set him down as a retired groceryman—wholesale, perhaps, but none the less a groceryman. Yet touch him upon the subject of his profession, and the *bonhomie* lapsed away from him at once." And Norris continued, "This elderly man of letters, who had seen the rise and fall of a dozen schools, was above the influence of fads, and he whose books were among the classics even before his death was infallible in his judgments of the work of the younger writers. All the stages of their evolution were known to him—all their mistakes, all their successes. He understood; and a story by one of them, a poem, a novel, that bore the stamp of his approval, was 'sterling.'" But the public, in 1898, had lost its taste for sterling. It had ceased to buy Howells' novels, let alone those of the young men he kept recommending in his many critical articles. Instead it was buying the romances of F. Hopkinson Smith and Kate Douglas Wiggin, brassy sentiment covered with a thin silver wash.

Norris had dressed in tails to spend his first evening at the Howells'; he liked to be the dandy when he had money for good clothes. He was a big, engaging young man of twenty-eight with prematurely gray hair and a wide cupid's-bow mouth that curled into consciously boyish smiles. Unlike the other Naturalists, he had been the rather spoiled child of a wealthy family; and he had formed a high opinion of himself that kept him from feeling professional jealousy and therefore permitted him to have a high opinion of others. Howells liked him so much at their first meeting that he consented to read the manuscript of the Zolaesque novel that his visitor had lately finished after working on it at intervals for four years. It was called *McTeague* and it was the story of an unlicensed San Francisco dentist who had murdered his miserly wife. A few evenings later Norris came back to hear the master's judgment. This time he was received by Howells in lounging slippers and they sat for a long time by the open fire talking about the novel. It wouldn't be popular, Howells said, but he gave it the stamp of his approval; it was sterling.

Most of the magazines were shocked by *McTeague* when it was published in February 1899. The *Independent* called it a dangerous book that had "no moral, esthetical or artistic reason for being." The *Bookman* condemned it as "the unexpected revival of realism in its most unendurable form." Other critics were incensed by a page in *McTeague* that described a little boy wetting his pants; they said that Norris had mentioned the unmentionable. There was much in the book that worried Howells, too, but he reviewed it with something close to enthusiasm. It prompted him to raise a serious question in the weekly column he was writing for *Literature*. The question was "whether we shall abandon the old-fashioned American ideal"—to which Howells himself had always clung—"of a novel as something which may be read by all ages and sexes, for the European notion of it as something fit only for age and experience, and for men rather than women; whether we shall keep to the bonds of the provincial proprieties, or shall include within the imperial territory of our fiction the passions and motives of the savage world which underlies as well as environs civilization." Howells did not try to answer the question, but he did say with a sense of prophecy, "The time may come at last when we are to invade and control Europe in literature. I do not say that it has come, but if it has we may have to employ European means and methods."

McTeague was not the first novel in the manner of the French Naturalists to be written in the United States, for there must have been others that remained in manuscript, like the wicked book by Dreiser's two St. Louis friends. It was not even the first Naturalistic novel to be published here, for Stephen Crane's *Maggie, a Girl of the Streets* had been issued by D. Appleton and Company in 1896, after being privately printed in 1893. But *Maggie*, though it dealt with poverty and prostitution from a Naturalistic point of view, was not so much American as metropolitan; it was an episode that might have taken place in any of the world's large cities. *McTeague* was localized; it was the first novel that applied Zola's massive technique, his objective approach, and his taste for the grotesquely common to a setting that everyone recognized as American.

Today it has lost its power to shock, but it retains more vitality and clearsightedness than any of Norris's later novels. The others, even *The Octopus*, are full of romantic situations in the taste of the time; we read them today as period pieces. And the author himself, when we follow his career in Franklin Walker's biography, arouses a good deal of affectionate amusement mingled with our respect for what he achieved. He was a giant who never grew up. He never got over his dependence on his strong-minded mother; every illness sent him scurrying home to her apron strings. Harry Thurston Peck, the editor of the *Bookman*, said of Norris in a letter, "The author of the terrible 'McTeague' is a pleasant, cultivated young gentleman, inclined to be obstreperous—and humorless—in arguments on realism, but in every other respect a very pleasant boy." He also thought that his face suggested "photographs of Hawthorne or of some classic actor." Another observer thought that he resembled "an old-time tragedian . . . Edwin Booth, perhaps." The truth was that Norris's writing was full of stage effects and that he never lost the actor's habit of looking at himself admiringly in the successive roles he played: the art student, the French dandy with sideburns and a cane, the fraternity brother, the breezy Westerner, the man about town, the Anglo-Saxon imperialist and explorer, the romantic lover, the struggling writer, the great novelist. Yes, even the last was a role; for his letters give the impression that Norris stood back and applauded himself as the author of books on big themes that he chose for their bigness, no matter how foreign they might be to his own experience.

About the time that *McTeague* appeared, he was getting launched on the biggest theme of all. "Tell Burgess I'm full of ginger and red pepper," he said in a letter, "and am getting ready to stand up on my hind legs and yell *big*." At the end of March 1899, he wrote to Howells thanking him for his review of *McTeague*. "I have the idea of another novel or rather series of novels buzzing in my head these days," he added. "I think there is a chance for somebody to do some great work with the West and California as a background, and which will be at the same time thoroughly American. My idea is to write three novels around the one subject of *Wheat*. First, a story of California (the producer), second, a story of Chicago (the distributor), third, a story of Europe (the consumer) and in each keep to the idea of this huge Niagara of wheat rolling from West to East. I think a big epic trilogy *could* be made out of such a subject, that at the same time would be modern and distinctly American. The idea is so big that it frightens me at times but I have about made up my mind to have a try at it." He was in fact already working on his plans, and early in April he went to California in a search for characters, incidents, and local color.

The first volume of the trilogy was published just two years later, in April 1901. *The Octopus* was on all counts his most ambitious novel, the most carefully composed, the broadest and most colorful in its background, the closest in its theme to great historical events. It was written after a period of sudden booms and depressions, when big business was swallowing little businesses and millions of individuals felt themselves the victims of impersonal corporations or uncontrollable forces. Norris gave expression to their sense of injustice and bewilderment; and he also introduced new technical methods, especially in his collective treatment of the California ranchers. His chapters on the barn dance and the rabbit hunt were almost the first portrayals in American fiction of a group that exulted and suffered as one man. *The Octopus*, in one of his favorite phrases, was a book "as big as all outdoors"; but its bigness was achieved at the expense of many strained effects and more concessions than he had made in *McTeague* to the bad taste of the day. At the end it declined into muzzy sentiments and fine writing. There is one long passage describing a dinner given by a railroad tycoon, with ortolan patties and Londonderry pheasants served at the exact moment when Mrs. Hooven, robbed of her home by the railroad, was dying of starvation in a vacant lot—one passage of twenty pages that belongs in an old-fashioned servant girls' weekly.

Howells admired *The Octopus* with reservations; after the comparatively unpretentious honesty of *McTeague*, he seems to have felt that it made too many compromises. But there were still more compromises in the second volume of the trilogy, *The Pit*, which appeared in January 1903 after being serialized in the *Saturday Evening Post*. With its effort to romanticize the big gambler on the Chicago Board of Trade, and with its secondary plot about the wife who discovers that she really loves him after being tempted to run away with a freshwater esthete, who in turn is merely funny instead of being the sinister figure that Norris tried to present, it becomes a provincial melodrama rather than a second canto in the epic of the wheat. *The Pit* seems to indicate that the author had made his peace with genteel society. Perhaps the indication is false, for Norris was dissatisfied with this latest work. Perhaps the next book would have been better; but he died suddenly of peritonitis in the autumn of 1902, before *The Pit* was published and before he had even begun to collect material for the third volume of his trilogy.

It is easy now to see the faults of his work. He was a borrower of literary effects; he took those he needed wherever he found them, in Kipling, Stevenson, Tolstoy, Zola, or Maupassant. He depended on instinct rather than intelligence for his choice of borrowings, since he always thought viscerally, with his heart and bowels instead of his brain. In that respect he resembled the first Roosevelt; and Henry Adams' judgment on the President applies to the novelist equally: "We are timid and conventional, all of us, except T. R., and he has no mind." But T. R. was often timid and conventional in politics, for all his bluster, just as Norris was often conventional in writing his big dramatic scenes and timid in his moral judgments. One remembers how Presley, the poet in *The Octopus* who often speaks for the author, sets out to rescue the penniless Hooven family, finds that the daughter has become a prostitute, and runs away from her in sick terror, feeling that with her first step into sin she has passed beyond all human help. Norris's moral rebellion, like T. R.'s political rebellion, stayed within the limits of what was then good form.

He had no feeling for any but the most obvious social values; I think it was Henry James who said that Norris's pictures of Chicago society would have been good satires if he had known they were satires. He was proud of not writing careful prose. He didn't live long enough to learn many subtleties of character or the use in portraying them of many shades between black and white. Yet it may be that his faults and failures helped to keep him close to a public that had missed the ironies in Henry B. Fuller's work and felt that Stephen Crane was cold, European, and possibly corrupt. They were the faults of his time and they contributed, in their way, to his timely influence on American writing. His great virtues were also of a sort that the public could learn to respect: freshness, narrative vigor, a marvelous eye for the life around him and courage to portray it in its drama and violence, besides the ability to construct his novels like Zola's in massive blocks. During a literary career of only six years, he managed to impress his personality, some of his particular virtues, and many of his shortcomings on the whole Naturalistic school that would follow him.

After half a century we can look back in an objective or Naturalistic spirit at the work of the writers inspired by Norris. We can describe their principles, note how these were modified in practice, and reach some sort of judgment on their achievements.

Naturalism in literature has been defined by Oscar Cargill as pessimistic determinism, and the definition is true so far as it goes. The Naturalists were all determinists in that they believed in the omnipotence of natural forces. They were pessimists in that they believed in the absolute incapacity of men and women to shape their own destinies. They regarded the individual as merely "a pawn on a chessboard"; the phrase recurs time and again in their novels. They felt that he could not achieve happiness by any conscious decision and that he received no earthly or heavenly reward for acting morally; man was, in Dreiser's words, "the victim of forces over which he has no control."

In some of his moods, Frank Norris carried this magnification of forces and minification of persons to an even greater extreme. "Men were nothings, mere animalculae, mere ephemerides that fluttered and fell and were forgotten between dawn and dusk," he says in the next-to-last chapter of *The Octopus*. "Men were naught, life was naught; FORCE only existed— FORCE that brought men into the world, FORCE that made the wheat grow, FORCE that garnered it from the soil to give place to the succeeding crop." But Norris, like several other Naturalists, was able to combine this romantic pessimism about individuals with romantic optimism about the future of mankind. "The individual suffers, but the race goes on," he says at the very end of the novel. "Annixter dies, but in a far distant corner of the world a thousand lives are saved. The larger view always and through all shams, all wickednesses, discovers the Truth that will, in the end, prevail, and all things, surely, inevitably, resistlessly work together for good." This was, in its magniloquent way, a form of the belief in universal progress announced by Herbert Spencer, but it was also mingled with native or Emersonian idealism, and it helped to make Naturalism more palatable to Norris's first American readers.

Zola had also declared his belief in human perfectibility, in what he called "a constant march toward truth"; and it was from Zola rather than Spencer or any native sources that Norris had borrowed most of his literary doctrines. Zola described himself as "a positivist, an evolutionist, a materialist." In his working notes, which Norris of course had never seen, but which one might say that he divined from the published text of the novels, Zola had indicated some of his aims as a writer. He would march through the world observing human behavior as if he were observing the forms of animal life. "Study men as simple elements and note the reactions," he said. And again, "What matters most to me is to be purely naturalistic, purely physiological. Instead of having principles (royalism, Catholicism) I shall have laws (heredity, atavism)." And yet again, "Balzac says that he wishes to paint men, women, and things. I count men and women as the same, while admitting their natural differences, and *subject men and women to things.*" In that last phrase, which Zola underlined, he expressed the central Naturalistic doctrine: that men and women are part of nature and subject to the same indifferent laws.

The principal laws, for Zola, were those of heredity, which he assumed to be as universal and unchanging as the second law of thermodynamics. He fixed upon the hereditary weakness of the Rougon-Macquart family as a theme that would bind together his vast series of novels. Suicide, alcoholism, prostitution, and insanity were all to be explained as the result of the same hereditary taint. "Vice and virtue," he said (or quoted from Taine), "are products like vitriol and sugar." Norris offered the same explanation for the brutality of McTeague. "Below the fine fabric of all that was good in him," Norris said, "ran the foul stream of hereditary evil, like a sewer. The vices and sins of his father and of his father's father, to the third and fourth and five hundredth generation, tainted him. The evil of an entire race flowed in his veins. Why should it be? He did not desire it. Was he to blame?" Others of the Naturalistic school, and Norris himself in his later novels, placed more emphasis on environmental forces. When Stephen Crane sent a copy of *Maggie* to the Reverend Thomas Dixon, he wrote on the flyleaf: "It is inevitable that this book will greatly shock you, but continue, pray, with great courage to the end, for it tries to show that environment is a tremendous thing and often shapes lives regardlessly. If I could prove that theory, I would make room in Heaven for all sorts of souls (notably an occasional street girl) who are not confidently expected to be there by many excellent people." Maggie, the victim of environment, was no more to blame for her transgressions than McTeague, the victim of hereditary evil. Nobody was to blame in this world where men and women are subject to the laws of things.

A favorite theme in Naturalistic fiction is that of the beast within. As the result of some crisis—usually a fight, a ship-wreck, or an expedition into the Arctic—the veneer of civiliza-tion drops away and we are faced with "the primal instinct of the brute struggling for its life and for the life of its young." The phrase is Norris's, but it might have been written by any of the early Naturalists. When evolution is treated in their novels, it almost always takes the opposite form of devolution or degeneration. It is seldom that the hero evolves toward a superhuman nature, as in Nietzsche's dream; instead he sinks backward toward the beasts. Zola set the fashion in *L'Assommoir* and *La Bête Humaine* and Norris followed him closely in the novel he wrote during his year at Harvard, *Vandover and the Brute*. Through yielding to his lower in-stincts, Vandover loses his humanity; he tears off his clothes, paddles up and down the room on his hands and feet, and snarls like a dog.

A still earlier story, "Lauth," was written at the University of California after Norris had listened to the lectures of Pro-fessor Joseph LeConte, a famous evolutionist. The action takes place in medieval Paris, where Lauth, a student at the Sor-

bonne, is mortally wounded in a brawl. A doctor brings him
back to life by pumping blood into his veins, but the soul had
left the body and does not return. Without it, Lauth sinks back
rapidly through the various stages of evolution: he is an ape,
then a dog, then finally "a horrible shapeless mass lying upon
the floor. It lived, but lived not as do the animals or the trees,
but as the protozoa, the jellyfish, and those strange lowest
forms of existence wherein the line between vegetable and
animal cannot be drawn." That might have been taken as a
logical limit to the process of devolution; but Jack London,
who was two parts Naturalist, if he was also one part socialist
and three parts hack journalist, tried to carry the process even
farther, into the realm of inanimate nature. Here, for example, is the description of a fight in *Martin Eden*:

> Then they fell upon each other, like young bulls, in all the
> glory of youth, with naked fists, with hatred, with desire to
> hurt, to maim, to destroy. All the painful, thousand years'
> gains of man in his upward climb through creation were lost.
> Only the electric light remained, a milestone on the path of the
> great human adventure. Martin and Cheese-Face were two
> savages, of the stone age, of the squatting place and the tree
> refuge. They sank lower and lower into the muddy abyss, back
> into the dregs of the raw beginnings of life, striving blindly
> and chemically, as atoms strive, as the star-dust of the heavens
> strives, colliding, recoiling and colliding again and eternally
> again.

It was more than a metaphor when London said that men
were atoms and stardust; it was the central drift of his philosophy. Instead of moving from the simple to the complex, as
Herbert Spencer tells us that everything does in this world,
the Naturalists kept moving from the complex to the simple,
by a continual process of reduction. They spoke of the nation as
"the tribe," and a moment later the tribe became a pack.
Civilized man became a barbarian or a savage, the savage
became a brute, and the brute was reduced to its chemical
elements. "Study men as simple elements," Zola had said; and
many years later Dreiser followed his advice by presenting
love as a form of electromagnetism and success in life as a
question of chemical compounds; thus, he said of his brother
Paul that he was "one of those great Falstaffian souls who, for

lack of a little iron or sodium or carbon dioxide in his chemical compost, was not able to bestride the world like a Colossus."

There was a tendency in almost all the Naturalistic writers to identify social laws with biological or physical laws. For Jack London, the driving force behind human events was always biology—"I mean," says his autobiographical hero, Martin Eden, "the real interpretative biology, from the ground up, from the laboratory and the test tube and the vitalized inorganic right on up to the widest esthetic and social generalizations." London believed that such biological principles as natural selection and the survival of the fittest were also the laws of human society. Norris fell into the same confusion between the physical and the social world when he pictured the wheat as "a huge Niagara . . . flowing from West to East." In his novels wheat was not a grain improved by men from various wild grasses and grown by men to meet human needs; it was an abstract and elemental force like gravity. "I corner the wheat!" says Jadwin, the hero of *The Pit*. "Great heavens, it is the wheat that has cornered me." Later, when he is ruined by the new grain that floods the market, Jadwin thinks to himself, "The Wheat had grown itself: demand and supply, these were the two great laws that the Wheat obeyed. Almost blasphemous in his effrontery, he had tampered with these laws, and roused a Titan. He had laid his puny human grasp upon Creation and the very earth herself, the great mother, feeling the touch of the cobweb that the human insect had spun, had stirred at last in her sleep and sent her omnipotence moving through the grooves of the world, to find and crush the disturber of her appointed courses."

Just as the wheat had grown itself, so, in the first volume of Norris's trilogy, the Pacific and Southwestern Railroad had built itself. This octopus that held a state in its tentacles was beyond human contol. Even Shelgrim, the president of the railroad, was merely the agent of a superhuman force. At the end of the novel he gives a lecture to Presley which overwhelms the poet and leaves him feeling that it rang "with the clear reverberation of truth." "You are dealing with forces," Shelgrim says, "when you speak of Wheat and the Railroads, not with men. There is the Wheat, the supply. It must be carried to the People. There is the demand. The Wheat is one force, the Railroad, another, and there is the law that governs them—supply and demand. Men have little to do with the whole business." If the two forces came into conflict—if the employees of the railroad massacred the wheat ranchers and robbed them of their land—then Presley should "blame conditions, not men."

The effect of Naturalism as a doctrine is to subtract from literature the whole notion of human responsibility. "Not men" is its constant echo. If Naturalistic stories had tragic endings, these were not to be explained by human wills in conflict with each other or with fate; they were the blind result of conditions, forces, physical laws, or nature herself. "There was no malevolence in Nature," Presley reflects after meeting the railroad president. "Colossal indifference only, a vast trend toward appointed goals. Nature was, then, a gigantic engine, a vast, cyclopean power, huge, terrible, a leviathan with a heart of steel, knowing no compunction, no forgiveness, no tolerance; crushing out the human atom standing in its way, with nirvanic calm." Stephen Crane had already expressed the same attitude toward nature in a sharper image and in cleaner prose. When the four shipwrecked men in "The Open Boat" are drifting close to the beach but are unable to land because of the breakers, they stare at a windmill that is like "a giant standing with its back to the plight of the ants. It represented in a degree, to the correspondent, the serenity of nature amid the struggles of the individual—nature in the wind, and nature in the visions of men. She did not seem cruel to him, then, nor beneficent, nor treacherous, nor wise. But she was indifferent, flatly indifferent."

These ideas about nature, science, and destiny led to the recurrent use of words and phrases by which early Naturalistic fiction can be identified. "The irony of fate" and "the pity of it" are two of the phrases; "pawns of circumstance" is another. The words that appear time and again are "primitive," "primordial" (often coupled with "slime"), "prehensile," "apelike," "wolflike," "brute" and "brutal," "savage," "driving," "conquering," "blood" (often as an adjective), "master" and "slave" (also as adjectives), "instinct" (which is usually "blind"), "ancestor," "huge," "cyclopean," "shapeless," "abyss," "biological," "chemic" and "chemism," "hypocrisy," "taboo," "unmoral." Time and again we read that "The race is to the swift and the battle to the strong." Time and again we are told about "the law of claw and fang," "the struggle for existence," "the blood of his Viking ancestors," and "the foul stream of hereditary evil." "The veneer of civilization" is always being "stripped away," or else it "drops away in an instant." The characters in early Naturalistic novels "lost all resemblance to humanity," reverting to "the abysmal brute." But when they "clash together like naked savages," or even like atoms and stardust, it is always the hero who "proves himself the stronger"; and spurning his prostrate adversary he strides forward to seize "his mate, his female." "Was he to blame?" the author asks his readers; and always he answers, "Conditions, not men, were at fault."

All those characteristics of the earlier American Naturalists might have been deduced from their original faith in Darwinian evolution and in the need for applying biological and physical laws to human affairs. But they had other characteristics that were more closely connected with American life in their own day.

The last decade of the nineteenth century, when they started their literary careers, was an age of contrasts and sudden changes. In spite of financial panics, the country was growing richer, but not at a uniform rate for all sections: the South was hopelessly impoverished and rural New England was returning to wilderness. Cities were gaining in population, partly at the expense of the Eastern farms, industry was thriving at the expense of agriculture, and independent factories were being combined into or destroyed by the trusts. It was an age of high interest rates, high but uncertain profits, low wages, and widespread unemployment. It was an age when labor unions were being broken, when immigrants were pouring through Ellis Island to people the new slums, and when the new American baronage was building its magnificently ugly châteaux. "America," to quote again from Dreiser's memoirs, "was just entering upon the most lurid phase of that vast, splendid, most lawless and most savage period in which

the great financiers were plotting and conniving at the enslave-
ment of the people and belaboring each other." Meanwhile the
ordinary citizen found it difficult to plan his future and even
began to suspect that he was, in a favorite Naturalistic phrase,
"the plaything of forces beyond human control."

The American faith that was preached in the pulpits and
daily reasserted on editorial pages had lost its connection with
American life. It was not only an intolerable limitation on
American writing, as all the rebel authors had learned; it also
had to be disregarded by anyone who hoped to rise in the
business world and by anyone who, having failed to rise,
wanted to understand the reasons for his failure. In its simplest
terms, the American faith was that things were getting better
year by year, that the individual could solve his problems by
moving, usually westward, and that virtue was rewarded with
wealth, the greatest virtue with the greatest wealth. Those
were the doctrines of the editorial page; but reporters who
worked for the same newspaper looked around them and decided that wealth was more often the fruit of selfishness and
fraud, whereas the admirable persons in their world—the kind,
the philosophic, the honest, and the open-eyed—were usually
failures by business standards. Most of the early Naturalistic
writers, including Stephen Crane, Harold Frederic, David
Graham Phillips and Dreiser, were professional newspapermen; while the others either worked for short periods as
reporters or wrote series of newspaper articles. All were more
or less affected by the moral atmosphere of the city room; and
the fact is important, since the newspapermen of the 1890's
and 1900's were a special class or type. "Never," says Dreiser,
speaking of his colleagues on the Pittsburgh *Dispatch*, "had I
encountered more intelligent or helpful or companionable al-
beit more cynical men than I met here"; and the observation
leads to general remarks about the reporters he had known:

> One can always talk to a newspaper man, I think, with the
> full confidence that one is talking to a man who is at least free
> of moralistic mush. Nearly everything in connection with those
> trashy romances of justice, truth, mercy, patriotism, public
> profession of all sorts, is already and forever gone if they have
> been in the business for any length of time. The religionist is

seen by them for what he is: a swallower of romance or a masquerader looking to profit and preferment. Of the politician, they know or believe but one thing: that he is out for himself.

Essentially the attitude forced upon newspapermen as they interviewed politicians, evangelists, and convicted criminals was the same as the attitude they derived or might have derived from popular books on evolution. Reading and experience led to the same convictions; that Christianity was a sham, that all moral professions were false, that there was nothing real in the world but force and, for themselves, no respectable role to play except that of detached observers gathering the facts and printing as many of them as their publishers would permit. They drank, whored, talked shop, and dreamed about writing cynical books. "Most of these young men," Dreiser says, "looked upon life as a fierce, grim struggle in which no quarter was either given or taken, and in which all men laid traps, lied, squandered, erred through illusion: a conclusion with which I now most heartily agree." His novels one after another would be based on what he had learned in his newspaper days.

In writing their novels, most of the Naturalists pictured themselves as expressing a judgment of life that was scientific, dispassionate, and, to borrow one of their own phrases, completely unmoral; but a better word for their attitude would be "rebellious." Try as they would, they could not remain merely observers. They had to revolt against the moral standards of their time; and the revolt involved them more or less unconsciously in the effort to impose new standards that would be closer to what they regarded as natural laws. Their books are full of little essays or sermons addressed to the reader; in fact, they suggest a Naturalistic system of ethics complete with its vices and virtues. Among the vices, those most often mentioned are hypocrisy, intolerance, conventionality, and unwillingness to acknowledge the truth. Among the virtues, perhaps the first is strength, which is presented as both a physiological and a moral quality; it implies the courage to be strong in spite of social restraints. A second virtue is naturalness, that is, the quality of acting in accordance with one's nature and physical instincts. Dreiser's Jennie Gerhardt was among the first of the purely natural heroines in American literature, but she had many descendants. A third virtue is complete candor about the world and oneself; a fourth is pity for others; and a fifth is tolerance, especially of moral rebellion and economic failure. Most of the characters presented sympathetically in Naturalistic novels are either victors over moral codes which they defy (like Cowperwood in *The Financier* and Susan Lenox in the novel by David Graham Phillips about her fall and rise) or else victims of the economic struggle, paupers and drunkards with infinitely more wisdom than the respectable citizens who avoid them. A great deal of Naturalistic writing, including the early poems of Edwin Arlington Robinson, is an eloquent hymn to loneliness and failure as the destiny, in America, of most superior men.

There are other qualities of American Naturalism that are derived not so much from historical conditions as from the example of the two novelists whom the younger men regarded as leaders or precursors. Norris first and Dreiser after him fixed the patterns that the others would follow.

Both men were romantic by taste and temperament. Although Norris was a disciple of Zola's, his other favorite authors belonged in one way or another to the romantic school; they included Froissart, Scott, Dickens, Dumas, Hugo, Kipling, and Stevenson. Zola was no stranger in that company, Norris said; on one occasion he called him "the very head of the Romanticists."—"Terrible things must happen," he wrote, "to the characters of the naturalistic tale. They must be twisted from the ordinary, wrenched from the quiet, uneventful round of everyday life and flung into the throes of a vast and terrible drama that works itself out in unleashed passions, in blood and sudden death. . . . Everything is extraordinary, imaginative, grotesque even, with a vague note of terror quivering throughout like the vibration of an ominous and low-pitched diapason." Norris himself wished to practice Naturalism as a form of romance, instead of taking up what he described as "the harsh, loveless, colorless, blunt tool called Realism." Dreiser in his autobiographical writings often refers to his own romantic temper. "For all my modest repute as a realist," he says, "I seem, to my self-analyzing eyes, somewhat more of a romanticist." He speaks of himself in his youth as "a creature of slow and uncertain response to anything practical, having an eye single to color, romance, beauty. I was but a half-baked poet, romancer, dreamer." The other American Naturalists were also romancers and dreamers in their fashion, groping among facts for the extraordinary and the grotesque. They believed that men were subject to natural forces, but they felt those forces were best displayed when they led to unlimited wealth, utter squalor, collective orgies, blood, and sudden death.

Among the romantic qualities they tried to achieve was "bigness" in its double reference to size and intensity. They wanted to display "big"—that is, intense—emotions against a physically large background. Bigness was the virtue that Norris most admired in Zola's novels. "The world of M. Zola," he said, "is a world of big things; the enormous, the formidable, the terrible, is what counts; no teacup tragedies here." In his own novels, Norris looked for big themes; after his trilogy on Wheat, he planned to write a still bigger trilogy on the three days' battle of Gettysburg, with one novel devoted to the events of each day. The whole notion of writing trilogies instead of separate novels came to be connected with the Naturalistic movement, although it was also adopted by the historical romancers. Before Norris there had been only one planned trilogy in serious American fiction: The *Littlepage Manuscripts*, written by James Fenimore Cooper a few years before his death; it traces the story of a New York State landowning family through a hundred years and three generations. After Norris there were dozens of trilogies, with a few tetralogies and pentalogies: to mention some of the better known, there were Dreiser's trilogy on the career of a financier, T. S. Stribling's trilogy on the rise of a poor-white family, Dos Passos's trilogy on the United States from 1900 to 1930, James T. Farrell's trilogy on Studs Lonigan, and Eugene O'Neill's trilogy of plays, *Mourning Becomes Electra*. Later O'Neill set to work on a trilogy of trilogies, a drama to be complete in nine full-length plays. Farrell wrote a pentalogy about the boyhood of Danny O'Neill and then attacked another theme that would require several volumes, the young manhood of Bernard Clare. Trilogies expanded into whole cycles of novels somehow related in theme. Thus, after the success of *The Jungle*, which had dealt with the meat-packing industry in Chicago, Upton Sinclair wrote novels on other cities (Denver, Boston) and other industries (oil, coal, whiskey, automobiles); finally he settled on a character, Lanny Budd, whose adventures were as endless as those of Tarzan or Superman. Sinclair Lewis dealt one after another with various trades and professions: real estate, medicine, divinity, social service, hotel management, and the stage; there was no limit to the subjects he could treat, so long as his readers' patience was equal to his own.

With their eyes continually on vast projects, the American Naturalists were careless about the details of their work and indifferent to the materials they were using; often their trilogies resembled great steel-structural buildings faced with cinder blocks and covered with cracked stucco ornaments. Sometimes the buildings remained unfinished. Norris set this pattern, too, when he died before he could start his third novel on the Wheat. Dreiser worked for years on *The Stoic*, which was to be the sequel to *The Financier* and *The Titan*; but he was never satisfied with the various endings he tried, and the book had to be completed by others after his death. Lewis never wrote his novel on labor unions, although he spent months or years gathering material for it and spoke of it as his most ambitious work. In their effort to achieve bigness at any cost, the Naturalists were likely to undertake projects that went beyond their physical or imaginative powers, or in which they discovered too late that they weren't interested.

Meanwhile they worked ahead in a delirium of production, like factories trying to set new records. To understand their achievements in speed and bulk, one has to compare their output with that of an average novelist. There is of course no average novelist, but there are scores of men and women who earn their livings by writing novels, and many of them try to publish one book each year. If they spend four months planning and gathering material for the book, another four months writing the first draft (at the rate of about a thousand words a day) and the last four months in revision, they are at least not unusual. Very few of the Naturalists would have been satisfied with that modest rate of production. Harold Frederic wrote as much as four thousand words a day and often sent his manuscripts to the printer without corrections. At least he paused between novels to carry on his work as a foreign correspondent; but Jack London, who wrote only one thousand words a day, tried to meet that quota six days a week and fifty-two weeks a year; he allowed himself no extra time for planning or revision. He wrote fifty books in seventeen years and didn't pretend that all of them were his best writing. "I have no unfinished stories," he told an interviewer five years before his death. "Invariably I complete every one I start. If it's good, I sign it and send it out. If it isn't good, I sign it and send it out." David Graham Phillips finished his first novel in 1901 and published sixteen others before his death in 1911, in addition to the articles he wrote for muckraking magazines. He left behind him the manuscripts of six novels (including the two-volume *Susan Lenox*) that were published posthumously. Upton Sinclair set a record in the early days when he was writing half-dime novels for boys. He kept three secretaries busy; two of them would be transcribing their notes while the third was taking dictation. By this method he once wrote eighteen thousand words in a day. He gained a fluency that helped him later when he was writing serious books, but he also acquired a contempt for style that made the books painful to read, except in their French translations. Almost all the Naturalists read better in translation; that is one of the reasons for their international popularity as compared with the smaller audience that some of them found at home.

The Naturalistic writers of all countries preferred an objective or scientific approach to their material. As early as 1864 the brothers Goncourt had written in their journal, "The novel of today is made with documents narrated or selected from nature, just as history is based on written documents." A few years later Zola defined the novel as a scientific experiment; its purpose, he said in rather involved language, was to demonstrate the behavior of given characters in a given situation. Still later Norris advanced the doctrine "that no one could be a writer until he could regard life and people, and the world in general, from the objective point of view—until he could remain detached, outside, maintain the unswerving attitude of the observer." The Naturalists as a group not only based their work on current scientific theories but tried to copy scientific methods in planning their novels. They were writers who believed, or claimed to believe, that they could deliberately choose a subject for their work instead of being chosen by a subject; that they could go about collecting characters as a biologist collected specimens; and that their fictional account of such characters could be as accurate and true to the facts as the report of an experiment in the laboratory.

It was largely this faith in objectivity that led them to write about penniless people in the slums, whom they regarded as "outside" or alien subjects for observation. Some of them began with a feeling of contempt for the masses. Norris during his college years used to speak of "the canaille" and often wished for the day when all radicals could be "drowned on one raft." Later this pure contempt developed into a contemptuous interest, and he began to spend his afternoons on Polk Street, in San Francisco, observing with a detached eye the actions of what he now called "the people." The minds of the people, he thought, were simpler than those of persons in his own world; essentially these human beings were animals, "the creatures of habit, the playthings of forces," and therefore they were ideal subjects for a Naturalistic novel. Some of the other Naturalists revealed the same rather godlike attitude toward workingmen. Nevertheless they wrote about them, a bold step at a time when most novels dealt only with ladies, gentlemen, and faithful retainers; and often their contemptuous interest was gradually transformed into sympathy.

Their objective point of view toward their material was sometimes a pretense that deceived themselves before it deceived others. From the outside world they chose the subjects that mirrored their own conflicts and obsessions. Crane, we remember, said his purpose in writing *Maggie* was to show "that environment is a tremendous thing and often shapes lives regardlessly." Yet, on the subjective level, the novel also revealed an obsessive notion about the blamelessness of prostitutes that affected his career from beginning to end; it caused a series of scandals, involved him in a feud with the vice squad in Manhattan, and finally led him to marry the madam of a bawdy house in Jacksonville. Norris's first novel, *Vandover and the Brute*, is an apparently objective study of degeneration, but it also mirrors the struggles of the author with his intensely Puritan conscience; Vandover is Norris himself. He had drifted into some mild dissipations and pictured them as leading to failure and insanity. Dreiser in *Sister Carrie* was telling a story that he felt compelled to write—"as if I were being used, like a medium," he said—though it now seems obvious that the story was suggested by the adventures of one of his sisters. In a sense he was being used by his own memories, which had become subconscious. There was nothing mystic to Upton Sinclair about his fierce emotion in writing *The Jungle*; he knew from the beginning that he was telling his own story. "I wrote with tears and anguish," he says in his memoirs, "pouring into the pages all that pain which life had meant to me. Externally, the story had to do with a family of stockyards workers, but internally it was the story of my own family. Did I wish to know how the poor suffered in Chicago? I had only to recall the previous winter in a cabin, when we had only cotton blankets, and cowered shivering in our separate beds. . . . Our little boy was down with pneumonia that winter, and nearly died, and the grief of that went into the book." Indeed, there is personal grief and fury and bewilderment in all the most impressive Naturalistic novels. They are at their best, not when they are scientific or objective, in accordance with their own theories, but when they are least Naturalistic, most personal and lyrical.

If we follow William James and divide writers into the two categories of the tough and the tender-minded, then most of the Naturalists are tender-minded. The sense of moral fitness is strong in them; they believe in their hearts that nature *should* be kind, that virtue *should* be rewarded on earth, that men *should* control their own destinies. More than other writers, they are wounded by ugliness and injustice, but they will not close their eyes to either; indeed, they often give the impression of seeking out ugliness and injustice in order to be wounded again and again. They have hardly a trace of the cynicism that is often charged against them. It is the quietly realistic or classical writers who are likely to be cynics, in the sense of holding a low opinion of life and human beings; that low estimate is so deeply ingrained in them that they never bother to insist on it—for why should they try to make converts in such a hopeless world? The Naturalists are always trying to convert others and themselves, and sometimes they build up new illusions simply to enjoy the pain of stripping them away.

It is their feeling of fascinated revulsion toward their subject matter that makes some of the Naturalists hard to read; they seem to be flogging themselves and their audience like a band of Penitentes.

So far I have been trying to present the positive characteristics of a movement in American letters, but Naturalism can also be defined in terms of what it is not. Thus, to begin a list of negations, it is not journalism in the bad sense, merely sensational or entertaining or written merely to sell. It has to be honest by definition, and honesty in literature is a hard quality to achieve, one that requires more courage and concentration than journalists can profitably devote to writing a novel. Even when an author holds all the Naturalistic doctrines, his books have to reach a certain level of observation and intensity before they deserve to be called Naturalistic. Jack London held the doctrines and wrote fifty books, but only three or four of them reached the required level. David Graham Phillips reached it only once, in *Susan Lenox*, if he reached it then.

Literary Naturalism is not the sort of doctrine that can be officially sponsored and taught in the public schools. It depends for too many of its effects on shocking the sensibilities of its readers and smashing their illusions. It always becomes a threat to the self-esteem of the propertied classes. *Babbitt*, for example, is Naturalistic in its hostile treatment of American businessmen. When Sinclair Lewis defended Babbittry in a later novel, *The Prodigal Parents*, his work had ceased to be Naturalistic.

For a third negative statement, Naturalism is not what we have learned to call literature "in depth." It is concerned with human behavior and with explanations for that behavior in terms of heredity or environment. It presents the exterior world, often in striking visual images; but unlike the work of Henry James or Sherwood Anderson or William Faulkner—to mention only three writers in other traditions—it does not try to explore the world within. Faulkner's method is sometimes described as "subjective Naturalism," but the phrase is self-contradictory, almost as if one spoke of "subjective biology" or "subjective physics."

Naturalism does not deal primarily with individuals in themselves, but rather with social groups or settings or movements, or with individuals like Babbitt and Studs Lonigan who are regarded as being typical of a group. The Naturalistic writer tries not to identify himself with any of his characters, although he doesn't always succeed; in general his aim is to present them almost as if they were laboratory specimens. They are seldom depicted as being capable of moral decisions. This fact makes it easy to distinguish between the early Naturalists and some of their contemporaries like Robert Herrick and Edith Wharton who also tried to write without opimistic illusions. Herrick and Wharton, however, dealt with individuals who possessed some degree of moral freedom; and often the plots of their novels hinge on a conscious decision by one of the characters. Hemingway, another author whose work is wrongly described as Naturalistic, writes stories that reveal some moral quality, usually stoicism or the courage of a frightened man.

Many Naturalistic works are valuable historical documents, but the authors in general have little sense of history. They present each situation as if it had no historical antecedents, and their characters might be men and women created yesterday morning, so few signs do they show of having roots in the past. "Science" for Naturalistic writers usually means laboratory science, and not the study of human institutions or patterns of thought that persist through generations.

With a few exceptions they have no faith in reform, whether it be the reform of an individual by his own decision or the reform of society by reasoned courses of action. The changes they depict are the result of laws and forces and tendencies beyond human control. That is the great difference between the Naturalists and the proletarian or Marxian novelists of the 1930's. The proletarian writers—who were seldom proletarians in private life—believed that men acting together could make a new world. But they borrowed the objective and exterior technique of the Naturalists, which was unsuited to their essentially religious purpose. In the beginning of each book they portrayed a group of factory workers as the slaves of economic conditions, "the creatures of habit, the playthings of forces"; then later they portrayed the conversion of one or more workers to communism. But conversion is a psychological, not a biological, phenomenon, and it could not be explained purely in terms of conditions or forces. When the conversion took place, there was a shift from the outer to the inner world, and the novel broke in two.

It was not at all extraordinary for Nauralism to change into religious Marxism in the middle of a novel, since it has always shown a tendency to dissolve into something else. On the record, literary Naturalism does not seem to be a doctrine or attitude to which men are likely to cling through their whole lives. It is always being transformed into satire, symbolism, lyrical autobiography, utopian socialism, communism, Catholicism, Buddhism, Freudian psychology, hack journalism, or the mere assembling of facts. So far there is not in American literature a single instance in which a writer has remained a Naturalist from beginning to end of a long career; even Dreiser before his death became a strange mixture of Communist and mystic. There are, however, a great many works that are predominantly Naturalistic; and the time has come to list them in order to give the basis for my generalities.

I should say that those works, in fiction, were *Maggie* and *George's Mother*, by Stephen Crane, with many of his short stories; *The Damnation of Theron Ware*, by Harold Frederic; *Vandover*, *McTeague*, and *The Octopus* (but not *The Pit*), by Frank Norris; *The Call of the Wild*, which is a sort of Naturalistic Aesop's fable, besides *The Sea Wolf* and *Martin Eden*, by Jack London; *The Jungle*, by Upton Sinclair, as far as the page where Jurgis is converted to socialism; *Susan Lenox*, by David Graham Phillips; all of Dreiser's novels except *The Bulwark*, which has a religious ending written at the close of his life; all the serious novels of Sinclair Lewis between *Main Street* (1920) and *Dodsworth* (1929), but none he wrote afterwards; Dos Passos's *Manhattan Transfer* and *U. S. A.*; James T. Farrell's work in general, but especially *Studs Lonigan*; Richard Wright's *Native Son*; and most of John Steinbeck's early novels, including *In Dubious Battle* and all but the hortatory passages in *The Grapes of Wrath*. There are also autobiographies, and one of them is *The Education of Henry Adams*, which presents the author's life as determined by the conflict between unity and multiplicity and by the law of historical acceleration. The book can be read as a Naturalistic novel, and in fact its technique is more fictional, in the good sense, than Dreiser's technique in *The "Genius."* In poetry there is Robinson's early verse, as far as *Captain Craig*, and there is Edgar Lee Masters' *Spoon River Anthology*. In the drama there are the early plays of Eugene O'Neill, from *Beyond the Horizon* to *Desire under the Elms*. Among essays there are H. L. Mencken's *Prejudices* and Joseph Wood Krutch's *The Modern Temper*, which is the most coherent statement of the Naturalistic position. There are other Naturalists in all fields, especially fiction—as note F. Scott Fitzgerald's *The Beautiful and Damned*—and other Naturalistic books by several of the authors I have mentioned; but these are the works by which the school is likely to be remembered and judged.

And what shall we say in judgment?—since judge we must, after this long essay in definition. Is Naturalism true or false in its premises and good or bad in its effect on American literature? Its results have been good, I think, insofar as it has forced its adherents to stand in opposition to American orthodoxy. Honest writing in this country, the only sort worth bothering about, has almost always been the work of an opposition, chiefly because the leveling and unifying elements in our culture have been so strong that a man who accepts orthodox judgments is in danger of losing his literary personality. Catullus and Villon might be able to write their poems here; with their irregular lives they wouldn't run the risk of being corrupted by the standards of right-thinking people. But Virgil, the friend of Augustus, the official writer who shaped the myth of the Roman state—Virgil would be a dubious figure as an American poet. He would be tempted to soften his values in order to become a prophet for the masses. The American myth of universal cheap luxuries, tiled bathrooms, and service with a smile would not serve him as the basis for an epic poem.

The Naturalists, standing in opposition, have been writers of independent and strongly marked personalities. They have fought for the right to speak their minds and have won a measure of freedom for themselves and others. Yet it has to be charged against them that their opposition often takes the form of cheapening what they write about; of always looking for the lowdown or the payoff, that is, for the meanest explanation of everything they describe. There is a tendency in literary Naturalism—as distinguished from philosophical Naturalism, which is not my subject—always to explain the complex in terms of the simple: society in terms of self, man in terms of his animal inheritance, and the organic in terms of the inorganic. The result is that something is omitted at each stage in this process of reduction. To say that man is a beast of prey or a collection of chemical compounds omits most of man's special nature; it is a metaphor, not a scientific statement.

This scientific weakness of Naturalism involves a still greater literary weakness, for it leads to a conception of man that makes it impossible for Naturalistic authors to write in the tragic spirit. They can write about crimes, suicides, disasters, the terrifying, and the grotesque; but even the most powerful of their novels and plays are case histories rather than tragedies in the classical sense. Tragedy is an affirmation of man's importance; it is "the imitation of noble actions," in Aristotle's phrase; and the Naturalists are unable to believe in human nobility. "We write no tragedies today," says Joseph Wood Krutch in his early book, *The Modern Temper*, which might better have been called "The Naturalistic Temper." "If the plays and novels of today deal with littler people and less mighty emotions it is not because we have become interested in commonplace souls and their unglamorous adventures but because we have come, willy-nilly, to see the soul of man as commonplace and its emotions as mean." But Krutch was speaking only for those who shared the Naturalistic point of view. There are other doctrines held by modern writers that make it possible to endow their characters with human dignity. Tragic novels and plays have been written in these years by Christians, Communists, Humanists, and Existentialists, all of whom believe in different fashions and degrees that men can shape their own fates.

For the Naturalists, however, men are "human insects" whose brief lives are completely determined by society or nature. The individual is crushed in a moment if he resists; and his struggle, instead of being tragic, is merely pitiful or ironic, as if we had seen a mountain stir itself to overwhelm a fly. Irony is a literary effect used time and again by all the

Naturalistic writers. For Stephen Crane it is the central effect on which almost all his plots depend: thus, in *The Red Badge of Courage*, the boy makes himself a hero by running away. In "A Mystery of Heroism," a soldier risks his life to bring a bucket of water to his comrades, and the water is spilled. In "The Monster," a Negro stableman is so badly burned in rescuing a child that he becomes a faceless horror; and the child's father, a physician, loses his practice as a reward for sheltering the stableman. The irony in Dreiser's novels depends on the contrast between conventional morality and the situations he describes: Carrie Meeber loses her virtue and succeeds in her career; Jennie Gerhardt is a kept woman with higher principles than any respectable wife. In Sinclair Lewis the irony is reduced to an obsessive and irritating trick of style; if he wants to say that a speech was dull and stupid, he has to call it "the culminating glory of the dinner" and then, to make sure that we catch the point, explain that it was delivered by Mrs. Adelaide Tarr Gimmitch, "known throughout the country as 'the Unkies' Girl.' " The reader, seeing the name of Gimmitch, is supposed to smile a superior smile. There is something superior and ultimately tiresome in the attitude of many Naturalists toward the events they describe. Irony—like pity, its companion—is a spectator's emotion, and it sets a space between ourselves and the characters in the novel. They suffer, but their cries reach us faintly, like those of dying strangers we cannot hope to save.

There is nothing in the fundamental principles of Nauralism that requires a novel to be written in hasty or hackneyed prose. Flaubert, the most careful stylist of his age, was the predecessor and guide of the French Naturalists. Among the Naturalistic writers of all countries who wrote with a feeling for language were the brothers Goncourt, Ibsen, Hardy, and Stephen Crane. But it was Norris, not Crane, who set the standards for Naturalistic fiction in the United States, and Norris had no respect for style. "What pleased me most in your review of 'McTeague,' " he said in a letter to Isaac Marcosson, "was 'disdaining all pretensions to style.' It is precisely what I try most to avoid. I detest 'fine writing,' 'rhetoric,' 'elegant English'—tommyrot. Who cares for fine style! Tell your yarn and let your style go to the devil. We don't want literature, we want life." Yet the truth was that Norris's novels were full of fine writing and lace-curtain English. "Untouched, unassailable, undefiled," he says of the Wheat, "that mighty world force, that nourisher of nations, wrapped in Nirvanic calm, indifferent to the human swarm, gigantic, resistless, moved onward in its appointed grooves." He never learned to present his ideas in their own clothes or none at all; it was easier to dress them in borrowed plush; easier to make all his calms Nirvanic and all his grooves appointed.

Yet Norris wrote better prose than most of his successors among the American Naturalists. With a few exceptions like Dos Passos and Steinbeck, they have all used language as a blunt instrument; they write as if they were swinging shillelaghs. O'Neill was a great dramatist, but he never had an ear for the speech of living persons. Lewis once had an ear, but in later life he listened only to himself. He kept being arch and ironical about his characters until we wanted to snarl at him, "Quit patronizing those people! Maybe they'd have something to say if you'd only let them talk." Farrell writes well when he is excited or angry, but most of the time he makes his readers trudge through vacant lots in a Chicago South Side smog. Dreiser is the worst writer of all, but in some ways the least objectionable; there is something native to himself in his misuse of the language, so that we come to cherish it as a sign of authenticity, like the tool marks on Shaker furniture. Most of the others simply use the oldest and easiest phrase.

But although the Naturalists as a group are men of defective hearing, they almost all have keen eyes for new material. Their interest in themes that others regarded as too unpleasant or ill-bred has immensely broadened the scope of American fiction. Moreover, they have had enough vitality and courage to be exhilarated by the American life of their own times. From the beginning they have exulted in the wealth and ugliness of American cities, the splendor of the mansions and the squalor of the tenements. They compared Pittsburgh to Paris and New York to imperial Rome. Frank Norris thought that his own San Francisco was the ideal city for storytellers; "Things happen in San Francisco," he said. Dreiser remarked of Chicago, "It is given to some cities, as to some lands, to suggest romance, and to me Chicago did that hourly . . . Florence in its best days must have been something like this to young Florentines, or Venice to the young Venetians." The Naturalists for all their faults were embarked on a bolder venture than those other writers whose imaginations can absorb nothing but legends already treated in other books, prepared and predigested food. They tried to seize the life around them, and at their best they transformed it into new archetypes of human experience. Just as Cooper had shaped the legend of the frontier and Mark Twain the legend of the Mississippi, so the Naturalists have shaped the harsher legends of an urban and industrial age.

Sister Carrie's Brother

WHEN HE finished *Sister Carrie*, his first novel, Theodore Dreiser was a big, shambling youngster of twenty-nine with an advancing nose, a retreating chin, and a nature full of discordancies. He was dreamy but practical, rash but timid, persistent in his aims but given to fits of elation or dejection. His manners must have been frightful, in spite of the hours he had spent in his boyhood poring over *Hill's Manual of Etiquette*. He was full of understanding and sympathy for the weakness of others, including drunkards, wastrels, and criminals, but often he failed to show generosity toward those he regarded as rivals, with the result that his career was full of sudden friendships and estrangements.

He was an appealing young man in many ways and yet, on the basis of what he afterwards wrote about himself, he could hardly be called an admirable character. He was possessed by cheap ambitions; his early picture of the good life was to own what he called "a lovely home," with cast-iron deer on the lawn; to drive behind "a pair of prancing bays," and to spend his evenings in "a truly swell saloon," with actors, song writers, and Tammany politicians, amid "the laughter, the jesting, the expectorating, and back-slapping geniality." His taste was worse than untrained; it was actively bad except in fiction, and when he was offered the choice between two words, two paintings, two songs, or two pieces of furniture, he took the one that looked or sounded more expensive. In his "affectional relations," as he called them, he was a "varietist," to use his expensive word for a woman-chaser; and he makes it clear that he treated some women abominably after he caught them. If the character of Eugene Witla in *The "Genius"* is a self-portrait, as it seems to be, then his neighbors must have said rightly that his first wife was a saint to put up with him.

Yet Dreiser painted the portrait knowing that it would be recognized; and in other books he described his transgressions in the first person. Once in his life he stole money; he needed a

This essay appeared in the *New Republic* in two parts: "Sister Carrie's Brother," 116, May 26, 1947, 23–25, and "The Slow Triumph of Sister Carrie," 116, June 23, 1947, 24–27.

new overcoat and held out twenty-five dollars from his weekly collections for a Chicago furniture house. That petty crime must have been the hardest to confess to his reader, but he told the story in all its details, including his terror and shame when the theft was discovered. In writing of himself or his background he had a massive honesty that was less a moral than a physiological quality. It was his whole organism, not his conscious mind or his moral code, that made him incapable of any but minor falsehoods. Several times he tried writing false stories for money, but the words wouldn't come; and later in his career he found it physically impossible to finish some of the novels he had started, if their plots took a turn that seemed alien to his experience. He wasn't satisfied with easy answers. "Chronically nebulous, doubting, uncertain," he says of himself, "I stared and stared at everything, only wondering, not solving." It would take him thirty years to find—in his own life—the right ending for his last novel, *The Bulwark*.

There were always persons who believed in him and came to his help at critical points in his career. There was his mother first of all, a woman who could read a little, but couldn't sign her name until Dorsch, as she called him, and his youngest sister learned to write in the second grade of a German-language parochial school; they taught her to form the letters. But the mother understood her Dorsch sympathetically; and later when he confided to her that he wanted to be a writer more than anything else in the world, she made her painful little sacrifices so that he could read and study. Then there was the teacher at the Warsaw, Indiana, high school who was so impressed by this earnest and fumbling student that later she rescued him from his underpaid work at the warehouse in Chicago where he was showing symptoms of tuberculosis; she arranged to have him admitted to the University of Indiana and paid most of his expenses for his one college year out of her slender purse.

There was a copyreader on the Chicago *Globe*, a quietly raging cynic who took a fancy to Dreiser, insisted that he be hired, and taught him to write signed stories. There were various newspaper editors, including Joseph B. McCullagh of the St. Louis *Globe-Democrat*, who trained him and pushed him ahead. There was Arthur Henry, formerly of the Toledo

Blade, who encouraged him to write *Sister Carrie;* the writing faltered and stopped for two months when Henry went away, then started again when Henry returned, read the early chapters and said, yes, it was going fine. There was most of all his brother Paul, who helped him in his recurrent fits of depression; he would go searching for Theodore, find him hiding in a cheap lodging house, force money on him, and invent a job that he could fill. Then, in later years, there were all the publishers (including Horace Liveright) who offered him large sums in the form of advances against royalties on novels that in most cases were never written; who gave him the money as a business venture, partly, but also as a token of respect for the work he had done.

Largely as a result of the interventions that saved him time and again, Dreiser came to have a mystical faith in his star. What he said of Eugene Witla might have been applied to himself: "All his life he had fancied that he was leading a more or less fated life, principally more. He had thought that his art was a gift, that he had in a way been sent to revolutionize art in America, or carry it one step forward." It was, however, only during his periods of elation that Dreiser regarded himself as a favored ambassador of fate. When he became dejected, "he fancied," as Dreiser said of Witla and presumably of himself, that "he might be the sport or toy of untoward and malicious powers, such as those which surrounded and accomplished Macbeth's tragic end, and which might be intending to make an illustration of him." Hurstwood, in *Sister Carrie,* was such an "illustration"; his story was based on Dreiser's fancies of sinking into the depths. Cowperwood, the financier of a later trilogy, was Dreiser riding the storm and battling among the Titans.

Believing himself to be a marked man, he displayed a curious self-confidence. James Oppenheim wrote a poem about the time when he and Dreiser watched an amazing sunset over the Hudson. "Could you describe that, Dreiser?" he asked. "Yes, that or anything," was the answer. Dreiser could describe anything, from the stupid to the sublime, because in a sense he could describe nothing; he never learned to look for the exact phrase. One sometimes feels that he would have been a great philosopher if he had acquired the art of thinking systematically, instead of merely brooding over ideas, and a great writer if he had ever learned to write. Or might one call him a great inarticulate writer? There are moments when Dreiser's awkwardness in handling words contributes to the force of his novels, since he seems to be groping in them for something on a deeper level than language; there are crises when he stutters in trite phrases that are like incoherent cries.

His memoirs make it clear that what he respected in himself was the intensity of his emotions and his sense of what he calls, in another trite phrase, "the mystery and terror and wonder of life." He often heard voices. One of them—it was the voice of Chicago—spoke to him in his youth, and later he transcribed its words into a sort of elemental poetry. "I am the pulsing urge of the universe," it said to him. "All that life or hope is or can be or do, this I am, and it is here before you! Take of it! Live, live, satisfy your heart!"

A phrase often applied to Dreiser by others is "standing alone" or "marching alone." "It was Dreiser standing alone who won the battle against the censors," I heard a publisher say. In his Nobel Prize address, Sinclair Lewis told the Swedish Academy that Dreiser "more than any other man, marching alone, usually unappreciated, often hated, has cleared the trail from Victorian and Howellsian timidity and gentility in American fiction to honesty and boldness and passion of life." Although Dreiser deserved the tribute, its phrasing was inaccurate. He marched forward and at last won the battle, but he was seldom alone, except in the fits of dejection when he hid away from the world. Even then there was always someone who sought him out, gave him money or encouragement, and insisted that he go back to writing. Indeed, these helpers appeared so often at critical moments that one is tempted, like Dreiser himself, to regard them as emissaries of the powers that watched over him.

There were, however, less supernatural reasons for the support he received, and they also help to explain the abuse and hatred that made it necessary. In those days a new social class was appearing in the larger American cities. It consisted of young, ambitious, yearning, rootless men, chiefly from the Middle West, who were indifferent to the past and felt that their aspirations had never been portrayed in American literature. They knew that Dreiser was one of them, in his faults as well as his virtues, and they sensed that he would be loyal to his class. It was class loyalty that they expected of him, not personal gratitude. If he wrote great novels, they would not deal with foreigners and aristocrats, or with bygone days, and they would not be written politely for women and preachers. Instead the books would describe persons like those who helped him, like his brothers and sisters, his teachers, his newspaper friends, and his publishers, who would be appearing for the first time in serious fiction. It was the new men who recognized his integrity and chose him—elected him, one might say—to be their literary representative.

The post was dangerous. Later, when he fought their battles, Dreiser would be exposed to attacks from all those who disliked the vulgarity and what seemed to be the dubious moral standards of the new class from which he came. Instead of "marching alone," he would stand in a double relationship to American society: he would be the spokesman for one group and the scapegoat of others.

ii

In the summer of 1900 Dreiser joined forces with Frank Norris for a battle against the genteel tradition in American letters. Norris was then thirty years old, was newly married, and was working hard to finish his biggest novel, *The Octopus*. Meanwhile he was supporting himself by reading manuscripts for the new publishing house of Doubleday, Page and Company, which had issued his *McTeague* the year before. One of the manuscripts he carried home was that of a first novel called *Sister Carrie*. "I have found a masterpiece," he said to his first caller in the office one morning. "The man's name is Theodore Dreiser."

"I know him," the caller interrupted.

"Then tell him what I think of it. It's a wonder. I'm writing him to call."

A few weeks earlier Dreiser had found a masterpiece too. He had read *McTeague* and had been excited to learn that another novelist was trying to present an unretouched picture of American life. When he went to see Norris in the Doubleday office, he found that they were almost of an age—Norris was one year older—and that they shared the same literary convictions. There was, however, an essential difference between them. Norris had reached the convictions by an intellectual process, largely as a result of reading Zola and deciding that Zola's methods could be applied to American material. Dreiser insists that he hadn't read Zola when he wrote his first novel. He had become a Naturalist almost without premeditation, as a result of everything his life had been or had lacked. Unlike Norris he couldn't choose among different theories or move from the drably pitiful to the boisterous to the sentimental. He wrote what he did because he had to write only that or keep silent.

It was his friend Arthur Henry who first persuaded him to write fiction. They used to work at the same table, encouraging each other, and they each finished five or six stories. Dreiser's stories were accepted, not by genteel magazines like the *Century* and *Scribner's*, but by the new ten- and fifteen-cent monthlies that were less concerned with ideality and good manners. Henry then insisted that he write a novel. Dreiser protested that he couldn't afford the time, that he was too busy earning a living, that no novel of his would be published—and besides, he didn't have a plot; but still he kept pleasantly brooding over the notion. One day in October 1899, he found himself writing two words on a clean sheet of paper: "Sister Carrie."

"My mind was a blank except for the name," he told his first biographer, Dorothy Dudley. "I had no idea who or what she was to be." Then suddenly he pictured Carrie Meeber on the train to Chicago; it was a vision that came to him, he said, "as if out of a dream." But the dream was also a memory, for much of his own life went into the novel. In one sense Carrie was Dreiser himself, just as Flaubert once said that *he* was Mme. Bovary; the little Midwestern girl had Dreiser's mixture of passivity and ambition, as well as his romantic love for cities. More definitely she resembled one of his sisters, the one who ran off to Chicago, met a successful business man, the father of two or three grown children—like Hurstwood in the novel—and eloped with him to New York. Hurstwood's degradation after losing Carrie was another memory, connected with Dreiser's misfortunes in 1895, after he lost his job on the

New York *World*. Unable to find other work, he had lived in cheap lodging houses and—before he was rescued by his brother Paul—had pictured himself as sinking toward squalor and suicide. But there was more of Dreiser in the book than simply the two chief characters: there was his obsessive fear of poverty, there was his passion for gaslight and glitter, and there was his hatred for the conventional standards by which his big family of brothers and sisters had been judged and condemned. Most of all there was his feeling for life, his wonder at the mysterious fall and rise of human fortunes.

Sister Carrie had the appearance of being a Naturalistic novel and would be used as a model for the work of later Naturalists. Yet it was, in a sense, Naturalistic by default, Naturalistic because Dreiser was writing about the life he knew best in the only style he had learned. There is a personal and compulsive quality in the novel that is not at all Naturalistic. The book is felt rather than observed from the outside, like *McTeague*; and it is based on dreams rather than documents. Where *McTeague* had been a conducted tour of the depths, *Sister Carrie* was a cry from the depths, as if McTeague had uttered it.

It was a more frightening book to genteel readers than *McTeague* had been. They were repelled not only by the cheapness of the characters but even more by the fact that the author admired them. They read that Hurstwood, for example, was the manager of "a gorgeous saloon . . . with rich screens, fancy wines and a line of bar goods unsurpassed in the country." They found him an unctuous and offensive person, yet they also found that Dreiser described him as "altogether a very acceptable individual of our great American upper class— the first grade below the luxuriously rich." Genteel readers didn't know whether to be more offended by the judgment or by the language in which it was expressed; and they felt, moreover, that Hurstwood and his creator belonged to a new class that threatened the older American culture. Most of all they resented Carrie Meeber. They had been taught that a woman's virtue is her only jewel, that the wages of sin are death; yet Carrie let herself be seduced without a struggle, yielding first to a traveling salesman, then to Hurstwood; and instead of dying in misery she became a famous actress.

McTeague had offended the proprieties while respecting moral principles; every misdeed it mentioned had been punished in the end. *Sister Carrie*, on the other hand, was a direct affront to the standards by which respectable Americans had always claimed to live.

The battle over Carrie started even before the book was published. Dreiser had first given the manuscript to Henry Mills Alden, the editor of *Harper's Magazine*, who had already bought some of his articles. Alden said he liked the novel, but he doubted that any publisher would take it. He turned it over to the editorial readers for Harper and Brothers, who sent it back to the author without comment. Next the manuscript went to Doubleday, Page and Company, where it had the good fortune to be assigned to the man who could best appreciate what Dreiser was trying to do. "It *must* be published," Norris kept repeating to anyone who would listen. His enthusiasm for *Sister Carrie* won over two of the junior partners, Henry Lanier and Walter Hines Page; and with some misgiving they signed a contract to bring it out that fall. Then Frank Doubleday, the senior partner, came back from Europe and carried the proof sheets home with him to read over the weekend. Mrs. Doubleday read them too, and liked them not at all, but her part in the story is not essential. Her husband could and did form his own opinion of *Sister Carrie*. He detested the book and wanted nothing to do with it as a publisher.

There has been a prolonged argument over what happened afterwards, but chiefly it is an argument over words like "suppression"; most of the facts are on record. Doubleday spoke to his junior partners, who had great respect for his business judgment, and they summoned Dreiser to a conference. Norris managed to see him first. "Whatever happens," he said in effect, "make them publish *Sister Carrie*; it's your right." Dreiser then conferred with the junior partners, who tried to persuade him to surrender his contract. "Crushed and tragically pathetic," as Lanier remembers him, he kept insisting that the contract be observed.

It was a binding document and it *was* observed, to the letter. *Sister Carrie* was printed, if only in an edition of roughly a thousand copies. It was bound, if in cheap red cloth with dull black lettering. It was listed in the Doubleday catalogue. It was even submitted to the press for review, if only, in most cases, through the intervention of Frank Norris. When orders came in for it, they were filled. It wasn't "suppressed" or "buried away in a cellar," as Dreiser's friends afterwards complained, but neither was it displayed or advertised or urged on the booksellers. I think it was in the travels of Ibn Batuta that I read the account of some Buddhist fishermen whose religion forbade them to deprive any creature of life, even a sardine. Instead of killing fishes they merely caught them in nets and left them to live as best they could out of water. That is about what happened to *Sister Carrie*, which wasn't, incidentally, the first or the last book to receive such treatment from publishing houses that changed their collective minds. One couldn't quite say that it was killed; it was merely deprived of light and air and left to die.

Favorable reviews might have rescued it, but with two or three exceptions the reviews were violently adverse and even insulting. "The story leaves a very unpleasant impression," said the Minneapolis *Journal*. "You would never dream of recommending to another person to read it," said the *Post-Intelligencer* in Seattle. *Life*, the humorous weekly, was serious about Carrie and warned the girls who might think of following in her footsteps that they would "end their days on the Island or in the gutter." *Sister Carrie*, said the Chicago *Tribune*, "transgresses the literary morality of the average American novel to a point that is almost Zolaesque." The *Book Buyer* accused Dreiser of being "the chronicler of materialism in its basest forms. . . . But the leaven of the higher life remains," it added, "nowhere stronger than with us."

The book-buying public, most of which yearned for the leaven of the higher life, had no quarrel with the reviewers. The Doubleday records show that 1,008 copies of the book were bound, that 129 were sent out for review, and that only 465 were sold. After five years the other 423 copies, with the plates from which they had been printed, were turned over to a firm that specialized in publishers' remainders. That was the end of the story for Doubleday, but not for Dreiser. As soon as he could scrape together five hundred dollars, he bought the plates of his own novel. He succeeded in having it reprinted by the B. W. Dodge Company in 1907 and by Grosset and Dunlap in 1908. Later it would be reissued in successively larger editions by three other publishers—in 1911 by Harper and Brothers, the firm that had first rejected it, then in 1917 by Boni and Liveright, and in 1932 by the Modern Library—and it would also be translated into most of the European languages. For Dreiser the battle over *Sister Carrie* lasted for more than a quarter-century and ended with his triumph over the genteel critics.

Yet the first years were full of disasters, in spite of the help that Dreiser and his book received from Frank Norris. One English publisher remembered Norris as a man who was "more eager for Dreiser's *Carrie* to be read than for his own novels." Besides trying to get American reviews for the book, Norris kept writing about it to England. A London edition of *Sister Carrie* appeared in 1901 and was enthusiastically praised. "At last a really strong novel has come from America," exclaimed the *Daily Mail*; and there were echoes of the judgment in other English papers.

There was a different sort of echo in New York, a buzz of angry gossip about English critics and their fantastic notions of American fiction. Without the London edition, *Sister Carrie* might have been forgotten for years, but now it was arousing a quiet wave of condemnation among persons who had never seen a copy of the novel. Dreiser found that magazine editors were suddenly uninterested in his articles and stories, which had once been widely published; the new ones were coming back with rejection slips. One editor said, "You are a disgrace to America." The *Atlantic Monthly* wrote him that he was "morally bankrupt" and could not publish there. At the office of *Harper's Monthly* Dreiser happened to meet William Dean Howells, who had always been friendly since the day when Dreiser had interviewed him for another magazine. This time Howells was cold. "You know, I don't like *Sister Carrie*," he said as he hurried away. It was the first occasion on which he had failed to support a new work of honest American fiction.

In 1900 Howells had surrendered to the trend of the times. The great house of Harper, which had dominated American publishing, went bankrupt in that year, and Howells feared that he had lost his principal source of income. But the firm was soon reorganized, with new capital furnished through the elder J. P. Morgan and new editors for most of its magazines. Colonel Harvey, the new president, was determined to make the house yield dividends. He had an overnight conference with Howells, asked him to continue writing for *Harper's Magazine* on a yearly salary and told him, incidentally, that the battle for realism was lost.

Howells, who had been battling for realism since 1885, sadly agreed with Colonel Harvey. Whatever fire there had been in his critical writing was also lost after 1900, though perhaps that was merely because he was growing old. He still had his style, which was better than that of any other living American writer except Mark Twain. He had his almost official position as dean of American letters, but he was no longer the friend and patron of young writers in revolt.

The failure of *Sister Carrie* in its first edition was part of a general disaster that involved the whole literary movement of the 1890's. One after another the leaders of the movement had died young or else had surrendered to genteel conservatism. The first of them to go was the novelist H. H. Boyesen, a pioneer of social realism and once a famous figure, although his name is seldom mentioned now except in literature courses; Boyesen died in 1895. Next to go, in 1898, was Harold Frederic, the peppery rebel from upstate New York, who, in *The Damnation of Theron Ware*, had written the first American novel that questioned the virtue of the Protestant clergy. Stephen Crane, the one genius of the group, died in 1900, the victim of consumption, malaria, hard work, and hard living.

The dramatist James A. Herne had tried and failed to be the American Ibsen; but at least he had written the immensely popular *Shore Acres* and other plays that introduced daily American life to the American stage. He died in 1901, worn out and discouraged after the presidential campaign of the preceding year, in which he had fought for Bryan and against the annexation of the Philippines. Then Norris died in the autumn of 1902, at the beginning, so it seemed, of a grandly successful career; but he had already given signs, in *The Pit*, of abandoning his Naturalistic doctrines.

All these, except Herne, were comparatively young men

and there were very few left to carry on the literary movement they had started. Hamlin Garland, after fulminating against the conservatives in art and politics, had gone over to the enemy by easy stages. Editors had taken him out to dinner and convinced him that his passion for reform was weakening his novels as works of art. Unfortunately Garland was no artist; when he lost his crusading passion he lost everything. Henry B. Fuller, the Chicago realist, remained faithful to his own standards; but his novels hadn't sold and he wrote very little for a dozen years after 1900. It was not only the rebel authors, almost all of them, who had died or fallen silent or surrendered. The little magazines that flourished in New York, Chicago, and San Francisco during the 1890's had also disappeared and the new publishing houses had become conventional or had gone out of business. Serious writing on American themes declined into a sort of subterranean existence. Speaking generally, the best American books of the following decade would either be privately printed, like *The Education of Henry Adams*, or else they would be written in Europe.

Meanwhile Dreiser himself had narrowly escaped the fate of his brothers in arms. After *Sister Carrie* was accepted, he had begun working simultaneously on two other novels, in a frenzy of production, but slowly he had been overcome by the feeling that he was unwanted and a failure. He had destroyed one of his two manuscripts, put the other aside, sent his wife to her family in Missouri, and retired to a furnished room in Brooklyn, where he sat day after day brooding over the aimlessness of life and trying to gather enough courage to commit suicide. This time again he was rescued by his brother Paul, who gave him new clothes and sent him to a sanitarium. After his recovery he became a magazine editor and climbed rapidly in his profession, until, as head of the Butterick publications, he was earning twenty-five thousand dollars a year. It was a long time, however, before he felt strength enough in himself to write another novel.

The story of *Sister Carrie* had a curious sequel. Imperceptibly the standards of the American public had been changing in the years after 1900 and Dreiser himself had been gaining a sort of underground reputation based on his one book. When his second novel, *Jennie Gerhardt*, appeared in 1911 it was a critical and even to some extent a popular success. The struggle for Naturalism came into the open again. Dreiser had new allies in the younger writers, and by 1920 they had ceased to be rebels; instead they were the dominant faction. It was a long and finally a triumphant chapter in the history of American letters that began with the lost battle over *Sister Carrie.*

Sherwood Anderson's Book of Moments

REREADING Sherwood Anderson after many years, one feels again that his work is desperately uneven, but one is gratified to find that the best of it is as new and springlike as ever. There are many authors younger in years—he was born in 1876—who made a great noise in their time, but whose books already belong among the horseless carriages in Henry Ford's museum at Greenfield Village. Anderson made a great noise too, when he published *Winesburg, Ohio* in 1919. The older critics scolded him, the younger ones praised him as a man of the changing hour, yet he managed in that early work and others to be relatively timeless. There are moments in American life to which he gave not only the first but the final expression.

He soon became a writer's writer, the only storyteller of his generation who left his mark on the style and vision of the generation that followed. Hemingway, Faulkner, Wolfe, Steinbeck, Caldwell, Saroyan, Henry Miller . . . each of these owes an unmistakable debt to Anderson, and their names might stand for dozens of others. Hemingway was regarded as his disciple in 1920, when both men were living on the Near North Side of Chicago. Faulkner says that he had written very little, "poems and just amateur things," before meeting Anderson in 1925 and becoming, for a time, his inseparable companion. Looking at Anderson he thought to himself, "Being a writer must be a wonderful life." He set to work on his first novel, *Soldier's Pay*, for which Anderson found a publisher after the two men had ceased to be friends. Thomas Wolfe proclaimed in 1936 that Anderson was "the only man in America who ever taught me anything"; but they quarreled a year later, and Wolfe shouted that Anderson had shot his bolt, that he was done as a writer. All the disciples left him sooner or later, so that his influence was chiefly on their early work; but

Introduction to Sherwood Anderson, *Winesburg, Ohio*, Viking Compass Edition, New York, 1960. A portion of the essay was published as "Anderson's Lost Days of Innocence," *New Republic*, 143, February 15, 1960, 16–18.

still it was decisive. He opened doors for all of them and gave them faith in themselves. With Whitman he might have said:

I am the teacher of athletes,
He that by me spreads a wider breast than my own proves the
 width of my own,
He most honors my style who learns under it to destroy the teacher.

As the disciples were doing, most of Anderson's readers deserted him during the 1930's. He had been a fairly popular writer for a few years after *Dark Laughter* (1925), but his last stories and sketches, including some of his best, had to appear in a strange collection of second-line magazines, pamphlets, and Sunday supplements. One marvelous story called "Daughters" remained in manuscript until six years after his death in 1941. I suspect that the public would have liked him better if he had been primarily a novelist, like Dreiser and Lewis. He did publish seven novels, from *Windy McPherson's Son* in 1916 to *Kit Brandon* in 1936, not to mention the others he started and laid aside. Among the seven *Dark Laughter* was his only best seller, and *Poor White* (1920), the best of the lot, is studied in colleges as a picture of the industrial revolution in a small Midwestern town. There is, however, not one of the seven that is truly effective as a novel; not one that has balance and sustained force; not one that doesn't break apart into episodes or nebulize into a vague emotion.

His three personal narratives—*A Story-Teller's Story* (1924), *Tar: A Midwest Childhood* (1926), and *Sherwood Anderson's Memoirs* (1942)—are entertainingly inaccurate; indeed, they are almost as fictional as the novels, and quite as deficient in structure. They reveal that an element was missing in his mature life, rich as this was in other respects. They do not give us—and I doubt whether Anderson himself possessed —the sense of moving ahead in a definite direction. All the drama of growth was confined to his early years. After finding his proper voice at the age of forty, Anderson didn't change as much as other serious writers; perhaps his steadfastness should make us thankful, considering that most Americans change for the worse. He had achieved a quality of emotional rather than factual truth and he preserved it to the end of his career, while

doing little to refine, transform, or even understand it. Some
of his last stories—by no means all of them—are richer and
subtler than the early ones, but they are otherwise not much
different or much better.

He was a writer who depended on inspiration, which is to
say that he depended on feelings so deeply embedded in his
personality that he was unable to direct them. He couldn't say
to himself, "I shall produce such and such an effect in a book
of such and such a length"; the book had to write or rather
speak itself while Anderson listened as if to an inner voice. In
his business life he showed a surprising talent for planning and
manipulation. "One thing I've known always, instinctively," he
told Floyd Dell, "—that's how to handle people, make them
do as I please, be what I wanted them to be. I was in business
for a long time and the truth is I was a smooth son of a bitch."
He never learned to handle words in that smooth fashion.
Writing was an activity he assigned to a different level of
himself, the one on which he was emotional and unpractical.
To reach that level sometimes required a sustained effort of
the will. He might start a story like a man running hard to
catch a train, but once it was caught he could settle back and let
himself be carried—often to the wrong destination.

He knew instinctively whether one of his stories was right
or wrong, but he didn't always know why. He could do what
writers call "pencil work" on his manuscripts, changing a word
here and there, but he couldn't tighten the plot, delete weak
passages, sharpen the dialogue, or give a twist to the ending; if
he wanted to improve the story, he had to wait for a return of
the mood that had produced it, then write it over from beginning to end. There were stories like "Death in the Woods"
that he rewrote a dozen times, at intervals of years, before he
found what he thought was the right way of telling them.
Sometimes, in different books, he published two or three ver-
sions of the same story, so that we can see how it grew in his
subconscious mind. One characteristic of the subconscious is a
defective sense of time: in dreams the old man sees himself as a
boy, and the events of thirty or forty years may be jumbled
together. Time as a logical succession of events was Anderson's
greatest difficulty in writing novels or even long stories. He
got his tenses confused and carried his heroes ten years forward

or back in a single paragraph. His instinct was to present everything together, as in a dream.

When giving a lecture on "A Writer's Conception of Realism," he spoke of a half-dream that he had "over and over." "If I have been working intensely," he said, "I find myself unable to relax when I go to bed. Often I fall into a half-dream state and when I do, the faces of people begin to appear before me. They seem to snap into place before my eyes, stay there, sometimes for a short period, sometimes longer. There are smiling faces, leering ugly faces, tired faces, hopeful faces. . . . I have a kind of illusion about this matter," he continued. "It is, no doubt, due to a story-teller's point of view. I have the feeling that the faces that appear before me thus at night are those of people who want their stories told and whom I have neglected."

He would have liked to tell the stories of all the faces he had ever seen. He was essentially a storyteller, as he kept insisting, but his art was of a special type, belonging to an oral rather than a written tradition. It used to be the fashion to compare him with Chekhov and say that he had learned his art from the Russians. Anderson insisted that, except for Turgenev, he hadn't read any Russians when the comparisons were being made. Most of his literary masters were English or American: George Borrow, Walt Whitman, Mark Twain (more than he admitted), and Gertrude Stein. D. H. Lawrence was a less fortunate influence, but only on his later work. His earliest and perhaps his principal teacher was his father, "Irve" Anderson, who used to entertain whole barrooms with tales of his impossible adventures in the Civil War. A great many of the son's best stories, too, were told first in saloons. Later he would become what he called "an almighty scribbler" and would travel about the country with dozens of pencils and reams of paper, the tools of his trade. "I am one," he said, "who loves, like a drunkard his drink, the smell of ink, and the sight of a great pile of white paper that may be scrawled upon always gladdens me"; but his earlier impulse had been to speak, not write, his stories. The best of them retain the language, the pace, and one might even say the gestures of a man talking unhurriedly to his friends.

Within the oral tradition, Anderson had his own picture of

what a story should be. He was not interested in telling conventional folk tales, those in which events are more important than emotions. American folk tales usually end with a "snapper"—that is, after starting with the plausible, they progress through the barely possible to the flatly incredible, then wait for a laugh. Magazine fiction used to follow—and much of it still does—a pattern leading to a different sort of snapper, one that calls for a gasp of surprise or relief instead of a guffaw. Anderson broke the pattern by writing stories that not only lacked snappers, in most cases, but even had no plots in the usual sense. The tales he told in his Midwestern drawl were not incidents or episodes, they were *moments*, each one of them so timeless that it contained a whole life.

The best of the moments in *Winesburg, Ohio* is called "The Untold Lie." The story, which I have to summarize at the risk of spoiling it, is about two farmhands husking corn in a field at dusk. Ray Pearson is small, serious, and middle-aged, the father of half a dozen thin-legged children; Hal Winters is big and young, with the reputation of being a bad one. Suddenly he says to the older man, "I've got Nell Gunther in trouble. I'm telling you, but keep your mouth shut." He puts his two hands on Ray's shoulders and looks down into his eyes. "Well, old daddy," he says, "come on, advise me. Perhaps you've been in the same fix yourself. I know what everyone would say is the right thing to do, but what do you say?" Then the author steps back to look at his characters. "There they stood," he tells us, "in the big empty field with the quiet corn shocks standing in rows behind them and the red and yellow hills in the distance, and from being just two indifferent workmen they had become all alive to each other."

That single moment of aliveness—that sudden reaching out of two characters through walls of inarticulateness and misunderstanding—is the effect that Anderson is trying to create for his readers or listeners. There is more to the story, of course, but it is chiefly designed to bring the moment into relief. Ray Pearson thinks of his own marriage, to a girl he got into trouble, and turns away from Hal without being able to say the expected words about duty. Later that evening he is seized by a sudden impulse to warn the younger man against being tricked into bondage. He runs awkwardly across the fields,

crying out that children are only the accidents of life. Then he
meets Hal and stops, unable to repeat the words that he had
shouted into the wind. It is Hal who breaks the silence. "I've
already made up my mind," he says, taking Ray by the coat
and shaking him. "Nell ain't no fool. . . . I want to marry
her. I want to settle down and have kids." Both men laugh, as
if they had forgotten what happened in the cornfield. Ray
walks away into the darkness, thinking pleasantly now of his
children and muttering to himself, "It's just as well. Whatever I told him would have been a lie." There has been a
moment in the lives of two men. The moment has passed and
the briefly established communion has been broken, yet we feel
that each man has revealed his essential being. It is as if a gulf
had opened in the level Ohio cornfield and as if, for one
moment, a light had shone from the depths, illuminating
everything that happened or would ever happen to both of
them.

That moment of revelation was the story Anderson told
over and over, but without exhausting its freshness, for the
story had as many variations as there were faces in his dreams.
Behind one face was a moment of defiance; behind another, a
moment of resignation (as when Alice Hindman forces herself
"to face bravely the fact that many people must live and die
alone, even in Winesburg"); behind a third face was a moment of self-discovery; behind a fourth was a moment of
deliberate self-delusion. This fourth might have been the face
of the author's sister, as he describes her in a chapter of
Sherwood Anderson's Memoirs. Unlike the other girls she had
no beau, and so she went walking with her brother Sherwood,
pretending that he was someone else. "It's beautiful, isn't it,
James?" she said, looking at the wind ripples that passed in the
moonlight over a field of ripening wheat. Then she kissed him
and whispered, "Do you love me, James?"—and all her loneliness and flight from reality were summed up in those words.
Anderson had that gift for summing up, for pouring a lifetime
into a moment.

There must have been many such moments of truth in his
own life, and there was one in particular that has become an
American legend. After serving as a volunteer in the
Spanish-American War; after supplementing his one year in

high school with a much later year at Wittenberg Academy; and after becoming a locally famous copywriter in a Chicago advertising agency, Anderson had launched into business for himself; by the age of thirty-six he had been for some years the chief owner and general manager of a paint factory in Elyria, Ohio. The factory had prospered for a time, chiefly because of Anderson's talent for writing persuasive circulars, and he sometimes had visions of becoming a paint baron or a duke of industry. He had other visions too, of being sentenced to serve out his life as a businessman. At the time he was already writing novels—in fact he had four of them under way —and he began to feel that his advertising circulars were insulting to the dignity of words. "The impression got abroad —I perhaps encouraged it," Anderson says, "—that I was overworking, was on the point of a nervous breakdown. . . . The thought occurred to me that if men thought me a little insane they would forgive me if I lit out, left the business in which they invested their money on their hands." Then came the moment to which he would always return in his memoirs and in his fiction. He was dictating a letter: "The goods about which you have inquired are the best of their kind made in the —" when suddenly he stopped without completing the phrase. He looked at his secretary for a long time, and she looked at him until they both grew pale. Then he said with the American laugh that covers all sorts of meanings, "I have been wading in a long river and my feet are wet." He went out of the office for the last time and started walking eastward toward Cleveland along a railroad track. "There were," he says, "five or six dollars in my pocket."

So far I have been paraphrasing Anderson's account—or two of his many accounts, for he kept changing them—of an incident that his biographers have reconstructed from other sources. Those others give a different picture of what happened at the paint factory on November 27, 1912. Anderson had been struggling under an accumulation of marital, artistic, and business worries. Instead of pretending to be a little crazy so that investors would forgive him for losing their money, he was actually—so the medical records show—on the brink of nervous collapse. Instead of making a conscious decision to abandon his wife, his three children, and his business career, he acted as if in a trance. There was truly a decision, but it was made by something deeper than his conscious will; one feels that his whole being, psyche and soma together, was rejecting the life of a harried businessman. He had made no plans, however, for leading a different life. After four days of aimless wandering, he was recognized in Cleveland and taken to a hospital, where he was found to be suffering from exhaustion and aphasia.

Much later, in telling the story time after time, Anderson forgot or concealed the painful details of his flight and presented it as a pattern of conduct for others to follow. What we need in America, he liked to say, is a new class of individuals who, "at any physical cost to themselves and others"—Anderson must have been thinking of his first wife—will "agree to quit working, to loaf, to refuse to be hurried or try to get on in the world." In the next generation there would be hundreds of young men, readers of Anderson, who rejected the dream of financial success and tried to live as artists and individuals. For them Anderson's flight from the paint factory became a heroic exploit, as memorable as the choice made by Ibsen's Nora when she walked out of her doll's house and slammed the door. For Anderson himself when writing his memoirs, it was the central moment of his career.

Yet the real effect of the moment on his personal life was less drastic or immediate than one would guess from the compulsive fashion in which he kept writing about it. He didn't continue wandering from city to city, trading his tales for bread and preaching against success. After being released from the hospital, he went back to Elyria, wound up his business affairs, then took the train for Chicago, where he talked himself into a job with the same advertising agency that had employed him before he went into business for himself. As soon as he had the job, he sent for his wife and children. He continued to write persuasive circulars—corrupting the language, as he said—and worked on his novels and stories chiefly at night, as he had done while running a factory. It would be nearly two years before he separated from his first wife. It would be ten years before he left the advertising business to support himself entirely by writing, and then the change would result from a gradual process of getting published and finding readers, instead of being the sequel to a moment of truth.

Those moments at the center of Anderson's often marvelous stories were moments, in general, without a sequel; they existed separately and timelessly. That explains why he couldn't write novels and why, with a single exception, he never even wrote a book in the strict sense of the word. A book should have a structure and a development, whereas for Anderson there was chiefly the blinding flash that revealed a life without changing it.

The one exception, of course, is *Winesburg, Ohio*, and that became a true book for several reasons: because it was conceived as a whole, because Anderson had found a subject that released his buried emotions, and because most of the book was written in what was almost a single burst of inspiration, so that it gathered force as it went along. It was started in the late autumn of 1915, when he was living alone in a rooming house at 735 Cass Street, on the Near North Side of Chicago, and working as always at the Critchfield Agency. Earlier that year he had read two books that impressed him deeply: *Spoon River Anthology*, by Edgar Lee Masters, and *Three Lives*, the early volume of stories by Gertrude Stein. The first may have suggested the possibility of writing about the buried selves of people in another Midwestern town, while the other pointed the way toward a simpler and more repetitive style, closer to the rhythms of American speech, than that of Anderson's first novels, *Windy McPherson's Son* and *Marching Men*. Both of these had recently been accepted for publication, but he did not feel that he had really expressed himself in either book. Then came another of those incandescent moments that seemed to reveal his inner self. Twenty years later he described the moment in a letter, probably changing the facts, as he had a weakness for doing, but remembering how he felt:

> I think the most absorbingly interesting and exciting moment in any writer's life must come at the moment when he, for the first time, knows that he is a real writer. . . . I remember mine. I walked along a city street in the snow. I was work-

ing at work I hated. Already I had written several long novels. They were not really mine. I was ill, discouraged, broke. I was living in a cheap rooming house. I remember that I went upstairs and into the room. It was very shabby. I had no relatives in the city and few enough friends. I remember how cold the room was. On that afternoon I had heard that I was to lose my job.

. . . There was some paper on a small kitchen table I had bought and brought up into the room. I turned on a light and began to write. I wrote, without looking up—I never changed a word of it afterwards—a story called "Hands." It was and is a very beautiful story.

I wrote the story and then got up from the table at which I had been sitting, I do not know how long, and went down into the city street. I thought that the snow had suddenly made the city very beautiful. . . . It must have been several hours before I got the courage to return to my room and read my own story.

It was all right. It was sound. It was real. I went to sit by my desk. A great many others have had such moments. I wonder what they did. For the moment I thought the world very wonderful, and I thought also that there was a great deal of wonder in me.

"Hands" is still sound and real; as Henry James said of *The Scarlet Letter*, "it has about it that charm, very hard to express, which we find in an artist's work the first time he has touched his highest mark." It was, however, the second of the Winesburg stories to be written, since the first was "The Book of the Grotesque," which serves as a general prologue. "Paper Pills" was the third, and the others followed in roughly the same order in which they appear in the book. All the stories were written rapidly, often like "Hands" in a single night, each of them being, as Anderson said, "an idea grasped whole as one would pick an apple in an orchard." He was dealing with material that was both fresh and familiar. The town of Winesburg was based on his memories of Clyde, Ohio, where he had spent most of his boyhood and where his mother had died at the same age as Elizabeth Willard. The hero, George Willard, was the author in his late adolescence, and the other characters were either remembered from Clyde or else, in many cases, suggested by faces glimpsed in the Chicago streets. Each face revealed a moment, a mood, or a secret that lay deep in Anderson's life and for which he was finding the right words at last.

As the book went forward, more and more names and places were carried from one story or chapter to another, so that Winesburg itself acquired a sort of corporate being. Counting the four parts of "Godliness," each complete in itself, there would be twenty-five stories in all. None of them taken separately—not even "Hands" or "The Untold Lie"—is as effective as the best of Anderson's later work, but each of them contributes to all the others, as the stories in later volumes are not expected to do. There was a delay of some months before the last three chapters—"Death," "Sophistication," and "Departure"—were written with the obvious intention of rounding out the book. It is a function they effectively perform: first George Willard is released from Winesburg by the death of his mother, then he learns how it feels to be a grown man, then he leaves for the city on the early-morning train, and everything recedes as into a framed picture. "When he aroused himself and looked out of the car window the town of Winesburg had disappeared and his life there had become but a background on which to paint the dreams of his manhood."

In structure the book lies midway between the novel proper and the mere collection of stories. Like several famous books by more recent authors, all early readers of Anderson—like Faulkner's *The Unvanquished* and *Go Down, Moses*, like Steinbeck's *The Pastures of Heaven*, like Caldwell's *Georgia Boy*—it is a cycle of stories held together by their background, their prevailing mood, and their central character, but also by an underlying plot that is advanced or in some way enriched by each story. One might summarize the plot of *Winesburg* by saying that it deals with persons who have been distorted not, as Anderson tells us in his prologue, by their having seized upon a single truth, but rather by their inability to express themselves. Since they cannot truly communicate with others, they have become emotional cripples. Most of the grotesques are attracted one by one to George Willard; they feel that he might help them. In those moments of truth that Anderson loves to describe, they try to explain themselves to George, believing that he alone in Winesburg has an instinct for finding the right words and using them honestly. They urge him to preserve and develop his gifts. "You must not become a mere peddler of words," Kate Swift the teacher insists, taking hold of his shoulders. "The thing to learn is to know what people are thinking about, not what they say." Dr. Parcival tells him, "If something happens perhaps you will be able to write the book I may never get written." All the grotesques hope that George Willard will some day speak what is in their hearts and thus reestablish their connection with mankind. George is too young to understand them at the time, but the book ends with what seems to be the implied promise that he will become the voice of inarticulate men and women in all the forgotten towns. If that is what it truly implies, and if Anderson himself was fulfilling the promise, then *Winesburg, Ohio* is far from the pessimistic or morbidly sexual work it was once attacked for being. Instead it is a work of love, an attempt to break down the walls of loneliness, and, in its own fashion, a celebration of village life in the lost days of innocence.

Pound Reweighed

I AM disturbed—well, call it angry—about some late phases of the perennial Ezra Pound affair. No, I am not angry about Pound himself, or his racial and monetary theories, or his conduct during World War II, when he broadcast for Mussolini without ceasing to insist that he was defending the United States Constitution. He paid for his conduct by being penned in a sort of gorilla cage in an Army prison camp near Pisa, and later by spending twelve years in an insane asylum. Meanwhile he clung to his theories and, wrongheaded as they are, he has earned the right to hold them. He now has the appeal for us of the obstinate dissenter, the village atheist, the individual out of step with the times—suspecting as we do that the times are as crazy as Pound, in a more dangerous fashion. He also has the appeal of a man who was obsessed with poetry before he became obsessed with currency reform, and who has exerted more influence on the poetry of our time than anyone else living or dead.

Pound has been a marvelous teacher, for those writers who were ready and qualified to learn from him. These have included, to mention only a few, William Carlos Williams, who met him when both men were students at the University of Pennsylvania; Hilda Doolittle ("H.D."), to whom he was briefly engaged, and her Bryn Mawr classmate Marianne Moore; in London T. S. Eliot, through whom he influenced a whole generation of poets, and Wyndham Lewis, his fellow editor of *Blast;* in Paris Ernest Hemingway, who applied some of Pound's theories in his early prose, then E. E. Cummings, then Archibald MacLeish; and in London and Rapallo W. B. Yeats, who said that Pound was largely responsible for the change from his earlier to his later style. I am omitting all the famous authors whose work he affected less or not at all, but whom he befriended by helping to find them an audience or a publisher: Frost, Lawrence, especially Joyce. During his London and Paris years, 1908–24, he served as a general

A shorter version of the present essay, with the same title, appeared in the *Reporter,* 24, March 2, 1961, 35–36, 38–40.

impresario for the new literature, but chiefly he was a theorist and a schoolmaster, or better a *chef d'école*.

And what were the doctrines expounded by this master of literary schools? Perhaps his central axiom was that poetry is a highly conscious art and indeed a science to be studied almost like chemistry. Its aim, he seemed to say, is to portray the inner nature and condition of man in absolutely accurate language. The best language to use in poetry is that of modern prose—preferably without relative clauses—but poetry should achieve a much higher degree of concentration than prose by omitting any and every word that can be spared. Pound further maintained that the essence of poetry is the image, defined as a complicated state of being or feeling presented in an instant of time. There need be no logical or narrative connection between one image and another. All the connecting passages are extraneous matter that, Pound believed, can be ruthlessly pared away. An image is best expressed in its own inherent rhythm, and poets should seek for that rhythm instead of falling back into the rocking-horse beat of conventional English verse. The great poet is always an explorer seeking for new images, new rhythms, and new methods of presentation. Having made a discovery he should leave it to be exploited by lesser poets, while he goes marching ahead into the unknown.

Pound as a schoolmaster is sometimes given credit for being more original than he was in fact. Many of his doctrines were those of other rebel poets: for example, E. A. Robinson had always written verse that could be parsed as straightforward prose. T. E. Hulme, a young English philosopher killed in the Great War, was largely responsible for Pound's theory of the hard, dry, accurate image. It was, however, Pound himself who carried each theory to an extreme, then expressed it in a simple declarative sentence that stuck in the mind. Thus, "Literature is news that STAYS news." "Poetry is the most concentrated form of verbal expression." "Bad art is inaccurate art. It is art that makes false reports."

Pound was also the man who kept exploring the literatures of other ages and countries in search of new devices that could be used in English poems. Anglo-Saxon alliterative verse,

Greek quantitative verse, and Chinese verse in contrasting flat statements with a metaphorical value: he carried them all to modern London. I like to think of him as a tramp freighter, S.S. *Tenacity*, steaming through oceans of time and space, now coasting past the isles of Greece, now harbored in Alexandria or Byzantium, now spending a season in Ostia when it was the port of Augustan Rome, now landing a crew in Tuscany or Provence, now moored to a dock in Le Havre while collecting Paris wares for transport across the Channel, now rounding the Cape of Good Hope for a voyage to China and Japan, but returning, in those days, almost always with a cargo to be seized upon by other writers. "There are very few living poets," W. H. Auden said, "even if they are not conscious of having been influenced by Pound, who could say, 'My work would be exactly the same if Mr. Pound had never lived.' "

As a poet in his own right, he was less impressive than as a teacher. I am thinking of the years before 1920, during which he published book after book, each in a new style, each based on a new voyage of exploration. It is mildly exciting even today to reread them in their original editions. The translations are admirable, especially those from Provençal, Italian, and Chinese. The original poems are witty and personal, though they have rather less to say, their general message being that the poet lives in a garret, has a mistress—romantic word!—writes deathless verses, and despises all sorts of respectable citizens. In the mass of dated or mannered work, there are two or three almost perfect love poems—"Doria," "A Virginal"—there are a few Mediterranean landscapes rendered as if in marble, and there is the "Mauberley" sequence, which served as his embittered farewell to England. This much, and I grant a little more, of his earlier work is literature in Pound's definition of the word: news that *stays* news.

The controversy over Pound, so far as it is not a question of his public conduct, has been more and more confined to the immense poem that he started about 1920 and designed as his masterpiece: the *Cantos*. It has appeared at intervals in generous installments until it has become the longest poem of modern times and the hardest to read, though not the most unified. From one installment to another, the poem has changed with the years as the poet himself has changed. In the earlier and best cantos, numbered one to thirty, it seemed to be concerned with recurrent patterns in history. The later cantos, beginning with a group published in 1933, are more concerned with fiscal and administrative problems and with a campaign to save the world by overthrowing the banking system, which Pound calls "the usurocracy." On this subject he is crotchety and vindictive, but one can read him without losing one's temper. No, what I am angry about is the critics of Pound and their almost concerted attempt to make us believe that his unended diatribe against bankers—especially Jewish bankers—is the greatest poem of modern times, as well as being the longest; that it is superior to the best productions of Yeats, Eliot, Valéry, Rilke, perhaps of everyone else since Dante; and that his *Cantos* should be studied religiously by everyone who wants to write or teach or merely appreciate poetry.

I suppose that such an attempt was inevitable, given the conditions that prevail in the critical world. The standard critical method has come to be explication or exegesis, and this is a method that quickly exhausts its subject matter. There is hardly anything more to be explicated in Melville, Conrad, Eliot, or Faulkner, the favorite subjects for dissection of the last fifteen years, and even Joyce will soon be reduced to boiled-white bones. But Pound, but the *Cantos*. . . . Here is a relatively untouched body of work, one from which most of the professorial critics have been frightened away by its impenetrability. Moreover, the *Cantos* has (sing.) the great advantage—unlike *Ulysses*—of being a purely bookish work, based on the author's reading and having few troublesome contacts with life, so that most of the researches—difficult and extensive as they are—can be completed without one's leaving a good university library. If the explicators succeed in demonstrating that the *Cantos* is a masterpiece, they will gain credit for being original scholars, men of independent minds—and not only credit but leading posts in English departments.

Perhaps I am being unjust to the best Pound scholars. All I really know is that books and critical essays about him are multiplying, while his own published work is growing by accretion. In the last few years there have been several items of Poundiana, of which I shall mention only these five:

A Casebook of Ezra Pound, edited by William Van

O'Connor and Edward Stone, is a fair-minded selection chiefly
of magazine articles for and against the poet. Although it is
designed for use in college English courses, most of the articles
deal with his politics or personality rather than with his poems.

A Primer of Ezra Pound, by M. L. Rosenthal, is a brief
and reverent discussion of the poetry. It shies away from
Pound's opinions, remarking only that "His specific commit-
ments to Mussolini's methods and his anti-Semitism . . . remain the terrible aberrations of a man of genius."

Pound himself has made two contributions to the argument. *Thrones, 96–109 de los cantares* is the latest installment
of his poem. It has all the faults of earlier installments, with
fewer lyric passages to offset them. By now the typesetters are
becoming so confused by Pound's mannerisms that they are
afraid to correct his mistakes in spelling. At one point I
counted three mistakes in as many lines: "kolschoz" (for kol-
khoz), "quidity," and "sovreignty," with "Alcot" four lines
below.

*Impact: Essays on Ignorance and the Decline of American
Civilization*, edited by Noel Stock, is a selection of Pound's
prose writing on politics since 1930. This carries exactly the
same message as the *Cantos*, but has the great disadvantage,
for Pound's reputation, of being intelligible.

Finally there is a long biography, called simply *Ezra
Pound*, by Charles Norman. It brings together all the facts that
can be obtained from the fairly obvious sources and makes a
fascinating story. Mr. Norman is a little confused, however, by
the contrast—which he exaggerates—between the poet and the
politician. He keeps extravagantly praising the first and indig-
nantly blaming the second, often in the same paragraph.

I should also mention an older book, *The Poetry of Ezra
Pound*, by Hugh Kenner, since it is still the most complete—
and most admiring—treatment of the *Cantos* up to and including the Pisan sequence. Mr. Kenner was the first to discover,
for himself at least, that the work is a masterpiece of structure.
"Sheer architectonics," he says, "despite the superficial fragmentary look of the page, can scarcely have been carried much
further in poetry." Moreover, the *Cantos* invites comparison
with Dante, since there has been "no effort at moral definition

of comparable scope since the *Commedia*." After those high words I can only offer, in a modest way, a report of my own *periplum*, as Pound would call it, my voyage round the jagged contours of his masterpiece.

The *Cantos* is an unfinished work on which Pound has been engaged for the last half century. He calls it an epic and defines an epic as "a long poem containing history." So far 107 sections of the poem, numbered 1–71 and 74–109, have been published. Cantos 72 and 73 have been kept in manuscript, perhaps because, as Mr. Norman suggests, they present the poet's conclusions too bluntly. At the present stage of the work it is impossible for an ordinary reader to discern the architectonic structure that Mr. Kenner claims to be unexcelled. Nobody else has even conjectured how Pound will be able to finish the structure in 120 cantos, as it is said he is planning to do. Nobody else has tried to explain why the poem shouldn't have ended with the Pisan sequence (Cantos 74–84), or why, on the contrary, it shouldn't go on forever.

It makes greater demands on one's learning and perseverance than any other poem that has ever been written. The reader is expected, for example, to guess at the meaning of quotations and monologues in nine foreign languages: Greek, Latin, Italian, French, Old French, Provençal, Spanish, German, and Chinese (besides one name in Persian script and, in Canto 93, a group of Egyptian hieroglyphs). The reader is also expected to plow his way through many long or obscure works in order to grasp the force and appositeness of the quotations. Some of those works Pound himself found it hard to procure: for example, the letter books of the Venetian foreign office and *The Works of John Adams*, in ten volumes that provide the substance of Cantos 62–71.

In addition to undertaking such studies, the ideal reader— or "suitably sensitized apprehensor," as Mr. Kenner calls him —will make himself as familiar with the details of Pound's literary career as if they were incidents from the *Odyssey*. Even then he will understand many passages only after learning to recognize Pound's friends and minor acquaintances.

Thus, we read at the end of Canto 89:

> *I want Frémont looking at mountains*
> *or, if you like, Reck, at Lake Biwa*

Frémont would be the American explorer—but Reck? We find the answer in Mr. Norman's biography: Michael Reck is a young man who visited Pound at St. Elizabeth's Hospital and afterward wrote him a letter about the temple near Kyoto where Ernest Fenellosa is buried. From the temple Reck enjoyed a vista of Lake Biwa, which he described as "a great blue surrounded by mountains." That clears up the last line of Canto 89—but what about the general notion of writing long poems that can be fully understood only after one has become acquainted with the poet's life, read his correspondence, published or unpublished, and studied all the books he happened to acquire? And what does Pound offer us in return for such labors?

In some ways he offers a great deal; in others, less than we have a right to expect. The *Cantos* does not present "an action of considerable magnitude," as Aristotle said that an epic must do; in fact it presents no action whatever. It does offer hundreds of incidents, all fragmentary, and thousands of separate sharp images, but usually there appears to be no connection between one incident or image and the one that follows. There are names, again by the thousands, but no true characters. Even the hero, who appears under many of the names—as Ulysses, as Hanno the Carthaginian explorer, as Sigismundo Malatesta, and as a number of early American statesmen—is only a series of faceless masks for the poet himself. Emotions are often celebrated or condemned—for example, there is a fine canto in praise of love and part of another in dispraise of pity—but they are seldom or never evoked from the reader. There are no recurrent patterns of meter or rhyme or refrain or strophe to create and satisfy one's expectations. In a poem where everything is freedom and surprise, one expects anything, and nothing at all is truly surprising.

Mr. Kenner holds that these deficiencies are virtues in fact. Does the poem lack "a subject-matter, a plot, a line of philosophic development"? Why, Mr. Kenner answers, it was "Pound's principal achievement" to do away with all that outworn machinery. "In the *Cantos* the place of a plot is taken by large-scale interlocking rhythms of recurrence." I should take exception to that last phrase. There are hundreds of interlocking repetitions in the *Cantos*, but they do not occur at rhythmical—that is, more or less regular—intervals. Rhythm, as Pound once defined it brilliantly, "is a form cut into TIME, as a design is predetermined SPACE." The *Cantos* has neither rhythmical pattern, in that sense, nor spatial design; what it has is a mass of disconnected items set side by side in an irregular fashion. But let's get back to Mr. Kenner. "The fragmenting of the aesthetic idea into allotropic images," he says in his logotropic style, "as first theorized by Mallarmé"— but first applied on a large scale by Pound—"was a discovery whose importance for the artist corresponds to that of nuclear fission for the physicist." Old-style novels or epics are no longer worth writing. "Paraphrasable plot," Mr. Kenner keeps insisting, is "irrelevant" and "obsolete."

Of course plot will never be obsolete. Plot, or story, is simply people engaged in an action, as a result of which *something is changed*. A four-line poem can have a plot—as do many of Mallarmé's quatrains—and is usually better for having it. An epic poem without a plot is what a whale would be without a backbone; it falls apart into fragments—witness the *Cantos*—or softens into a jelly. And the word "paraphrasable" —why should Mr. Kenner use it with an air of contempt? Of course the total effect of a good poem is not paraphrasable, because the poet has produced it with the right number of right words in the right order. Change the words or the order and part of the effect is destroyed. But almost everything else about a poem, including its meaning, can be paraphrased more or less effectively, and critics like Mr. Kenner spend much of their time doing exactly that.

The *Cantos* in particular is full of paraphrasable ideas, which Pound himself has paraphrased to some extent in his critical essays, but chiefly in his political prose. One doesn't object to the presence of such ideas in the poem, but one is permitted, I hope, to question their validity.

In the early cantos, for example, the central idea seems to be that human types and social situations are universal and permanent, so that characters from Greek legends or Chinese paleohistory can be interchanged with those of the Middle Ages or the early American republic. The Albigensian Crusade reenacts the Trojan War, and Helen is reborn in Eleanor of Aquitaine. There is also a second idea in the early cantos, which, as I said, are the best: that the present era, dominated by moneylenders and merchants of death, is ignoble as compared with the past.

In the later cantos—those published after 1933 and numbered 31–109—the ideas are more numerous and some of them, instead of being left for the reader to infer, are flatly stated. Most of the ideas are in the closely related fields of government, banking, and currency. Pound says, for example —or suggests by the items of fact and gossip chosen for presentation

—that Western civilization is at the mercy of an international conspiracy of bankers, or, as he calls them, usurers;

—that wars are caused by this "usurocracy" in order to run nations into debt and create opportunities for manipulating the currency;

—that the worst of the usurers are Jews, especially a few big Jews conducting a "vendetta on the goyim";

—that usury cheapens art, falsifies history, and reduces literature to lying journalism;

—that the usurocracy could be abolished by a simple reform in currency, namely, the issuance of stamped and dated scrip based on the goods available for consumption;

—but that such a reform would have to be instituted by a benevolent despot on the order of Mussolini or the best Chinese emperors;

—that Confucius laid down the lines of the good society;

—that American culture, great in the days of Jefferson and John Adams, declined after 1830 and perished in the Civil War, also caused by bankers. "The United States were sold to the Rothschilds in 1863."

What distresses me about this group of ideas is not so much their inhumanity as their extreme and almost childlike simplicity. To be exposed to such primer-book notions—to find them supported by an aggregation of facts or supposed facts torn loose from their historical contexts and jumbled together like the letters in a game of anagrams—is this our reward for plodding through the most difficult poem ever written? Nowhere in the *Cantos* do we find any deep conception of human nature or destiny or any complicated picture of social behavior. Nowhere do we find the Christian feeling that every individual—including the poet himself—shares in the guilt of all. T. S. Eliot, usually Pound's most effective supporter, once scolded him for this lack of humility. The Inferno that Pound presents in his poem, Eliot said, "is a Hell for the *other people*, the people we read about in the newspapers, not for oneself and one's friends."

Yeats offered what is, in effect, a more sweeping condemnation, though it occurs in an essay written before the first of the cantos. "We make," he said, "out of the quarrel with others, rhetoric; out of the quarrel with ourselves, poetry." Pound has never had, or at least has never revealed, any quarrel with himself. Others have been in the wrong; himself has been the upright one, the "better maker," the persecuted artist. There is, it is true, one passage at the end of Canto 81 in which he adjures himself to "Pull down thy vanity," but even in that justly celebrated lyric he ends by deciding that what he had done was never vanity; that his only mistake had been in what he failed to do. With that qualified exception, all his condemnation is reserved for the people we read about in the newspapers, especially bankers and their hired artists and politicians. He never tries to understand them. Instead—Yeats said in finally writing about the *Cantos*—he rages against them as at "malignants with inexplicable characters and motives, grotesque figures out of a child's book of beasts."

"We make out of the quarrel with others, rhetoric. . . ." There is a great deal of poetry in the *Cantos*, not only the fine lyrics about pity, love, and vanity, but scores of Mediterranean landscapes revealing fauns and nymphs dancing among the olive trees above a quiet sea: Pound's picture of the earthly paradise. The heart of the poem, however, is in that group of ideas chiefly about government, banking, and currency. Pound desperately believes in those ideas and wants us to accept them as our only hope of saving the world. He has been trying to combine his two roles of teacher and poet, but more and more, as his poem continues, the poet is being silenced by the teacher. In all the later cantos Pound is making rhetoric, not only as

Yeats defines it but also in the older meaning of the word: "the art of persuasion." It follows that the *Cantos* is not an epic in any valid sense. It is a didactic poem which, for all the contrasts in method, belongs to the same order as Pope's *Essay on Man*.

There is one more point to be made after my voyage through the *Cantos*. Although Pound's system of rhetoric has not proved effective in persuading any but a few scholarly critics and various members of right-wing groups, it is not something he happened upon by chance or wrongheadedness. It is truly a system, being based upon a theory of teaching which in turn is based upon a theory of knowledge, an epistemology. In philosophical terms Pound is a nominalist, a disciple of Aristotle and Duns Scotus, as well as of Confucius, but one who carries a few of their theories to simplified extremes. He insists that the only genuine knowledge is of separate *things* (including separate actions and sensations). He distrusts all generalities except his own. As Mr. Kenner praises him for doing, he believes that the only method "of making complete and qualified statements is to present a selection of EXAMPLES."

Let me present an example of my own. If Pound were asked to define "vegetable," which is a generic term, and if he strictly followed his own method, he would appear with a basketful of onions, beans, lettuce, and cauliflower. Then, fearing that his statement was not sufficiently complete or qualified, he would rush back to the market and reappear with another basket, this time piled with carrots, beets, turnips, and radishes. That is essentially what he calls his "ideogrammic method," and it is the system of rhetoric he follows in the *Cantos*. There his usual means of conveying ideas is by presenting basketsful of disconnected items from the history of various countries, including Italy, China, the United States, medieval England, and the Byzantine Empire. "The principle of the ideogrammic method," Mr. Kenner tells us, "is simply that things explain themselves by the company they keep. Individual opacities reach upward toward an intelligible point of union."

But that intelligible point of union—that meaning, to use a simpler word—is likely to be something else than a valid statement about men in themselves or men in history. There are obvious weaknesses in the ideogrammic method when carried to the extreme to which Pound carries it, and one of them is that it abolishes logical thinking. One cannot compare or evaluate statements that consist of vegetables by the basketful or historical items by the gross. One cannot test the statements for consistency with each other. "Things explain themselves by the company they keep," says Mr. Kenner. But when the "things" are chiefly historical items from a dozen cultures, who is going to decide which items belong together? Doesn't the statement extracted from the items depend, in the last analysis, on the poet's intuition or on his preconceived notion of what goes with what?

Then too, if he puts one item after another, isn't he suggesting that the first is the cause or explanation of the second? *Post hoc, ergo propter hoc.* There are examples of this simplest logical fallacy everywhere in the later cantos, as likewise in the political prose of *Impact.* Indeed, the verse and the prose are hard to distinguish, except that the verse is more ideogrammic and harder to read. "The state can lend," he says in one essay. "The fleet that was victorious at Salamis was built with money advanced to the shipbuilders by the State of Athens." The historical item is versified in Canto 74:

> *and the fleet that went out to Salamis*
> *was built by state loan to the builders*
> *hence the attack on classical studies*

—In other words, the study of Greek is being discouraged *because* students might discover that the Athenian state lent money to productive enterprises instead of borrowing money from the bankers. The inference is a little strained, but let it pass; there is more to come. In Canto 89 and elsewhere Pound suggests that the American Civil War was caused by the Bank of the United States:

> *Branch forced on Alabama,*
> *trade in bills Ersatz for products*
> *Hence WAR, 30 years later.*

The bankers (perhaps the Rothschilds, who bought the United States in 1863?) were also responsible for the death of Abraham Lincoln. In one of his essays Pound quotes from a speech of Lincoln's: ". . . and gave to the people of this Republic the greatest blessing they ever had—their own paper to pay their own debts." Obviously Pound thinks this remark frightened the bankers, for he adds on the following page, "Lincoln was assassinated after he made the statement quoted above." *Post hoc, ergo propter hoc.* Everything is the fault of the bankers, down to and beyond the Second World War, which began, Pound tells us more than once, "in 1694, with the foundation of the Bank of England." Hitler was a martyr to the bankers. It was England, ruled by the usurocracy, which started the more recent phase of the war by urging the Poles to resist his reasonable demands. Thus, in Canto 104,

> *The Pollok was hooked by a false promise:*
> > *"black sea"*
> *"help by the black sea"*

Poor stupid Poles who accepted the bankers' promise! Unfortunate Hitler, victim of a war he didn't want to fight. . . . I feel no resentment against Pound for presenting this eccentric picture of history. He believes in it as in everything else: his collection of ideas, his ideogrammic method of presenting them, his bold non sequiturs, and his mission of saving the world from usury, war, and bad art. After his years of confinement let him live in peace—and in honor too, for the debt that other poets owe him. The resentment I feel is only against the critics who have been proclaiming that Pound is a genius to set beside Dante and that his endless harangue against the bankers is a poetic masterpiece to be studied in every course in modern literature. There is time in college to study only so many masterpieces. The *Cantos* would have to take the place of something else, perhaps of other modern poetry, perhaps of Wordsworth or Milton. Students might conclude, in their practical way, that poetry was damned nonsense and that critics didn't know what they were talking about.

A Weekend with Eugene O'Neill

BACK IN THE early 1920's, Eugene O'Neill was the animating spirit of a group that surrounded the Provincetown Players. His success as a dramatist had enabled the Players to move to New York and had kept their venture alive in bad seasons. It had kept me alive, too, during a hard year when I was paid ten dollars a week to be a black ghost in *The Emperor Jones* and a white ghost in a revival of *Where the Cross Is Made*; I never aspired to play the part of any living person. Although I hadn't been eating much that year, I made a rather substantial wraith, even with streaks of aluminum paint over my ribs to make them look as if the flesh had rotted away. Then Gene stopped writing plays with ghosts in them and my stage career came to an end. It was a minor example of how his decisions affected all of us.

If the Provincetown Players drank at the Hell Hole—officially known as the Golden Swan—which stood at the southeast corner of Fourth Street and Sixth Avenue in Greenwich Village, that was also because of Gene. Before it became a speakeasy, the Hell Hole was a Raines Law hotel, which means that there were furnished rooms upstairs and that, in theory, it furnished meals to travelers. As legal proof of the theory, the same mummified sandwiches appeared Sunday after Sunday on the round tables in the back room. Not even the unfed stumblebums who slept there on winter nights would dust off the sandwiches and eat them. The Hell Hole before the First World War, when it stayed open all night, was one of the principal models that Gene copied for Harry Hope's saloon in *The Iceman Cometh*. It was the grubbiest drinking parlor west of the Bowery—the No Chance Saloon, Bedrock Bar, the End of the Line Café, the Bottom of the Sea Rathskeller, as Larry Slade calls it in the play. "Don't you notice the beautiful calm in the atmosphere?" he continues. "That's because it's the last harbor. No one here has to worry about where they're going next, because there is no farther they can go."

Reporter, 17, September 5, 1957, 33–36.

Larry Slade in life was Terry Carlin, a gaunt, benign Irishman who had retired from gainful occupation after a working career that lasted one day. It was a Saturday, Terry explained, and the gainful occupation was that of helping behind the bar, where he had slaved from noon to midnight in order to empty the till after the saloon was closed. But the proprietor emptied it first, and Terry, disillusioned, had sworn never to do another day's work in his life. He kept the oath and lived to be nearly eighty, on a chiefly liquid diet. During Prohibition he used to drink canned heat, strained through a not very clean blue bandanna—that is, till the afternoon when I heard him say dreamily, "I'll have to stop drinking wood alcohol. It's beginning to affect my eyesight." Terry was a mystic of sorts who had been a radical syndicalist in his early days and then a philosophical anarchist. He had also been a patron of the Hell Hole when anyone would buy him a drink, as Gene often did. At Provincetown in the summer of 1916, Terry had repaid the debt by introducing his desperately shy friend to the Players as a young man with a trunkful of unperformed plays.

Outside of a few drunken radicals or ex-radicals like Terry and Hippolyte Havel (Hugo Kalmar in *The Iceman Cometh*), the denizens of the Hell Hole were more practical than the characters in Gene's play. Some of the latter were invented and others were carried over from Jimmy the Priest's, a waterfront dive that had been one of Gene's earlier haunts. At the Hell Hole the regular patrons included sneak thieves and shoplifters, touts, a square-shooting Negro gambler down on his luck, and a few bedraggled prostitutes—until 1917, that is, when "us girls" were driven off the streets and saloonkeepers were told not to serve them. There was a famous West Side gang known as the Hudson Dusters. Not many of the antisocial characters at the Hell Hole had spunk enough to be gangsters, but Hudson Dusters or simply Dusters was what we always called them. Gene had been drinking with them since 1915, when he first lived in the Village. The Dusters pitied him, sometimes fed him when he was starving, and one of them offered to steal him an overcoat when he was shivering with cold. "Tell you what, Gene," said an amiable shoplifter, "You make a trip up Sixth Avenue right away. Go to any store, pick out any coat you like, and tell me where it hangs on the rack. I bring you the coat tomorrow."

Gene hadn't accepted the offer, but he liked to tell about it, and anyone could see that he was proud of being accepted by the Dusters as one of the crowd. He had earned a place there by his apprenticeship in raggedness and drunkenness and near starvation, as well as by his unfailing good manners. He felt —and perhaps the Dusters felt—that he was leagued with them in a sullen rebellion against property and propriety. To a lesser extent he was also leagued with the Greenwich Villagers, particularly if they were poor and eccentric and a little outside the law. I think that for him the world was divided into downtowners and uptowners, as for a later generation of rebels it would be divided into hipsters and squares. For some time after becoming a successful playwright, he entered the uptown world with trepidation and in disguise, almost like a scout in enemy country, fearful of being caught and condemned to death, or forced to abandon his loyalties. He wouldn't even go to see his own plays when they were produced on Broadway. In the plays he depicted uptowners as hypocritical and sex-obsessed, and also as representatives of the paternal authority that he defied. He wanted to fling the truth about them into their smug faces. He wanted to show the uptowners, including his father, what he could do to enforce his dreams, but he didn't want to win them over; he wanted to impress and overawe, not persuade. In the back room of the Hell Hole, which was lighted by two flickering gas jets, with the corners of the room in darkness so that it looked like an expressionistic setting for *The Lower Depths*, among the honest sneak thieves and panhandlers at the very end of the line, he was safe from his father's reproaches; he could take off his mask and be understood.

That was what I felt about O'Neill, but what did I really know about him? Today how much do I really remember? I had seen him perhaps a dozen times, in the street, in the back room of the Hell Hole, at the Provincetown Playhouse, and once in the cold-water flat of Spanish Willie Fernandez, a bootlegger and small-time politician who worshiped him. I had heard some of his stories about life on shipboard and in a tuberculosis sanitarium, but it seems to me now that I heard them from others, his good friends and mine. I know that he liked to sing chanteys, omitting the obscene stanzas, and that his favorites were "Whisky for My Johnny" and "Blow the Man Down." When ordering another round of drinks, he might sing in a low voice,

> *Whisky is the life of man,*
> *(Whisky—Johnny),*
> *Oh, I drink whisky when I*
> *ca-a-an*
> *(Whisky for my Johnny).*

In humming the other chantey, he would pause to say that the slow rise and fall of the refrain, "Way-O, blow the man down," was like the movement of a ship on an ocean swell, and he would illustrate his meaning with a wavelike gesture of his right hand. But did I really see him make the gesture or was it someone else who made it in telling me about an evening spent with Gene? Often we fall into the illusion that the good friends of our friends are our good friends too.

Searching through my mind, discarding the questionable pictures and the stories told by others, I find that most of what I truly remember about Gene is connected with a visit to the O'Neills' country house at the beginning of November 1923, when the other guests were Hart Crane, whom we had met that summer, and my first wife, Peggy Baird. And what remains is not a continuous memory but a series of pictures, as if one's mind were a theatre, and a spotlight moved to illuminate one corner of the stage and then another while leaving the intervening spaces in blackness.

Hart Crane and I are climbing out of a nearly empty Harlem Division local at Purdy's Station on a Friday evening just after dark. Nobody else gets off the train. Gene's second wife, Agnes Boulton, had taken Peggy to the country earlier in the week, and now they are waiting for us on the dimly lighted platform. There are hugs, twitters, and Hart's boom of greeting. Shivering a little in the country air, I look up at the shadowy presence of big trees to the south of the station. Just north of it a sinister-looking bridge crosses the railway. A very bright electric bulb is burning at the top of the embankment, against a starless sky. A long flight of steps rises through shadows toward the single light. It is a stage setting by Robert Edmond Jones and makes me feel like a ghost again in one of Gene's early plays.

Carrying our bags, we struggle up the steps to where the O'Neills' new touring car is waiting under the light. The chauffeur, whose name is Vincent Bedini, drives us eastward by narrow roads lined with stone walls. From time to time, far back from the road, we catch glimpses of big houses among the trees, sailing past us like brilliantly lighted wooden ships. At some point we cross the Connecticut state line.

The O'Neills have recently bought one of the big houses in Ridgefield, I think with part of a legacy from Gene's brother Jim, or Jamie, though there have also been big royalties from *Anna Christie* and smaller ones from *The Hairy Ape*. The house is an 1890-ish affair called Brook Farm by its former owners, with a wide tree-dotted lawn and more than forty acres of land. Gene meets us in the hallway and so does his new dog—an Irish wolfhound, we are informed, the color and texture of coarse sandpaper and the size of a three-month-old calf. "He's extinct," I say, patting his head. "The *Encyclopaedia Britannica* tells us that Irish wolfhounds are an extinct breed." Offstage the telephone rings. With his hind paws slipping a little on the pale yellow hardwood floor, the dog rises to his full height, which is greater than mine, puts his forepaws on my shoulders, and looks down into my eyes. Enter Mrs. Fifine Clark, the housekeeper, known as "Gaga" by the family; she says there is another call from New York, from the Theatre Guild. "I'll take it," Gene murmurs. He comes back with a brief report, "I said no." There aren't any other guests and we sit down to an excellent dinner without being offered a drink. The door to the hallway is closed against Finn, the dog, who hasn't learned table manners.

After luncheon on Saturday, Gene and I are alone in a window nook at the left rear of the enormous living room. Hart has disappeared, I don't know where, and the girls are in Agnes's bedroom exchanging confidences over glasses of whisky and water, I suspect, but there is no liquor downstairs. Gene picks up a heavy green medical-looking book from the table beside us; it is one of Wilhelm Stekel's treatises on sexual aberrations —perhaps *The Disguises of Love*, which has recently been translated from the German. There are enough case histories in the book, Gene says, to furnish plots to all the playwrights who ever lived. He turns the pages and shows me the clinical record of a mother who seduced her only son and drove him insane. Then he talks about the German Expressionists, Toller and Kaiser and Hasenclever, whose plays he has read because they are said to resemble his own. Gene thinks their work is bold and interesting, but much too easy. The word "easy," which seems to be his strongest expression of disapproval, reminds him of *Anna Christie*. "I never liked it so well," he says, "as some of my other plays. In telling the story I deliberately employed all the Broadway tricks I had learned in my stage training. Using the same technique, and with my early experience as a background, I could turn out dozens of plays like *Anne Christie*, but I won't ever try. It would be too easy."

Nodding politely, I look down at the polished beech floor, with tiny eyes here and there in the wood. I think it is the handsomest floor I have ever seen.

Gene has taken me upstairs to the room where he works, a big bedroom so meagerly furnished that it looks like an abbot's cell. (Croswell Bowen, who wrote one of the books about O'Neill, tells me there was a crucifix over the bed, but I don't remember seeing it.) There are no books or pictures in the room. Between the two north windows is a dark mahogany secretary with drawers at the bottom, a cabinet at the top, and a drop-leaf table for writing. There are no papers on the writing surface. Gene opens the doors of the cabinet and takes out two or three medium-sized bound ledgers: "I write in these," he says. Each ledger contains several plays. Opening one of them, he shows me the text of *The Emperor Jones*, written with a very fine pen, in characters so small that they are illegible without a reading glass. There are no blank lines, and the text of the whole play fills only three pages of the ledger—or is it five? I think of the Lord's Prayer engraved on the head of a pin.

Gene tells me he is writing a play about New England, but he doesn't want to discuss it until it is finished. He is being extraordinarily kind to a shabby young man without a reputation. Partly that is because I am a friend of his friends, definitely not an uptowner, but there is something else involved—perhaps a need to explain himself to a new generation of writers, to a representative of the future by which he will be judged. I listen but do not respond, as I might well have done if he were French or English. In this country, as a result of the First World War, there has come to be a gulf between literary generations, besides that older gulf between fame and obscurity. Although Gene is only ten years older than I, he had come of age in a different world, and I feel we have very few admirations or even interests in common. Gene is trying to cross the two gulfs, but, in my defensive pride and foolish reticence, I do nothing to help him.

Rather late in a dry evening, Gene takes Hart and me down to the cellar, the only part of the house that seems to arouse his pride of ownership. He shows us the big coal furnace, with pipes radiating in all directions like the arms of an octopus. Standing under a bare electric light, he points to the cement floor and says that Vincent keeps it as clean as the living room. Vincent is a European who can't stand the way Americans let things go to waste. Last month he had gathered apples from the old orchard and made three barrels of cider. There they are—Gene points a finger into the shadows, where three fifty-gallon casks stand on a rack.

As a country boy I offer a disquisition on the virtues of hard cider, the wine of the Puritans, the interior sunlight of New England. "Let's broach a cask," Hart says. Gene demurs, but hesitantly; Vincent mightn't like it, he says, the cider is only three weeks old, and besides he doesn't know how a barrel should be tapped. Here I interrupt with my country knowledge. There is a spigot lying on the rack, I say, with a maul beside it. Cider doesn't have to ferment all winter; sometimes it tastes even better when the sugar hasn't quite worked out.

Gene goes upstairs to Gaga's kitchen and comes back with a white china pitcher and three glasses. By that time I have tapped a barrel, spilling more than a little cider on Vincent's clean floor. We stand with our full glasses under the bare electric light. "I can see the beaded bubbles winking at the brim," Hart says. Gene takes a sip of cider, holds it in his mouth apprehensively, gives his glass a gloomy look, then empties the glass in two deep nervous swallows. After a while we fill the pitcher again. When I go upstairs to bed, long after midnight, Gene is on his knees drawing another pitcher of cider, and Hart stands over him gesturing with a dead cigar as he declaims some lines composed that afternoon.

Soliloquy. I am lying awake while the clear gray morning light pours in through the bedroom windows. I am saying to myself that the O'Neills rattle around in this big country house like the last dried peas in a box—or better, like castaway sailors who have blundered into a deserted palace on the shore. But the sailors would laugh if they found wine in the cellar, where Gene hardly even smiles.

Peggy and I are running over the immense lawn in pursuit of the wolfhound. He mustn't be allowed to cross the road because, in spite of his amiable temper, the mere size of him terrifies the neighbors; he has developed a bad habit of killing chickens, and there have been threats that he would be shot. Finally he lets us catch him and lead him, or be dragged by him, back to the house. "The O'Neills—were kings in Ireland," I pant as we go. "It's like Gene—to buy—a dog of an extinct breed—the royal hunting dog of Irish kings—that kills the neighbors' chickens."

The big round table has been set for luncheon, with a plateful of hors d'oeuvres at each place. I look through the glass doors of the dining room and see the extinct dog walking gravely round the table, lowering, not raising, his head to empty each plate in turn. At luncheon Mrs. Clark gives soup to us instead. We are told at the last moment that Gene won't be down because he's working.

That evening we are in Woodstock, New York, sixty miles from Ridgefield as the crow flies. I know from one of Hart's published letters that we had been taken there in the O'Neills' touring car, which means that Vincent was at the wheel, but I don't remember by what roads, or how we crossed the Hudson, or anything that was said. A sort of curtain had fallen, to rise on another scene. My one intervening impression, a faint one, is that Agnes came along for the ride, then left rather hurriedly before dinner.

Now we are in a sort of eviscerated farmhouse, where ceilings and partitions have been ripped out to make an immensely high living room, with a balcony at one side and bedrooms opening out of it. There are six of us, all of an age except Niles Spencer's kid sister, who is pretty and sixteen. We have organized a game of hide-and-seek and go storming in and out of doors, up and down the balcony stairs, in alternate troughs and crests of laughter—first laughter pushed down, as into the hollow of a wave, then laughter splashing over us in breakers, with Hart's voice booming above them. For the Ridgefield pilgrims, it is as if a thin but perceptible mist of constraint, of jokes not made and differences of opinion that mustn't be aired, had suddenly been laughed away.

Hart stayed at the Woodstock farmhouse until after Christmas. Peggy and I went back to New York, where on Thursday of that week I wrote a letter to one of my literary friends. I told him briefly about the trip and said, "Eugene O'Neill, Mr. O'Neill the playwright, Gene . . . speaks a language so different from ours that we seemed to converse from different worlds." So the trip had ended for me in a failure of communication that was largely my fault.

There was, however, a sequel. All that Sunday, instead of working, Gene had kept on drawing pitchers of cider from the tapped barrel. While Agnes was away from Brook Farm he had called a taxi that took him to Purdy's, where he vanished. Agnes went to New York and spent a frantic week in search of him. Afraid of what the newspapers might say, she avoided the Bureau of Missing Persons; instead she made telephone calls to his friends and kept visiting his old haunts, including the Hell Hole.

On the last of her visits there, the proprietor confessed to her that Gene had sat in the back room and drunk himself into a coma. To avoid trouble with the police, he had been stashed away in the mysterious upstairs that none of us had seen, where Gene said that a crazy old woman wandered through the hallways, opening and closing doors. Agnes had him driven to Ridgefield, where in a few days he went back to work on *Desire Under the Elms*. That was not the last of his alcoholic misadventures, but his need to write plays proved stronger than his impulse toward self-destruction. A few years later, faced with the choice between writing and drinking, he stopped drinking for the rest of his life.

Robert Frost: A Dissenting Opinion

ROBERT FROST has been more heaped with academic honors than any other American poet, living or dead. Although he was never graduated from college, having left Dartmouth after two months and Harvard after two years—more credit to his dogged independence—he holds by a 1944 count no less than seventeen honorary degrees. He was twice made a Master of Arts (by Amherst and Michigan), three times a Doctor of the Humanities (by Vermont, Wesleyan, and St. Lawrence) and twelve times a Doctor of Letters (by Yale, Middlebury, Bowdoin, New Hampshire, Columbia, Williams, Dartmouth, Bates, Pennsylvania, Harvard, Colorado, and Princeton). He has been chosen as Phi Beta Kappa poet by Tufts, William and Mary, Harvard (twice), and Columbia. He has been a professor at Amherst; a poet in residence and a fellow in letters at Michigan; a Charles Eliot Norton professor, a Ralph Waldo Emerson fellow, and a fellow in American civilization at Harvard, all these being fairly lucrative appointments. He has been awarded four Pulitzer prizes, one more than E. A. Robinson and two more than Stephen Vincent Benét, the only other poets to be named more than once. He has also received the Loines award for poetry, the Mark Twain medal, the gold medal of the National Institute of Arts and Letters, and the silver medal of the Poetry Society of America. His work has been the subject of at least two full-length critical studies, many brochures, pamphlets, dissertations, bibliographies, and a memorial volume, *Recognition of Robert Frost*, not to mention hundreds of essays which, with some discordant notes in the early years, have ended as a vast diapason of praise.

And Frost deserves all these honors, both for his poetry in itself and for a long career devoted to the art of verse. In a country where poets go to seed, he has kept his talent ready to produce perfect blossoms (together with some that are misshapen or overgrown). It is a pleasure to name over the poems

"Frost: A Dissenting Opinion," *New Republic*, 111, September 11, 1944, 312–13; "The Case against Mr. Frost: II," *New Republic*, 111, September 18, 1944, 345–46.

of his youth and age that became more vivid in one's memory with each new reading: dramatic dialogues such as "The Death of the Hired Man" and "The Witch of Coös," among half a dozen others; descriptions or narrations that turn imperceptibly into Aesop's fables, as do "The Grindstone" and "Cow in Apple Time"; and, best of all, short lyrics such as "The Pasture," "Now Close the Windows," "The Sound of the Trees," "Fire and Ice," "Stopping by the Woods on a Snowy Evening" (always a favorite with anthologists), "To Earthward," "Tree at My Window," "Acquainted with the Night," "Neither Out Far Nor In Deep," "Beech," "Willful Homing," "Come In" . . . and I could easily add to the list. One of his best lyrics was written in 1892, when Frost was a freshman at Dartmouth; three or four others were included in his recent book, *The Witness Tree*, published just fifty years later; and these recent lyrics show more skill and density of expression than almost anything he had written before.

The same volume and the one that preceded it—*A Further Range*, published in 1936—also contain bad poems that have been almost equally admired: long monologues in pedestrian blank verse, spoken as if from a cracker barrel among the clouds, and doggerel anecdotes directed (or rather, indirected) against the New Deal; but a poet has the right to be judged by his best work, and Frost at his best has added to our never sufficient store of authentic poetry. If in spite of this I still say that there is a case against him and room for a dissenting opinion, perhaps I chiefly mean that there is a case against the zealous admirers who are not content to take the poet for what he is, with his integrity and his limitations, but insist on regarding him as a national sage. Still worse, they try to use him as a sort of banner for their own moral or political crusades.

We have seen the growth or revival in this country of a narrow nationalism that has spread from politics into literature (although its literary adherents are usually not political isolationists). They demand, however, that American writing should be affirmative, optimistic, not too critical, and "truly of this nation." They have been looking round for a poet to exalt; and Frost, through no effort of his own—but more through the weakness than the strength of his work—has been adopted as their symbol. Some of the honors heaped upon him are less poetic than political. He is being praised too often and with too great vehemence by people who don't like poetry, especially modern poetry. He is being presented as a sort of Sunday-school paragon, a saint among miserable sinners. And the result is that his honors shed little of their luster on other poets, who in turn feel none of the pride in his achievements that a battalion feels, for example, when one of its officers is cited for outstanding services. Frost's common sense and his "native quality" are used as an excuse for belittling and berating all his contemporaries, who have supposedly fallen into the sins of pessimism, obscurity, obscenity, and yielding to foreign influences; we even hear of their treachery to the American dream. Frost, on the other hand, is depicted as a loyal, autochthonous, and almost aboriginal Yankee. We are told not only that he is "the purest classical poet of America today"— and there is truth in Gorham B. Munson's early judgment— but also that he is "the one great American poet of our time" and "the only living New Englander in the great tradition, fit to be placed beside Emerson, Hawthorne and Thoreau."

But when he is so placed and measured against them, his stature seems diminished; it is almost as if a Morgan horse from Vermont, best of its breed, had been judged by the standards that apply to Clydesdales and Percherons. Height and breadth and strength: he falls short in all these qualities of the great New Englanders. And the other quality for which he is often praised, his utter faithfulness to the New England spirit, is hardly a virtue that they tried to cultivate. They realized that the New England spirit, when it stands alone, is inclined to be narrow and rigid and arithmetical. It has reached its finest growth only when cross-fertilized with alien philosophies. Hinduism, Sufism, Fourierism, and German Romanticism: each of these contributed its share to the New England renaissance of the 1850's. Even Thoreau, who died almost in sight of his birthplace, said that he had traveled much in Concord; he spoke of bathing his intellect "in the stupendous and cosmogonal philosophy of the Bhagvat-Geeta. . . . The pure Walden water," he went on to say, "is mingled with the sacred water of the Ganges." And even Hawthorne, who told us that "New England is quite as large a lump of earth as my heart can really take in," was eager for any new ideas that might help to explain the nature of New Englanders as individuals or as members of society. The books he borrowed from the Salem Athenaeum, during the twelve lonely years he spent at home after his graduation from college, included the complete works, in French, of Rousseau, Voltaire (several times), Pascal, Racine (several times), the *Essais* of Montaigne and, in English translation, the works of Machiavelli, as well as a great number of volumes on science, philosophy, government, general history, and the past of New England. Some of his weaker contemporaries were quite unbalanced by the foreign learning with which they overloaded their minds; but the stronger ones assimilated everything and, in the end, reasserted their New England natures, which had become immensely richer as a result of what they had learned.

Even Frost, as purely Yankee as his character seems today, was partly formed by his three years abroad. The turning point in his life was the moment when he was able to sell his first New Hampshire farm—which his grandfather had bought for him on condition that he live there for at least ten years—and when his wife said, "Let's go to England and live under thatch." In England after 1912 he made the reputation that enabled him to live by poetry and teaching. In England, too, he had the experience of meeting other poets who understood what he was trying to say: Lascelles Abercrombie, Rupert Brooke, Wilfred Wilson Gibson, and Edward Thomas. They were willing to learn from him, and Frost, in a sense, learned even more from them: that is, he learned to abandon the language of genteel verse and to use his own speech without embarrassment. It is interesting to compare *A Boy's Will*, published in London but written in New Hampshire before his English journey, with *Mountain Interval*, published in 1916 after his return to this country, but written chiefly in England. The poems in *A Boy's Will* gave his own picture of the world, but the picture was overlaid with conventional decorations: with phrases like "maidens pale," "sweet pangs," "airy dalliance," and "thine emulous fond flowers." On the other hand, the poems written in the English countryside used the language spoken by educated farmers north and east of Boston. Their speech had formerly been regarded as a mere dialect, to be misspelled for quaint or comic effects and to be used only in homely ballads like "Skipper Ireson's Ride" or in satirical comments like "The Biglow Papers"; but Frost in England had done what Hemingway would later do in Paris: he had refined his native idiom into a literary language capable of expressing the whole range of his emotions.

It was after his return that he carried the process further. Having learned to write as well as speak New Hampshire, he chose to think New Hampshire, in the sense of accepting its habits and customs as immutable laws. Unlike the great Yankees of an earlier age, he expressed hostility toward innovations in art, ethics, science, industry, or politics. He bridled when he heard "a New York alec" discussing Freudian psychology, which Frost for his part dismissed as "the new school of the pseudo-phallic." In his later poems he objects to researches in animal behavior (which he calls "instituting downward comparisons"), to new inventions (saying that ingenuity should be held in check), and even to the theory of evolution —or at least he ridicules one farmer who speaks of it admiringly, whereas he sympathizes with another who stops him on the road to say:

> *The trouble with the Mid-Victorians*
> *Seems to have been a man named John L. Darwin.*

New ideas seem worse to him if they come from abroad, and worst of all if they come from Russia. He is continually declaiming against Russians of all categories: the pessimistic Russians, the revolutionary Russians, the collectivistic Russians, the regimented Russians, the five-year-planning Russians; he seems to embrace them all in a global and historical dislike that extends from Dostoevsky to Dnieperstroy. He is horrified by the thought that New England might be exposed to the possibility of adopting any good or bad feature of the Russian program. Thus, after reading about a project for rural rehabilitation, he was quick to write:

> *It is in the news that all these pitiful kin*
> *Are to be bought out and mercifully gathered in*
> *To live in villages next to the theatre and store*
> *Where they won't have to think for themselves any more;*
> *While greedy good-doers, beneficent beasts of prey*

Swarm over their lives, enforcing benefits
That are calculated to soothe them out of their wits,
And by teaching them how to sleep the sleep all day,
Destroy their sleeping at night the ancient way.

Sometimes Frost decides that it would be a relief "To put these people at one stroke out of their pain"—these people being the marginal farmers; then next day he wonders how it would be if someone offered to end his own troubles. The upshot is that he proposes to do nothing whatever, being satisfied with the New England countryside as it is—or rather, as it was in his early manhood—and outraged by anyone who tries to improve it. Yet there are other poems in which he suggests that his faithfulness to "the ancient way" is more a matter of habit than conviction. In "The Black Cottage," he speaks of an old woman who had lost her husband in the Civil War, and who believed that the war had been fought for some deeper principle than freedom for the slaves or an inseparable union:

She wouldn't have believed those ends enough
To have given outright for them all she gave.
Her giving somehow touched the principle
That all men are created free and equal.
And to hear her quaint phrases—so removed
From the world's view today of all those things . . .

It is a Protestant clergyman who is telling us about her life, in one of Frost's dramatic monologues; but the poet seems to repeat his words with approval and to share his belief that freedom, union, and equality are all quaint words "so removed from the world's view today." The old woman was an orthodox Christian, and her presence in church kept the minister from changing any phrases in the creed. He goes on to say:

I'm just as glad she made me keep hands off,
For, dear me, why abandon a belief
Merely because it ceases to be true.
Cling to it long enough, and not a doubt
It will turn true again, for so it goes.

And that, too, seems to express Frost's attitude toward the old New England standards. He is more conventional than convinced, more concerned with prudence than with virtue, and very little concerned with sin or suffering; one might say that he is more Puritan, or even prudish, than he is Christian. All the figures in his poems are decently draped; all the love affairs (except in a very late narrative, "The Subverted Flower") are etherealized or intellectualized; and although he sometimes refers to very old adulteries, it is only after they have been wrapped in brown paper and locked away in cupboards. On the other hand, there is little in his work to suggest Christian charity or universal brotherhood under God. He wants us to understand once and for all that he is not his brother's keeper:

> *I have none of the tenderer-than-thou*
> *Collectivistic regimenting love*
> *With which the modern world is being swept.*

One of his narratives, "Two Tramps in Mud Time," has often been praised for the admirable lesson with which it ends; and yet a professor told me not long ago that his classes always seemed vaguely uncomfortable when they heard it read aloud. It was first published in 1934, and it deals with what seems to have been an incident of the depression years. The poet tells us how he was working in his dooryard on an April day between winter and spring; he was splitting great blocks of straight-grained beech with a lovely sense of satisfaction. Two tramps came walking down the muddy road. One of them said, "Hit them hard," and then lingered by the roadside, suggesting wordlessly that he might take the poet's job for pay. The poet assumed that they had spent the winter in a lumber camp, that they were now unemployed, and that they had slept "God knows where last night." In life the meeting may have had a different sequel. Perhaps the poet explained to the homeless men that he liked to split his own wood, but that he had other work for them to do; or perhaps he invited them into the kitchen for a slab of home-baked bread spread thickly with apple butter. In the poem, however, he lets them walk away without a promise or a penny; and perhaps that explains why a college class—west of the Alleghanies, at least—cannot hear it read without feeling uneasy. Instead of helping these men who wanted to work, not go on relief, Frost turns to the reader with a sound but rather sententious sermon on the ethical value of the chopping block:

> *But yield who will to their separation,*
> *My object in living is to unite*
> *My avocation and my vocation*
> *As my two eyes make one in sight.*
> *Only where love and need are one,*
> *And the work is play for mortal stakes,*
> *Is the deed ever really done*
> *For heaven and the future's sakes.*

The meter and tone of the passage remind us of another narrative poem written in New England almost a hundred years before; but "The Vision of Sir Launfal" came to a different conclusion:

> *Not what we give but what we share,*
> *For the gift without the giver is bare;*
> *Who gives himself with his alms feeds three,*
> *Himself, his hungering neighbor and me.*

What Frost sets before us is an ideal, not of charity or brotherhood, but of separateness. "Keep off each other and keep each other off," he tells us in "Build Soil." "We're too unseparate out among each other. . . . Steal away and stay away." In some of his poems he faintly suggests Emerson, and yet he is preaching only half the doctrine of self-reliance, which embraced the community as well as the individual. Emerson said, for example, "He only who is able to stand alone is qualified for society," thus implying that the self-reliant individual was to use his energies for social ends. Frost, on the other hand, makes no distinction between separateness and self-centeredness. In his poems, fine as the best of them are, the social passions of the great New Englanders have been diverted to smaller goals. One cannot imagine him thundering against the Fugitive Slave Law, like Emerson; or rising like Thoreau to defend John Brown after the Harper's Ferry raid; or even conducting a quietly persistent campaign against brutality on American ships, as Hawthorne did when he was consul at Liverpool. He is concerned chiefly with himself and his near neighbors, or rather with the Yankees among his neighbors—for although his section of New England is largely inhabited by Poles and French Canadians, there are only two poems in which these foreigners are mentioned. He says when splitting his straight-grained beech blocks:

> *The blows that a life of self-control*
> *Spares to strike for the common good*
> *That day, giving a loose to my soul,*
> *I spent on the unimportant wood;*

And one feels that the blows might symbolize the inward turning or backward turning of energies in a region that once had wider horizons. In another poem, the rambling monologue called "New Hampshire," Frost asks his readers:

> *. . . How are we to write*
> *The Russian novel in America*
> *As long as life goes so unterribly?*
> *There is the pinch from which our only outcry*
> *In literature to date is heard to come.*
> *We get what little misery we can*
> *Out of not having cause for misery.*

But the truth is that life in this country goes terribly and unterribly, depending on the point of view; we have more than our share of property and comfort, but also more than our share of suicides, nervous breakdowns in middle age (among the prosperous), and violence among all classes. Life doesn't go unterribly for Frost himself when he is writing his best lyrics; but at other moments he seems to suffer from nearsightedness or want of imagination. During his public career as a poet, there have been two crises in this country that went as deep as the conflict over slavery that engaged the best energies of the earlier New England writers. To the depression of the early 1930's, his answer was a group of poems in which he preached his doctrine of separateness, advising each of us to be a "Lone Striker." To the rise of fascism in Europe and the war spreading over the world, he also had a sort of answer; at least he wrote a philosophical poem called "The Lesson for Today," in which he undertook to discuss contemporary problems—but in what a curious fashion!

The poem was read before the Phi Beta Kappa Society of Harvard University on June 20, 1941, a year after the fall of France, nine months after the battle of England, and two days before the invasion of Russia. It is addressed, however, to a poet of Charlemagne's court, with whom Frost proposes to argue the question which century is darker, the ninth or the twentieth. "You and I," he says to this forgotten poet:

> *As schoolmen of repute should qualify*
> *To wage a fine scholastical contention*
> *As to whose age deserves the lower mark,*
> *Or should I say the higher one, for dark.*

After briefly noting the fact that every age has something to be sorry for, "A sordid peace or an outrageous war," Frost then picks out as the worst and sorriest feature of our own age, what?—not tyranny or heartlessness or insecurity, not invasions or massacres, but something, as he thinks, far deeper:

> *Space ails us moderns; we are sick with space.*
> *Its contemplation makes us out as small*
> *As a brief epidemic of microbes.*

And so, lost in space, he manages to overlook the misfortunes under his eyes. There is something appealing in the notion of a poet or philosopher retiring to his mountain farm and musing over the eternities; but when his musings in time of civil and universal war lead him to such a coldly inadequate conclusion, one decides that something is wanting in him, if not as a lyric poet, then certainly as a prophet (for he has his pretensions to prophecy) and even more as a literary idol to be set before the American nation—some absent quality, one might call it breadth or sympathy or imagination or simple curiosity about the fashion in which two-legged featherless creatures live and die.

Unlike some of his predecessors and contemporaries in New England, Frost does not strive for greater depth to compensate for what he lacks in breadth; he does not strike far inward into the wilderness of human nature. It is true that he often talks about the need for inwardness. He says, for example, in "Build Soil," which with all its limitations is the best of his long philosophical poems and perhaps the only one worth preserving:

> *We're always too much out or too much in.*
> *At present from a cosmical dilation*

> *We're so much out that the odds are against*
> *Our ever getting inside in again.*

And yet he sets limits on the exploration of himself, as he sets them on almost every other human activity; here again he displays the sense of measure and decorum that puts him in the classical, or rather the neoclassical, tradition. He is always building defenses against the infinite, walls that stand "Between too much and me." In the woods, there is a pile of rocks and an iron stake to mark the limit of his land; and here too,

> *One tree, by being deeply wounded,*
> *Has been impressed as Witness Tree*
> *And made commit to memory*
> *My proof of being not unbounded.*

The woods play a curious part in Frost's poems: they seem to be his symbol for the uncharted country within ourselves, full of possible beauty, but also full of horror. From the woods at dusk, he might hear the hidden music of the brook, "a slender, tinkling fall"; or he might see wood creatures, a buck and a doe, staring over the stone fence that marks the limit of the pasture lot. But he doesn't cross the fence, except in dreams; and then, instead of brook or deer, he is likely to meet a strange Demon rising "from his wallow to laugh." And so, for fear of the Demon, and also because of his moral obligations, he merely stands at the edge of the woods to listen:

> *Far in the pillared dark*
> *Thrush music went—*
> *Almost like a call to come in*
> *To the dark and lament.*
>
> *But no, I was out for stars:*
> *I would not come in.*
> *I mean not even if asked,*
> *And I hadn't been.*

But Hawthorne before him, thin and conventional as he was in many of his tales, still plucked up his courage and ventured into the inner wilderness; and Conrad Aiken's poems and stories (to mention only one example of New England work today) are written almost solely from within that haunted mid-region. To explore the real horrors of the mind is a long tradition in American letters, one that goes back to our first professional novelist, Charles Brockden Brown. It was continued by Poe and Melville and Henry James, and it extends in an almost unbroken line into the late work of Hemingway and Faulkner. But Frost, in several of his finest lyrics, is content to stop outside the woods, either in the summer dusk or on a snowy evening:

The woods are lovely, dark and deep.
But I have promises to keep,
And miles to go before I sleep,
And miles to go before I sleep.

If he does not strike far inwards, neither does he follow the other great American tradition (extending from Whitman to Dos Passos) of standing on a height to observe the panorama of nature and society. Let us say that he is a poet neither of the mountains nor of the woods, although he lives among both, but rather of the hill pastures, the intervales, the dooryard in autumn with the leaves swirling, the closed house shaking in the winter gales (and who else has described these scenes more accurately, in more lasting colors?). In the same way, he is not the poet of New England in its great days, or in its catastrophic late-nineteenth-century decline (except in some of his earlier poems); he is rather a poet who celebrates the diminished but prosperous and self-respecting New England of the tourist home and the antique shop in the old stone mill. And the praise heaped on Frost in recent years is somehow connected in one's mind with the search for authentic ancestors and the collecting of old New England furniture. One imagines a saltbox cottage restored to its original lines; outside it a wellsweep preserved for its picturesque quality, even though there is also an electric pump; at the doorway a coach lamp wired and polished; inside the house, a set of authentic Shaker benches, a Salem rocker, willow-ware plates and Sandwich glass; and, on the tip-top table, carefully dusted, a first edition of Robert Frost.

Van Wyck Brooks's "Usable Past"

AFTER VAN WYCK BROOKS finished the last volume of *Makers and Finders*, the most important work of his later years was his three books of memoirs. The first of these was *Scenes and Portraits* (1954), the second and liveliest was *Days of the Phoenix* (1957), and the third, more discursive, was *From the Shadow of the Mountain*, which appeared in 1961 when Brooks was seventy-five. Not one of them has received the attention that each deserves. It is a convenience and a pleasure to have them available in this one big volume.

I think of them together as Brooks's memoirs rather than his autobiography in the strict sense. Of course the work is autobiographical too; it tells us candidly what we need to know about the author's family, education, career, and guiding purposes. Still, it is less concerned with these or with his inner world—except in one moving chapter of *Days of the Phoenix* —than it is with the outer world, which for him consisted mostly of writers and painters. He looked at them all with an observant and hopeful eye. *Scenes and Portraits*, the title of the first book, might be applied to the work as a whole.

In rereading it we note again what we might have forgotten, that Brooks was a painterly writer, with a gift for rendering character by costume or gesture and atmosphere by his choice of images. One of the best of his many interiors painted in the Dutch style is Petitpas' restaurant in the Chelsea district of Manhattan, where old J. B. Yeats, the poet's father, used to preside over a tableful of writers without publishers and artists without a gallery. Among the occasional guests was Blaikie Murdoch, a Scotsman of wide and curious learning, who "followed his own personal notions of style," Brooks says, "sprinkling commas over his writing as a Parsee sprinkles red pepper

Introduction to Van Wyck Brooks, *An Autobiography*, New York, E. P. Dutton, 1965. The Introduction incorporated passages from two *Saturday Review* articles: "Van Wyck Brooks at Seventy-five," *SR* 44, February 18, 1961, pp. 15+; and "Van Wyck Brooks: A Career in Retrospect," *SR* 46, May 25, 1963, pp. 17–18+.

over meat. . . . Bald as a tonsured monk, with a mind as ripe
as old Roquefort cheese, Blaikie Murdoch was living in a
basement somewhere, cooking his meals on a gas-jet, not far
away; and, as he talked, he would stealthily manoeuvre stray
crusts of bread on the table into the yawning pockets of his old
brown jacket."

We remember Murdoch by those crusts of bread, as we
remember old Yeats by his impractical wisdom and his delight
in fine words, including the name of the disease from which he
was to die. When he heard that he was an "antique cardiac
arteriosclerotic," he said to Brooks, "I would rather be called
that than the King of the South of Egypt." Among the other
guests at Petitpas', we recognize Alan Seeger by "the long
black Paris student's cape" that he borrowed one winter when
he had no overcoat, and Brooks himself, then in his early
twenties, by his splendid waistcoats and the holes in the bot-
toms of his shoes. Every detail helps to recreate the atmosphere of a time when young writers were poor by choice as
well as necessity and when many of them wore poverty as a
uniform, but with a flower in the buttonhole.

Old Yeats, poor as the youngsters who surrounded him,
was a portrait painter without commissions, and he was also
Brooks's tutelary spirit. Once he said that the genius of his art
was "largely a genius for friendship." The best portraits are
painted, he explained, when friendship governs the relation of
the sitter to the painter. Brooks took the principle to heart, and
perhaps that is why he has devoted less space in this volume to
himself than to his friends. He gives us heroic portraits of
Max Perkins, Ned Sheldon, that brilliant playwright crippled
and blinded by arthritis, Waldo Frank, Sherwood Anderson,
and many others, including most of the rebels who surrounded
him when he was writing the early essays that announced a
second American renaissance. Meanwhile the author himself is
revealed not so much directly as by reflection, with his friendships serving as mirrors of his own idealistic, shy, loyal,
dogged, scrupulous, but not unworldly spirit. As for his career,
we see again that it had logical consistency and, almost to the
end, a continued growth of a sort not often found in the lives
of American writers.

For himself Brooks had only one ambition from the days when he went to high school in Plainfield, New Jersey. He wanted to be a writer, and he knew almost from the beginning what kind of writer: not a novelist, not a poet—though he wrote some early verses—but a critic. At first he thought of becoming an art critic on the model of Ruskin, but soon he began writing about books. "I was convinced," he says, "that criticism in some form was the most delightful activity one could dream of in this world. I even felt that everything might be expressed in criticism, as others have felt about music or fiction or sculpture." Gradually this private ambition developed into a public and largely unselfish one. That was for two good reasons: because he couldn't hope to become a critic of stature unless he had new, important, preferably native works to criticize, and because he couldn't succeed in his personal aim unless he helped to create an atmosphere in which other young writers might succeed. Thus, his career would depend in two ways on the general fate of American letters.

The fate seemed dubious in the years from 1904 to 1907, when Brooks was an undergraduate at Harvard. It was a time when the Eastern universities regarded themselves as trading posts beleaguered on the edge of Indian country, where they offered a stock of cultural goods to the younger natives. Almost all the goods had been freighted in from Europe. Students received the impression that there had once been an American literature of sorts, but that it lay "a generation or more behind us," as the poet George E. Woodberry told his Columbia classes. He expressed only a tempered admiration for that older literature, which had produced, he said, not one poet who was even of the rank of Thomas Gray. His judgment was echoed at other universities. When Barrett Wendell of Harvard wrote a book about American literature, he made his readers feel—so Howells said—that the subject was "not worth the attention of people meaning to be critical." Our past was thus abolished as a field of study, and hardly a course was offered at Harvard or elsewhere that dealt at length with American writers. As for the present, Woodberry disposed of its claims to attention in the article on American literature that he wrote for the eleventh edition (1910) of the *Encyclopedia*

Britannica. He concluded the article by saying that the social tradition and culture of the American people

> . . . make them impenetrable to the present ideas of Europe as they are current in literary forms. Nor has anything been developed from within that is fertile in literature. . . . The intellectual life is now rather to be found in social, political and natural science than elsewhere, the imaginative life is feeble, and when felt is crude; the poetic pulse is imperceptible.

Yet Harvard in those days was full of aspiring writers, some of whom would become Brooks's lifelong friends. They all wanted to produce enduring works, but they saw little hope of producing them in their native land where all the fruits seemed blighted. One of the aspirants, who looked forward to being an art critic, told Brooks in a letter that American criticism was virtually all "broken meat from the European table." The moral he drew was that one should "Sit at the first table, not the second," and he hurried off to Italy, where he planned to emulate Bernard Berenson. Other Harvard friends went to Paris or London or a German university; any city in Europe seemed to have a better climate for writing than New York. In those days Brooks himself believed "that the only chance an American had to succeed as a writer was to betake himself [to Europe] with all possible speed." He raced through college in three years, then traveled by steerage to England, where he nearly starved as a free-lance journalist and published his first book at the age of twenty-three.

As soon as the book appeared he went back to New York, in obedience to another and opposite belief that he held at the same time. "I was convinced as well," he says, "that a man without a country could do nothing of importance, that writers must draw sustenance from their own common flesh and blood and that therefore deracination also meant ruin. For me, at that time, the American writer could neither successfully stay *nor* go—he had only two alternatives, the frying-pan and the fire; and the question was therefore how to change the whole texture of life at home so that writers and artists might develop there."

His early ambition, without changing in essence, had found a new goal that would be retained for the rest of his life— though at different times he would follow different paths toward the same destination. Happily the question he tried to answer was not so broad and futile as it sounds. As a critic, a single dissenting voice, he realized that he couldn't do much "to change the whole texture of life at home." He might, however, do something to change our conception of the writer in America, and the writer's conception of his own task, always with the aim of encouraging himself and others to do better work, the best that was in them. To this aim he devoted himself with admirable consistency and—let it be recorded—with an amazing degree of success.

There is one field in which the success can be measured. When we think of the contempt for American authors, mixed with ignorance about them, that prevailed in universities during the reign of Barrett Wendell; when we contrast it with the reverence for many of the same authors that is now being proclaimed in hundreds of scholarly monographs each year, as well as being revealed statistically by the multiplication of courses in American literature—while living writers share in the glory reflected from the past by being invited to the campus as novelists or poets in residence—we might also remember that Brooks had more to do with creating the new attitude than anyone else in the country. Not a few of the academic critics who attacked him in later years were men whose careers would have been impossible if Brooks had not found them a subject and broken a path they could follow.

I said that he tried different methods of approaching what remained the same goal. In reality there were only two of the methods, and each of them belonged to a different stage of his career. In the earlier stage, which lasted from 1909 to 1926, he was the prophet of a new literature, and his method was a combination of exhortation, admonition, and holding up to scorn. America in 1915, he said, was "like a vast Sargasso Sea—a prodigious welter of unconscious life, swept by groundswells of half-conscious emotions." Ideally the country might have looked for direction to its poets and novelists and critics, who serve as "the pathfinders of society; to them belongs the vision without which the people perish." But the writers themselves were lost. "What immediately strikes one, as one surveys the history of our literature during the last half century, is the singular impotence of its creative spirit. That we have always had an abundance of talent is, I think, no less evident: what I mean is that so little of this talent really finds its way. . . . The chronic state of our literature is that of a youthful promise which is never redeemed."

I am quoting from three of Brooks's early essays: *America's Coming-of-Age* (1915), *Letters and Leadership* (1918), and *The Literary Life in America* (1921). Together they composed a manifesto for the new generation of writers, one that has been compared in its effects with Emerson's address "The American Scholar," delivered at Harvard in 1837. Emerson did more than anyone else to produce what was afterward known as the American renaissance. There was something Emersonian in Brooks's tone, and writing in the early days of a second renaissance, he found as many eager listeners.

He did not merely utter lamentations, which were justified at the time; he also diagnosed the weakness of American writing and offered a prescription for making it stronger. As compared with the writing "of almost any European country" —and the comparison with France and England was never far from Brooks's mind—its principal weakness was that "Our writers all but universally lack the power of growth, the endurance that enables one to continue personal work after the freshness of youth has gone." Instead of developing into great men of letters, they had surrendered easily to commercialism and convention, largely—Brooks told us in italics—because they had lacked "the sense that one is *working in a great line*." His prescription followed from the diagnosis: we should develop a tradition in American literature and, by studying its history, we should try to discover what he was the first to call a "usable past."

The two famous biographies that he wrote during this period were part of the search for that past, but they were also cautionary tales; they showed the consequences resulting from two different answers to his old question, whether American writers should live abroad or stay at home. *The Ordeal of Mark Twain* (1920) presented the example of a great American author who stayed at home and crippled his talent by yielding to native conventions. In later years Brooks revised the book to incorporate new facts, but he never changed his central judgment of Mark Twain's career. *The Pilgrimage of Henry James* (1925) told the story of another great author, one who lived abroad and who suffered equally—so Brooks insisted—through losing touch with his own people. About James he was never sure of having been completely fair. "I was to realize, looking back," he says, "that I had been quarreling with myself when I appeared to be quarreling with Henry James. For, like many of my friends, I too had been enchanted with Europe, and I had vaguely hoped to continue to live there. It struck me that if I was always 'straining to read the face of America,'—Paul Rosenfeld's phrase for my obsession—it was because of an over-determination, and perhaps the question of expatriation had so possessed my mind because this mind itself had been divided."

There was a time when "I was pursued especially," Brooks also says, "with nightmares in which Henry James turned great luminous menacing eyes upon me." That was during the prolonged nervous breakdown that he suffered after 1926, when his life became a succession of doctors, nursing homes with barred windows, and dreams of self-annihilation. "I could no longer sleep," he says, "I scarcely sat down for a year, I lived in a Plutonian psychical twilight." When he emerged from this "season in hell," as he calls it in that moving chapter of *Days of the Phoenix*, he was ready at the age of forty-five to start a new career.

Its goal would be the same as in his earlier career, that is, to give us a new picture of the American writer, of what he had done in the past and of what he might achieve. But Brooks had changed during his season in hell, and he was now temperamentally unable to follow his earlier method of combining exhortation with admonishment like a prophet in Israel. As for holding up to scorn or writing cautionary tales, both seemed alien to his new character, for the wound in himself had made him loath to expose the wounds in others. He looked eagerly now for things he could praise, especially in the lives of earlier American writers who had been long neglected. At the same time his experience in sanitariums had given him—or helped to give—more patience, a stronger sense of discipline, and a new habit of rising early in the morning, never later than six, and going straight to work. He was ready now to move toward his goal by a second method based on patient scholarship.

The five volumes of *Makers and Finders* took him nineteen years to write, or about four years for each volume. During that time he worked ten or twelve hours a day and read five thousand American books, some of which had not been opened by anyone else for more than half a century. What seems remarkable in this age of collective undertakings is that he did the work unaided by collaborators, research assistants, or even a secretary. He copied out all the quotations, and "I have not found one error in transcription," he said in a letter to a Harvard classmate, Samuel Eliot Morison, who had questioned some statements in *The Flowering of New England*. Besides Brooks's passion for the sort of accuracy that one couldn't demand of a hired assistant, he had another passion for being his own copyist. "It's the only way to get the feel of an author," he explained. "Passages copied by someone else don't have the same meaning." The manuscript of each volume was written in his small, nervous, angular, hard-to-decipher hand at the rate of never more than a page of three hundred and fifty words each day. It was the sort of purely individual project on a grand scale that has seldom been carried out since the days of Prescott, Parkman, and the other great New England historians.

The work as it progressed had an interesting critical reception. For *The Flowering of New England*, which was the first volume to appear, in 1936, though it came second in Brooks's plan for the series, there was something close to universal praise. Almost the only discordant voices were some of those on the political left, where one heard complaints that Brooks was no longer a leader and prophet, but had turned to "scholarly storytelling." The stories of course had a purpose, but the left-wing critics were slow to grasp it. Among the academic reviewers, Morison was the only one who thought that Brooks had been reckless with his facts. Brooks was disturbed by the charge and wrote his classmate a seven-page letter, not for publication, a copy of which was found among his own papers marked "*Important*—to keep."

> So far [one page of it reads], in going over my book, and the various criticisms of it, I have detected 14 mistakes. This includes two mistakes (the same mistake repeated) regarding the Franconia Notch, also the error about the sloop Harvard, and about H. G. Otis, who was not a merchant. . . . Some of these errors are exceedingly slight, and even on the ragged edge of truth. Observe, I am not defending this ragged edge. I did not say that Otis's punch-bowl held ten gallons. I had, and thought I conveyed, a different visual image in saying that "ten gallons of punch evaporated out of it," i.e., that the punch-bowl was refilled. Again, regarding the sloop Harvard, I did not specifically say that it was moored at the port, and I certainly thought it was, and I gladly accept the blame for my misstatement. (On looking through my notes, I find that I got this impression from Lowell's *Cambridge Thirty Years Ago*: "Cambridge has long had its port, but the greatest part of its maritime trade was, thirty years ago, entrusted to a single Argo, the sloop Harvard," etc.) The error was not in the transcription, but in a faulty inference from it. It seems to me, in the case in question, the inference was not unnatural, but I freely confess my error in 14 cases.
>
> Now why do I dwell on this? To show you that I am not disinclined to be careful about "pesky facts" and to ask you how you justify the charge that I "throw my facts about."

In truth the charge, though made in good faith, could not be justified except by adducing some inconsequential errors that Brooks was glad to correct, and it was seldom repeated in reviews of later volumes. The first of these, *New England: Indian Summer* (1940), had an autumnal rather than a springlike charm as compared with *The Flowering*, but this other quality was equally appreciated by its reviewers, some of whom babbled in a delirium of praise. There were attacks, however, in three or four scholarly journals, and there were more of these after *The World of Washington Irving* (1944), which Brooks regarded as the best of his books. Dealing as it did with the early writers of the Republic, many of whom had been forgotten even by scholars, it conveyed a happy feeling of exploration and rediscovery; but academic critics complained about Brooks's method. They said that he was wasting his time on minor figures, that he wasn't truly critical, and that in fact he wasn't writing a history of American literature of the sort that could be assigned to their students. The complaints were louder after *The Times of Melville and Whitman* (1947), and loudest after the series was completed with *The Confident Years* in 1952. By that time, moreover, the attacks on Brooks's method were being accompanied by others on his conception of American literature as a whole.

It has always seemed to me that the critics had reason, not for rushing into battle against Brooks, but for discussion and disagreement with him about that last grand question. At the end of *The Confident Years* he tries to define the American tradition that he has been presenting in narrative form all through the five volumes. It is, he tells us, a belief in the inherent goodness of men and in their capacity to govern themselves; it is "the tradition of Jefferson, Paine and Crève-coeur and the roundhead side in the English civil war,—with all the typical American institutions . . . and it was this that Europeans had in mind when they complained that American writers had never been 'American enough.' "

> From this [he continues] had sprung the great body of writers from Benjamin Franklin down to a regiment of poets, romancers, historians and thinkers who had given the country, in literature, a character of its own, and to deny this was to deny that America had a character, that it was anything but a congeries of exiles from Europe. This was the core of America, in fact,—to the world America meant this or nothing,—it was what the "Latin genius" was to France; and where else could one find the American "uniqueness" to fit the prescription of Eliot himself that "the culture of each country should be unique"?

But is Brooks defining the only American tradition in literature? One notes in this final chapter of *Makers and Find-ers* that he seems obsessed with T. S. Eliot, whom he accuses, in effect, of having betrayed the essential spirit of the nation. Might it not be more accurate to say that Eliot has followed one American tradition in preference to another? Brooks him-self has earlier made it clear that Eliot had many American predecessors, both in choosing to live abroad and in his attitude toward the art of letters. Other critics have traced his lineage as a writer through Henry James back to Hawthorne or, more circuitously, back to Poe by way of the French symbolists, who were proud of having adopted many of Poe's ideals. I am not the first to suggest that there are at least two traditions in American literature; perhaps there are several. If we prefer to have only two, there is the tradition that Brooks extols as being essentially American, the tradition of the sunny, expansive writers who believed in human improvability, and beside it another tradition that is dark, intensive, pessimistic about human nature, and preoccupied with form rather than message. Both have been long established in this country. If Brooks's tradition goes back to Franklin and Emerson, the other might be traced to Charles Brockden Brown, at the end of the eighteenth century, or even to Jonathan Edwards.

It was Brown who said in a letter: "An accurate history of the thoughts and feelings of any man, for one hour, is more valuable for some minds than a system of geography; and you, you tell me, are one of those who would rather travel into the mind of a ploughman than into the interior of America. I confess myself of your way of thinking." That suggests another way of distinguishing the two traditions: there are the writers in breadth and the writers in depth; there are the morning writers and—thinking of Brown and his successors—the twilight or nocturnal writers. In Philip Rahv's famous distinction, somewhat different from the one I have been suggesting, the literary Redskins are at war with the Palefaces. Most but not all of the writers whom Brooks praises for being essentially American are Redskins. The great men in his tradition are Emerson, Thoreau, Whitman, and after them Mark Twain (in *Huckleberry Finn*, but not later), William James, Parkman, Howells, Dreiser, and, among the generation of the 1920's, Thomas Wolfe. In the other tradition the great names are Hawthorne, Melville, Henry James, Henry Adams, and Faulkner.

And must we choose one side or the other? If there *are* two sides, that is, and only two—a questionable proposition—must we vote that only one of them is truly American, thus abandoning the writers on the other side to Europe or the feudal past or simple neglect? I have to confess that by temperament and training I feel more drawn to the writers in depth than to the expansive morning writers in the Emersonian line. But our literature is not so rich that it can afford to surrender any of its great men, Emerson *or* Hawthorne, Whitman or Melville, Parkman or Henry Adams, Brooks or Eliot; we need them all. By defining the American tradition restrictively, Brooks makes it seem poorer than it was in fact—and also poorer than he has made it seem in his five volumes of narrative. The academic critics had reason to argue with him on this point. Most of them, however, made the same sort of mistake as Brooks by rejecting another group of authors, exactly the ones that Brooks admires in his final chapter.

I have said too much about that one chapter and thus have neglected his real achievement in *Makers and Finders*. It was not to define the American tradition, bur rather to present it as a Tolstoyan novelist might do, in a grand historical pageant that flows on author by author, scene by scene, and volume after volume. For the first time he proved by narration, description, and quotation, rather than argument, that this country has had a continuous life and character in literature.

I have never been impressed by the academic complaints about Brooks's method, most of which were based on various misconceptions of his purpose as a historian. Academic critics like to feel that a work on American literature can be assigned to some familiar type; that its orientation is social or political or biographical or psychological, or that it is a history of ideas, or that it chooses the major authors and studies their work in depth. *Makers and Finders* belongs to none of these types, and in fact there is no real parallel in American or foreign scholarship for Brooks's attempt to recover a literary tradition where none had been thought to exist. Since the goal was new, he had to find a new method of reaching it, and this is what most of the critics have failed to understand.

Part of his method was to suggest, as a landscape painter might do, the special atmosphere of cities and sections where literary movements started or flourished or declined. One remembers particularly his pictures of Boston after the Civil War, in *New England: Indian Summer*, and of Philadelphia at the end of the eighteenth century, in *The World of Wash-*

ington Irving, but there are dozens of these effectively painted literary landscapes. A more important part of the method was to emphasize the interconnections among writers, the points at which they came together to form a field of radiating forces that was almost like a magnetic field. For an example of such emphasis, one might turn to *The Times of Melville and Whitman* and consider his treatment of Bayard Taylor, the flimsy poet and entertaining traveler who was long regarded as a rival of the great New Englanders. Brooks devotes eight pages to his literary career, about the same space that would be assigned to him by an old-fashioned literary historian. The new-fashioned historians, in their preoccupation with major writers, would give him no space whatever; perhaps they wouldn't mention his name. But men like Taylor are essential to Brooks's purpose, for, as he tells us in his memoirs, "It is the minor books or writers that body forth a culture, creating the living chain that we call tradition."

The facts to be mentioned about this minor but once famous writer are chosen with the "living chain" in mind. Brooks doesn't tell us the date of Taylor's birth (1825) or give us the titles of his principal works in verse or prose. What we learn about him is chiefly:

1. That he belonged to the staff of the New York *Tribune,* like many other talented authors of his time (and elsewhere in the book Brooks lists them by name).

2. That he made his reputation by walking through Europe and sending back letters to the American press. On his return he was invited to dine with Bancroft, Cooper, and Melville, while N. P. Willis wrote an introduction to his book of travels.

3. That he had grown up in southeastern Pennsylvania, which in some ways resembled rural New England as described in the novels of Harriet Beecher Stowe—"which the novels of Bayard Taylor in turn resembled,—though the people were less keen and their interests were narrower and simpler, as Taylor's novels were dimmer than Mrs. Stowe's." (One notes that Brooks's critical comments on his authors are often expressed as comparisons with other American authors of the same period.)

4. That Taylor was first inspired to travel by reading Washington Irving, N. P. Willis, and Longfellow's *Outre Mer*, and that later it was Irving who advised him to visit the Orient.

5. That he lectured on American literature in Weimar, Goethe's city, and introduced a distinguished audience to the works of Emerson, Longfellow, and Bryant.

There is no need to cite other facts of the same nature from the eight-page passage on Taylor, or to list the forty-two pages on which his name is mentioned elsewhere in the book, always in connection with other names, for I think that by now the nature of Brooks's emphasis is clear. What interests him in Taylor, as in many authors of second or third rank, is not their books primarily or their private lives, but chiefly their points of contact with fellow authors. I think it was Bernard DeVoto who complained that Brooks's subjects never fall in love and never have children unless the children are authors too. The omission of family matters weakens some of his portraits, but families are inessential to his purpose. He is trying to show that American writers, besides existing in the social world, also moved in a closed system of their own. By revealing their points of contact he creates, as it were, a medium in which the writers existed and in which they transmitted energy by collision, like so many planets or atoms. Many critics, including Eliot and his followers, have talked about the value of a literary tradition, but they have left its nature a little vague. Brooks was the first author in any language to make a tradition real and almost palpable by presenting it as a rich texture of meetings, readings, and ideas passed from one writer to another.

For all the critical attacks it had to withstand, *Makers and Finders* effected a deep change in our judgment of the American past and hence, I think, in our vision of the future. It will remain for a long time our greatest sustained work of literary scholarship. But Brooks's story doesn't end with the completion of the last volume a few days after his sixty-fifth birthday in February 1951. During the next twelve years he wrote ten other books, all conceived in the same spirit as *Makers and Finders*, though not, of course, on the same grand scale. He was continuing to revive our memories of neglected heroes. Except for the memoirs, my favorite among his later books is the one about that peppery, corncob-pipe-smoking Scotch Irishman, his old friend the painter John Sloan, who, in his good early work, was a novelist in color, just as Brooks himself is here again a landscape painter and portraitist in words. The landscapes are chiefly those of the New York art world in the pioneering days of the Armory Show.

After *John Sloan* I should place Brooks's defense and appreciation of William Dean Howells, a book that complements his earlier biographies of Mark Twain and Henry James in a way that *The Life of Emerson* had failed to do. Howells was a lifelong friend and rival of James, as well as the closest friend of Twain, and his career reveals still another approach to the provincial narrowness and iron conventions that had ruined so many American writers. Instead of fleeing to Europe with James, or letting himself be partly crippled by the conventions as Twain had been—or rising serenely above them with Emerson—Howells had flourished within the conventions while somehow preserving an integrity of purpose. He had also done more for his fellow writers, including the rebels of the 1890's, than anyone else of his time.

Brooks felt instinctively drawn to Howells and, in his later years, even came to resemble him. They were both short, solid men (though Brooks never let himself develop the paunch that Howells carried with dignity); they both had quiet good manners and dressed quietly well (Brooks with a half-inch of white cuff showing at the end of his sleeves); they both had very high foreheads and white soup-strainer mustaches (though Brooks's features were less old-Roman than Howells' and gave an impression of shy benignity). Both men were utterly devoted to the art and profession of writing books, and both suffered at the end from neglect. "I am comparatively a dead cult," Howells said in a letter, "with my statues cut down and the grass growing over them in the pale moonlight." Brooks for his part complained more than once of being "an infra-red type" surviving in an ultra-violet era of pessimism. Remembering the Chinese proverb, "A man is more the child of the age he lives in than he is of his own father and mother," he sometimes felt that the changing times had made him an orphan.

But the neglect was less harsh in Brooks's case than in that of Howells. It was softened by many public honors and, in a more gratifying fashion, by a stream of visits and letters from young writers who had been heartened by his work. One of them wrote, "I feel less like a nomad whenever I finish one of your books. Even at my loneliest, I feel sustained by the record of men before me who have struggled toward consciousness." A novelist said, "My work grows out of what went before. I feel I'm in the line." Another added, "One gains a real feeling of participation. . . . Our struggles of today fall into a new perspective." Brooks listened to these new voices as old J. B. Yeats had listened to Brooks, in the years when they sat together at the long table in Petitpas' garden.

Old Yeats's confident spirit pervades this volume of memoirs. Because of his wisdom, Brooks says, "J. B. Yeats was to leave behind him a great and lasting memory in many minds, for, whatever the virtues of Americans may be, wisdom is not one of them and most of his friends had never seen a wise man. . . . Who had ever heard of an American sage since the days of Emerson and Thoreau?" It becomes clear in retrospect that Brooks was trying to lead a sage's life. The story indirectly told but vividly suggested in his memoirs is that of an author who has followed a single line of development with complete integrity. It was in 1921 that Brooks asked a famous question: "Of how many of our modern writers can it be said that their work reveals a continuous growth, or indeed any growth, that they hold their ground tenaciously and preserve their sap from one decade to another?" Clearly there were no such American writers at the time, since Howells had died the year before and the new men were still too young for their careers to be judged. If there were a few such writers by 1960—Brooks himself among them—the change was partly owed to the work he had done for the literary profession in this country, by restoring its traditions and giving its members a past on which to build.

Three Cycles of Myth in American Writing

EVEN THE Mississippi wasn't always a legendary river, famous in song and story. Early travelers described it as "a furious, rapid, desolating torrent," and some of them believed that the country through which it flowed would never be fit for human habitation. Captain Frederick Marryat, late of the Royal Navy and a justly famous novelist in his time, took passage up the river in 1837. "There are," he reported, "no pleasing associations connected with the great common sewer of the Western America, which pours its mud out into the Mexican Gulf, polluting the clear blue sea for many miles beyond its mouth. It is a river of desolation."

Today the Mississippi has been surrounded with all the "pleasing associations" that Marryat missed because he came too early. Mark Twain was to be the man who transformed the river into a legend. Of course he had thousands of collaborators, including his boyhood friends in Hannibal, Missouri, and the tall talkers he met when he was an apprentice pilot— not to mention all the novelists, poets, historians, playwrights, and jazz singers who have written or bellowed out their praises of Old Man River—but Mark Twain was the first to give shape and color to the story. In *Life on the Mississippi* and even more in *Huckleberry Finn*, he created a myth, one that will live as long as cotton grows behind the levees or schoolboys dream of drifting southward on a raft.

Older than Mark Twain's version of the Mississippi story were myths of rural New England, of the Southern plantations, of the Eastern forest, and of the always receding frontier. Very few nations so young as nineteenth-century America have developed such an extensive mythology or one so expressive of an age and people. But it changed with the times, as the nation was also changing, and now the question is what new myths will be created to mirror the new suburban or industrial landscapes, the new adventures and defeats beyond the oceans, the representative characters, the deep fears and uneasy aspira-

"American Myths Old and New," a shorter version of this essay, appeared in *Saturday Review*, September 1, 1962.

tions of our day—and not only mirror all these but also make it possible for us to believe in ourselves as characters in the drama of American history.

Myths, for the present purpose, might be defined simply as familiar narratives that embody representative types of character and experience. Walt Whitman called them "national, original archetypes in literature" and said that they alone "put the nation in form, finally tell anything—prove, complete anything—perpetuate anything." Myths in this sense of the word can be recognized by their ability to live in the popular imagination quite independently of the incidents or books or ballads that gave birth to them. Myths are the wise Ulysses, the dutiful Aeneas, the fight at Roncesvalles, and—leaping over the centuries—they are Daniel Boone in the wilderness, the Texans at the Alamo, and Huck Finn drifting down the Mississippi.

Myths can be and often are false to history: for example, Skipper Floyd—or was it really Flood?—Ireson was a different figure in life from the protagonist of Whittier's poem. The real Flood Ireson never refused to rescue the crew of another fishing smack, and although he was tarred and feathered and carried in a cart, it wasn't by the women of Marblehead. Richard III of England lost the battle of Bosworth and his crown, but it wasn't "all for the lack of a horseshoe nail," as the old adage wanted us to believe. On the other hand, three hundred Spartans really defended the Pass of Thermopylae against the Persian hordes, and died to the last man, and their true exploit has also become a myth. Truth or falsity as judged by surviving records is not the test of a myth. The test is its ability to shape the popular mind, and hence we might say that the truth of a myth lies in the future.

One example should be familiar to every student of American history. During the 1830's the slave states of the American Union were quarreling with the free states and were becoming conscious of their separate identity. They tried—or, to be accurate, several of their novelists, poets, and journalists tried—to express that identity in the shape of a myth. They had been hearing from New England about the myth of the Puritans, and now they invented the counter myth of the Virginia Cavalier, the proud gentleman devoted to ideals of loyalty, honor, and personal courage. In order to find a historical basis for the myth, they claimed that Virginia had been settled by followers of King Charles I—the Cavaliers—whereas New England had been settled by his middle-class enemies, the Roundheads.

It is still an unsettled question how many of the English cavaliers emigrated to Virginia after the defeat of the king to whom they were loyal. There may have been only scores of them; there may have been hundreds or a very few thousands. On the whole, the myth of the Southern cavalier rests on shaky historical foundations. We might say, however, that when the myth began to be popular, during the 1830's, the proof of it did not lie in the past, in the records of colonial Virginia, but rather in the future. The proof was in the contribution made by the myth to the feeling of separate Southern nationality that led to the Civil War. The proof was also in the loyalty, honor, and personal courage of Virginia cavaliers like Robert E. Lee, Stonewall Jackson, and J. E. B. Stuart.

Myths, as we see, may be good or bad in their effects, or a mixture of good and bad. Sometimes they lead to complacency, national arrogance, or tribal hatreds. Very often they are used by political leaders to delude the public, and yet they form an essential and generally helpful part of every culture, ancient and modern. A country without them would seem inhumanly bare and baleful, like Captain Marryat's vision of the Mississippi. A nation without myths would scarcely be a nation, but only a mass of separate persons living in the same territory and obeying the same laws because they were afraid of the police. The separate persons would have no common ideals of character and conduct unless these were enforced by some sort of mythology. Walt Whitman was thinking about this problem when he said, in *Democratic Vistas*, "The literature, songs, esthetics, &c., of a country are of importance principally because they furnish the materials and suggestions of personality for the women and men of that country, and enforce them in a thousand effective ways." Therefore he called for a race of myth-making poets, able to shape the nation "with unconditional uncompromising sway. Come forth," he cried, "sweet democratic despots of the west!"

The democratic despots were slow to appear on this continent. America in the beginning had only the myths that the colonists carried with them from Europe. To the first settlers everything beyond their narrow clearings was not only strange but hostile and satanic. The New Englanders in particular regarded themselves as "a people of God settled in those which were once the Devil's territories; and it may easily be supposed," said the pious Cotton Mather, "that the Devil was exceeding disturbed when he perceived such a people here accomplishing the promise of old made unto our Blessed Jesus, that he should have the utmost parts of the earth for his possession." Cotton Mather and his friends believed that the forest, which they hated and feared—and destroyed as fast as the trees could be girdled, chopped down, and burned—was Satan's shadowy dominion. They believed that the Indian powwows or medicine men who lived in the forest were in league with Satan's other retainers, the witches and warlocks of northern Europe. Legends of witchcraft survived for a long time in New England, so that Nathaniel Hawthorne, who was born in 1804, remembered hearing them often by the kitchen fire. South of the Potomac feudal legends were more popular, especially those connected with courtly love, manor houses, and feuds between noble families. Yet both types of imported legends, Northern and Southern, slowly lost their hold on a new country which, as a whole, was neither feudal nor devil-fearing.

The colonists needed myths of their own, and, in the course of time, they created a fairly extensive native folklore. In a feeble but stubborn fashion, part of the lore has survived till our time, though chiefly in scattered regions like the Pennsylvania Dutch country, the Tennessee mountains, and the Ozarks, where it is still being tracked down and recorded by scholars. It must be added that the growth of folklore in the strict sense of an oral rather than a written tradition has been impeded in this country by the fact that Americans in the mass have been a literate people, with the habit of reading their stories instead of telling them by the fireside. Most of our mythology soon found its way into print; one might even say that most of it started there. More than in any other country it has been created by professional writers.

Those writers knew what they were doing, as anyone can learn for himself by studying their journals and correspondence. When they wrote to their friends about literary problems, they often used words like "legend," "mystery," "tradition," "picturesque," and "romance." All the words refer to the same quality, one that they felt was lacking in American life; Washington Irving defined it as "the color of romance and tradition." Hawthorne said that it was inconceivably difficult to write romances about a country "where there is no shadow, no antiquity, no mystery, no picturesque and gloomy wrong, nor anything but a commonplace prosperity, in broad and simple daylight, as is happily the case with my dear native land." Until the missing elements were supplied—if necessary by the private efforts of American writers—they doubted whether they could produce poems and stories equal to the best work of their English contemporaries.

That is one side of their effort to create myths—the selfish side, one might call it—but they also had other motives. Most of them were lonely men who felt themselves to be isolated from their practical-minded fellow citizens, and they were trying to arouse in Americans a sense of community and of common destinies on a deeper level than that of practical affairs. These writers loved their country—most of all when they were living in Europe—and they were trying to communicate a sense of its past trials and future greatness. With different motives working together, it is no wonder that our first successful authors, those who became widely known about 1820, were all professional mythopoeists.

Irving, for example, set out to people the Hudson Valley with ancestral ghosts and rather jovial demons. He invented some legends of the supernatural, heard others in Dutch villages along the river, and borrowed still others from European literature, as, for example, the plot of "Rip Van Winkle," which he found in a German book and moved to the Catskills. William Cullen Bryant devoted himself to the problem of putting American birds and flowers into poetry, where they had never been mentioned. He was the first poet to sing in honor of the bobolink and the fringed gentian. James Fenimore Cooper had a wooden style and no architectural talent, but his imagination was fired by the sea and the American wilderness. His great creation was the myth of the receding frontier. Some of his characters, including Long Tom Coffin in *The Pilot* and Natty Bumppo in the five Leatherstocking novels, were the first folk heroes in American fiction.

There would be many others before the nineteenth century had ended. One author after another contributed scenes and archetypical characters to American mythology. Hawthorne, for example, was a student of colonial times, bent on transforming the historical records into legends. Longfellow was fascinated by the same problem, and his work would bear a higher reputation today if we studied the substance of it as myth rather than sentiment or morality. Emerson turned away from the past to the present. His oration "The American Scholar" was a manifesto addressed to the new generation of writers. "I ask not for the great, the remote, the romantic; what is doing in Italy or Arabia; what is Greek art or Provençal minstrelsy," Emerson told them. "I embrace the common, I explore and sit at the feet of the familiar, the low. Give me insight into today, and you may have the antique and future worlds." One of his central problems was how to give a universal and eternal value to everyday experience. For him the meal in the firkin and the milk in the pan were the bread and wine of a new sacrament. Thoreau, who started as Emerson's disciple, wrote about his own township as if it were Athens in the time of Pericles. "I would fain set down something beside facts," he wrote in his journal. "Facts should be only as the frame to my picture; they should be material to the mythology which I am writing."

After the Civil War, Whitman complained that all the great literature of Europe was aristocratic or authoritarian. When he called for a new race of poets, in *Democratic Vistas*, he assumed that their principal function would be to furnish myths for a new continent and for democracy. The poets failed to come forth, but some of the myths were created in prose, as notably by Bret Harte in his stories about the California mining camps. Harte was followed by a school of local-color novelists, each romanticizing his own section of the country. Even William Dean Howells, the polite and rather timid realist, embodied in his work one famous American myth, that of the young girl or "tenderest society bud" who was distinguished, so it seems to us today, by her cast-iron innocence and inhuman refinement.

What we might call the first American mythology had taken a final shape by 1890. In retrospect it seems amazingly complete, including as it does a score of familiar backgrounds, each with its registered trademark. For New England the trademark was a low-roofed farmhouse with a well-sweep outside the kitchen door; for the tidewater South it was a high-porticoed mansion; for the Great Smokies it was a crazy-roofed cabin not far from a corn-liquor still. There were other trademarks as well, familiar to everyone who thumbed through the magazines or went to theatres: the Mississippi steamboat round the bend, the sod house on the prairie, the chuck wagon surrounded by cowboys squatting on their heels, the Indian village with dancing braves, and the gambling saloon near the California diggings. Against those familiar backgrounds moved a whole pantheon of mythological figures, at least twelve of which might be listed as the major gods of our first native Olympus. Here are the divine heroes and the one goddess who reigned over us like Zeus, Hermes, Artemis, and their kindred:

1. The sober-garbed and steeple-hatted Puritan, usually pictured on his way to the meeting house, with his Bible in one hand and his bell-mouthed musket in the other.

2. Contrasting with him, the plumed Virginia cavalier, spurring madly through the forest to defend his honor and rescue a damsel in distress.

3. The woods ranger in coonskin cap and fringed buckskin breeches, carrying a long rifle. Daniel Boone, Natty Bumppo, and Nick of the Woods are three of the many names to which he answered.

4. The backwoods boaster or Southwestern ring-tailed roarer, sometimes known as Davy Crockett. Half-horse, half-alligator, a little teched with the snapping turtle, he could grin the bark off'n a tree and hug a b'ar too close for comfort.

5. The Yankee to rhyme with lanky, a tall, loose-jointed figure with sallow cheeks, a sharp nose, and an eye to the main chance. First he was a schoolmaster called Ichabod Crane;

then he changed his name to Sam Slick and peddled wooden nutmegs. It was his brother Jonathan, equally shrewd but kinder-hearted, who grew a long chin beard and was caricatured in the newspapers as Uncle Sam.

6. The Southern colonel with black slouch hat and shoe-string tie, sitting behind tall white pillars in a rocking chair and calling, "Tom, you rascal, bring me another julep."

7. Uncle Tom, the faithful retainer, with his black head surrounded by a halo of white lamb's wool.

8. The slit-eyed, lean-jawed, soft-spoken gambler with two six-guns hidden beneath the frock coat made by the best Omaha tailor.

9. The bad man—Quantrill, Jesse James, Sam Bass—riding into town at the head of his outlaw band to rob a bank. He was whisky-eyed, unshaven, brutal, but he gave money to the poor and he never annoyed a woman.

10. The Indian chief in his bonnet of eagle feathers, his language consisting of "How" and "Ugh."

11. The Alger newsboy, doing and daring, rising by pluck and luck (and a willing smile) from rags to riches.

12. Finally the young girl who ruled over all the others by force of her unsullied innocence, so that the gambler blushed like a small boy when she spoke to him, the Southern colonel was ruled by her whims, the bad man fled, and the scarlet woman—on those few occasions when she appeared in American fiction—knelt to kiss the hem of her skirt.

Besides those major deities there were demigodlike figures not far behind them, including—to mention only a few—the Down East farmer who ordered his erring daughter into a snowstorm; the black-mustachioed villain with his city ways; the millionaire enslaved by his beautiful daughters; the bad boy that every American wished he could be once more; the widowed mother waiting for the mortgage to be foreclosed; the comic Irishman who outwitted the comic Dutchman and was in turn outwitted by the comic Jew; the abolitionist turned carpetbagger; the black mammy at her cabin door; the Eastern dude among cowboys; the half-witted old prospector; and —when some bolder author like Bret Harte dared to mention her—the dance-hall girl with a heart of twenty-four-karat gold.

In those days after the Civil War, it was the good women, wives and schoolmistresses, who bought the books and read the magazines; most men read only the newspapers. To be successful an author had to please a feminine audience. Women liked love stories and hence the magazines were full of them, while all the popular novels ended to the peal of a wedding march. On the other hand, romantic love was not a major theme either in American literature on its highest level or in familiar American folklore. After the first few chapters of our legendary novel, *Moby Dick*, it has no female characters except mother whales. There were not many women, either, in the great cycles of myth that dealt with the wilderness, the river, the cattle ranges, and the mining camps. All the cycles consisted of stories about men, working or wandering, hunting, fighting, enduring hardships, getting rich, or running away from civilization, but seldom or never passionately in love. Huck Finn was too young for love, but all the familiar heroes were boys at heart and old Leatherstocking died a bachelor.

Love was not the only topic that was seldom discussed in the American classical myths. As compared with the legendary epics of other nations, they treated a narrow range of subjects: for example, they were not much concerned with rivalries between countries or classes, with loyalty to rulers, or with the question of man's place in the universe, to mention themes that recur in epic poems from the *Iliad* to *Paradise Lost*. They did not express a strong sense of locality. Their heroes were lonely and often childless men who wandered farther than Ulysses, but always away from home.

Our myths were not tragic in the Greek sense of the word. The heroes were not punished for their pride, nor did they ever resign themselves to fate; when they found themselves in a tragic situation they pulled up stakes and moved farther west. Sometimes they couldn't move because they were surrounded by hostile Indians, but then they fought and triumphed over impossible odds by a mixture of courage, ingenuity, and blind luck. The U. S. Cavalry never failed to appear with gleaming sabers before the Redskins captured the wagon train. The heroes never lost hope, never smiled, and never stopped cracking jokes. Humor, dry or boisterous, was one quality of American myths and headlong action was an-

other; but what they most admirably expressed was the buoy-
ancy of a new nation, its faith in the individual, and its thirst
for perpetual movement and improvement.

By 1890 the country had changed and the old American gods
and heroes could no longer be followed as guides to daily
living. There were no more Indians to fight on the frontier
and in fact there was no frontier, in the sense of a continuous
line beyond which there were no permanent settlements. The
last big land rush had been the stampede across the Oklahoma
border in 1889. The gold rush at Cripple Creek, Colorado, in
1890 was the last really big one south of Canada. The new
pioneers would be the "back-trailers," as Hamlin Garland
called them, from the Plains States to Chicago and Boston and
New York. The new frontier was in the big cities.

Besides this movement from farms to factories and offices,
there were other changes produced by expansion and immigra-
tion. The center of American life had shifted from the seaboard, with its colonial traditions, to the Mississippi Valley.
English and Scottish were no longer regarded as the only true
native strains. Eventually there would be a change in popular
legends, to bring them closer to the new situation; but first
came a long war in American literature, a battle of the books
that began about 1885 and lasted for nearly half a century.
Although it used to be described as a quarrel between the
Idealists on one side and the Realists and Naturalists on the
other, it was also a struggle between rival mythologies.

The Idealists, who included most of the established writers
and the professors of literature, defended the older myths,
those with a rural background and a message of optimism. The
Naturalists were younger writers like Frank Norris, Theodore
Dreiser, and their friends, who believed that the old mythology should be abandoned. Their favorite targets for ridicule
were the Puritan, the Alger hero, and the young girl, but in
general they regarded all the deities of the old pantheon as
idols to be smashed. At the same time they were trying to
create new myths that would embody scientific laws—for they
were all disciples of Darwin and Herbert Spencer—besides

expressing the aspirations of new racial groups and portraying the urban and industrial America of their own generation.

Strange things happened to the older American heroes during this civil war in the literary world and after the victory of the Naturalistic writers. Thus, the sharp-witted Yankee peddler disappeared from fiction after a final visit to King Arthur's court. The Puritan became a blue-nosed Prohibitionist and, in popular books, a generally mean fellow. Uncle Tom was rejected by his own people. Other traditional characters survived and prospered, but only by moving to the city. There the slit-eyed gambler ran a night club—hundreds of night clubs in one moving picture after another—and kept his six-guns in the middle drawer of his executive-type desk. The bad man became a big-time mobster. Leatherstocking also moved to the city, where he wore a detective's badge and tracked down criminals as if they were hostile Indians. The young girl lost her innocence and, growing older, suffered a curious transformation. As the frigid, selfish wife and later as the possessive mother who kept her children tied to her silver-corded apron, she became the familiar villainess of American fiction.

New characters, mostly city dwellers, came forward to join the earlier heroes of legend. Among those who now took hold of the popular imagination were the wise girl making her lonely way in the metropolis (like Dreiser's Sister Carrie and David Graham Phillips' Susan Lenox, who fell and rose again); the robber baron winning and losing fortunes without regard for the law (as in Dreiser's *The Financier*); the political boss who looked like Mark Hanna and met his cronies in a smoke-filled room; the blond beast, Jack London's favorite character, seeking gold in the Northland as recklessly as his Viking ancestors; the criminal not to blame for his bad ancestry (like Norris's McTeague); and the pawn of circumstances (like Dreiser's Clyde Griffiths) whose blind yearnings led him into an American tragedy.

After the First World War, still other characters found their places in mythology. The flapper rushed on the scene and then rushed off again with her friend the smoothie from Princeton; later she would reappear briefly in bobby socks. The intellectual small-town housewife, or Carol Kennicott, lived on Main Street and yearned for higher things. George F. Babbitt sold real estate, crowded his house with gadgets, and talked in gold-filled platitudes. The tough and cynical front-page reporter tried to conceal his soft-boiled heart. The girl in the green hat, copied from English life by Michael Arlen, went from one love affair to another with the same brave, broken-hearted smile. In Hemingway's first novel she kept her British passport, but she became an American in John O'Hara's *Butterfield 8*. Poor thing, she paid a heavy price for her transatlantic voyage. Soon she was dying a series of painful deaths in dozens of novels about New York, Beverly Hills, the San Francisco Bay Area, and Nashville, Tennessee. Some doctoral candidate for a degree in American literature should trace her whole unedifying story.

Still another figure in the new pantheon was the Hemingway young man, hard-drinking and impassive, who roamed through Europe with the wary look of an Ojibway in the Michigan woods. He had less time for reading than the Thomas Wolfe young man, who spent his nights in the stacks of the Widener Library, where he pounced on books and devoured them like a tiger in the jungle. The Fitzgerald young man was betrayed by a princess in a golden tower. Besides these individual figures, our second mythology also included many of the corporate or collective legends in which the hero is a group, a business enterprise, or a locality. Perhaps the first of these, since it flourished in the muckraking days from 1900 to 1910, was the legend of the trust or "octopus" that strangled little businesses in its widespreading tentacles. By 1920 we also had the legend of the small and mean Midwestern town, as presented by Edgar Lee Masters in *The Spoon River Anthology*, by Sherwood Anderson in *Winesburg, Ohio*, and by Sinclair Lewis in *Main Street*. Then in succession came T. S. Eliot's legend of the spiritual wasteland, Scott Fitzgerald's legend of the jazz age, the Hemingway legend of the lost generation, the Erskine Caldwell legend of Tobacco Road, the Steinbeck legend of dispossessed Oklahoma farmers jolting westward to California, and the Southern cavalier legend, which, though it went back for more than a century, was raised to a new dimension by William Faulkner. It was during this period, too, that Troy was burned again in the shape of Atlanta and that King Priam, reincarnated as a Southern planter, was murdered in the midst of his retainers. Hundreds of authors working in collaboration had given us another Iliad, of sorts.

Looking back on their work, we can see that the authors of the interwar years were skillful and bold in presenting characters that became archetypes of American life. Their books performed the function that Whitman assigned to the literature and songs of a country: they furnished, as he said, "the materials and suggestions of personality for the women and men of that country," and enforced them "in a thousand suggestive ways." By 1940 many young Americans were behaving like Hemingway or Thomas Wolfe characters, as later their tragic hero would be Scott Fitzgerald. Life once again had copied fiction—and this time had copied it all the more readily because movies and the radio, coming before universal television, were already making fiction omnipresent. When one of our novelists created a new figure, not only was it reproduced in bulk by less original writers, but it was dramatized for Broadway, adapted for Hollywood, and readapted for the national networks—so that sometimes the hero of a serious novel, having descended toward a wider audience step after giant step, was heard five times a week in a radio serial and was seen (or a figure dimly inspired by him was seen) daily and Sunday in a comic strip.

Continually enriched by novelists and poets, always more widely diffused by new methods of communication, American mythology had broadened through the years until it appeared to offer a complete image of American life. That appearance, of course, was an illusion even in 1940. Not all of American life, and especially not its average level, had been expressed in mythological terms—and this for the simple reason that novelists and poets have always been less attracted by the average than by the intense and extraordinary. A more serious weakness of the literary imagination, when measured against American realities, is that it tends to be retrospective. The world most effectively described by novelists and poets is that of their youth, not the world of their mature years. They change with the times, but never as fast as the times, and the result is that literary mythologies are always out of date. That was true even in 1940, and it is vastly more true of the 1960's, when we are waiting to descry the outlines of what should become a third American mythology.

For there have been three distinct periods in the life of this republic, or at least in our values for living. During the first, American values were predominantly rural and the standards of conduct were those of an ideal country town like Concord, Massachusetts. During the second, which lasted from 1890 till the end of World War II, the values became urban or metro-politan and the standards of conduct were those of New York and Chicago. There has been another shift in emphasis since 1945. The central cities are declining not only in population but in their power to set fashions, while factories are employ-ing a smaller proportion of the labor force. In this new age the dominant values are suburban and the emerging standard of conduct is that of a sophisticated suburb like Westport, Con-necticut, or Mill Valley, California.

In the first age the representative American was born on a farm and probably lived on another farm west of his birth-place. In the second age he worked in or managed or sold goods from a factory. In the third age he has become an organization man employed in an office or a laboratory or in one of the service industries—the Culligan man, the Fuller Brush man—that is, unless he resigns from the organization and goes hitch-hiking over the country trying to recapture his own personality.

The American home in the first age was a log cabin or a farmhouse, in the second age it was a city apartment, and now—except for the poor and the rebels—it is a detached single dwelling in the suburbs, full of labor-saving machinery re-duced to a family scale. Rivalry in producing things, as we often read, has given way to rivalry in consuming them. In the first age the conflict portrayed in American fiction was often that of the single man against nature; in the second age it was that of the single man against society, fighting to change it or simply to rise in it. Now, in the third age, the conflict is more likely to be that of group against group, of generation against generation, or of man against himself.

In order for us to feel at home in the new landscape where,

old and young, we are all strangers; in order to form a new image of the nation, and chiefly in order for us to recognize ourselves as persons, we require, among other things, a new American mythology. "The experience of each age," as Emerson said, "requires a new confession and the world seems always waiting for its poet." This time the world has been waiting longer than it should, but there are signs in the fiction of the last few years that the new myths are beginning to appear. A few characters in postwar fiction have already become legends. That most of them are rebels is a fact in which I find no ground for complaint. The standards of an emerging society are revealed in its rebels as much as in its conformists, and the rebels are easier to remember. Who after all was the Man in the Gray Flannel Suit? The phrase survives, but the man himself has disappeared from our minds like gray flannel suits from Madison Avenue.

Some of the new figures we do remember are J. D. Salinger's troubled adolescent in a world where every adult is a phony, and Ralph Ellison's angry symbol of the American Negro as the *Invisible Man*, and Norman Mailer's hipster or "White Negro," and Saul Bellow's portrait, in *The Adventures of Augie March*, of a Jewish boy leaving the Chicago slums and wandering over three continents, not to win a fortune, but to find the answer to a simple question: Who am I? That question echoes through many other novels and helps to convey the puzzled spirit of the times, but it is still not enough. There has to be something more than a few rebellious characters asking representative questions before the new mythology comes into being, as it is certain to do, and I keep reading the new novels to find what shapes it will assume.*

---

* Since I wrote that last paragraph in 1962, fiction has provided some of the new figures, and they are not the ones I expected to find. My speculations had assigned too little importance to rebellious groups and their part in creating a new mythology. Suburban culture is increasingly dominant as cities spread out into the countryside like dough under a rolling pin, but it is under increasing attack. Curiously it is the inner cities, with their declining population, that have provided most of the new figures—which include the Schlemiel, usually Jewish, the Jive Artist, always black, and the simple-minded Graduate in a corrupt and complicated world. Of these only the last is a product of suburban culture, and he utterly rejects it.

Criticism: A Many-Windowed House

ALTHOUGH I have been a literary critic for more than forty years, I must confess that I have not devoted much time to the basic theories of my profession. Partly that oversight is due to indolence, but it is also the result of what might be called an incest taboo: I have tried to avoid critical endogamy and inbreeding. Instead of dealing critically with the critical critics of criticism, I have preferred to be a critic of poems and novels, or at most a literary historian. More recently, however, I have defied the taboo by reviewing several big critical works, and I have been dismayed to find that many of them were so badly written as to reveal a sort of esthetic deafness, that some of them were contemptuous of writers and writing —except as the raw material of critical works—and that most of them were episodes in the battle among critical systems, one or another of which we were being cannonaded into accepting as the only true critical faith.

When I tried to compare the systems in order to find a faith for myself, it seemed to me that each of them led to a different but equally specialized and partial standard for judging works of art. Thus, for historical critics the best book is the one that either sums up a historical movement or else has directly influenced history. For biographical critics it is the one most intimately connected with the author's life. For psychoanalytical critics it is the one that reveals how the author sublimated his antisocial desires. For expressionist critics of the Crocean school, the standard is sincerity and spontaneity of expression. For moral critics—who were dominant in this country as late as the 1920's—the best books are those which embody philosophical truths or inculcate the highest moral lessons. For political critics they are the books that advance a political cause, and this, during the 1930's, was usually that of international revolution. Each of these standards is inescapable, being derived from the method itself. Often the critic says, "I do not judge, I merely explain," yet the standard is revealed, if nowhere else, in his choice of books for explication.

Saturday Review, August 12, 1961, pp. 10–11, 46–47.

In the 1960's all those standards have fallen into critical disfavor. The presently accepted system of approaching works of art is one that attempts to purify criticism by purging it of everything that might be regarded as an extraneous element or, to use the fashionable word, as a fallacy. Out go the historical fallacy, the social fallacy, the moral fallacy, the personal fallacy, the genetic fallacy, the affective fallacy. Out goes the author's life; out goes his social background; out goes the audience for which he wrote; out goes the political meaning of his work; out goes its moral effect. What is supposed to remain after this cathartic process is the work itself, as pure act without antecedents or relevance or results: simply the words in their naked glory. They are the purified subject of the system known as textual or integral criticism, or less exactly—since the term has several meanings—as the "new" criticism.

Like all other systems, this one involves a standard of judgment derived from the method itself. Let me quote from an essay by John V. Hagopian, who is one of the ablest of the new critics. "The critic's duty," he says—and of course there is no question of the critic's or the reader's pleasure—"is to determine as nearly as he can what feeling-qualities are embodied in the form-content of the work, how they are embodied there, and how well. . . . He has no other task; evaluations of historical significance, autobiographical expression, moral goodness, or philosophical truths are purely gratuitous for criticism, even though"—a generous concession—"they may be valuable to other disciplines of the humanities." Then, after this rejection of other standards, Mr. Hagopian offers an effective but still, it seems to me, oversimplified standard of his own. "Given two literary works," he says, "which are equally successful in resolving an artistic problem, the critics can choose the more important one by determining which has integrated the greatest amount of complexity."

To put Mr. Hagopian's statement in slightly different words, the critic pretends that every work of literature is completely autonomous, and then judges it by the complexity of its inner relations. He could find worse standards. The new or integral system of evaluating works has yielded some precious illuminations and has proved to be an effective method of teaching literature. It does, however, involve a disturbing amount of make-believe. Let's pretend that the poem or story was written at no particular date in no particular country. Let's pretend that it has no relation with any other work by the same author, or with any tendencies prevailing among a group of authors. Let's pretend that it can be interpreted and judged with no material except the text itself, and perhaps a few commentaries by other textual critics.

All those pretenses are hard to maintain. Literature is not a pure art like music, or a relatively pure art like painting and sculpture. Its medium is not abstract like tones and colors, not inorganic like metal and stone. Instead it uses language, which is a social creation, changing over the years with the society that created it. The study of any author's language carries us straight into history, institutions, moral questions, personal stratagems, and all the other esthetic impurities or fallacies that many new critics are trying to expunge.

Nor is that the only reason why these critics cannot be consistent in applying their own standard of judgment. As soon as they admit that a given work of literature was not self-produced but had an author—as soon as they admit that he wrote other works, some of which preceded and some followed the work in question—they are violating the purity of their method and are becoming, if ever so faintly, biographical critics. As soon as they admit that the work may have been affected by other authors, or may have exerted an effect on them, they are becoming historical. As soon as they admit that the work was written for an audience, they are deviating into sociology. As soon as they admit that it had or might have had an effect on the conduct of that audience, they have to introduce moral notions; there is no escaping them. As soon as they discuss or even hint at the author's intentions, they are becoming psychological. Criticism too is a literary art, and like other forms of literature it is impure by definition.

Some critics have looked for a way out of this dilemma by denying that criticism is an art and by claiming a place for it among the sciences. In order to make it a science, however, they have to subject it to another process of purgation. This time they have to remove all its subjective elements, including the critic's feelings about the work and also including the author of the work, whose mere presence may be a source of nonconformity to scientific laws. Why not simply abolish the author—or, if he can't be abolished, why not rule him out of consideration?

That radical but, in the circumstances, necessary step was taken some years ago by Professors W. K. Wimsatt, Jr., and M. D. Beardsley. In an essay called "The Intentional Fallacy" they asserted that "The design or intention of the author is neither available nor desirable as a standard for judging the success of a work of art." They admitted that the psychology of composition was sometimes a valid and useful study, but they described it as "an art separate from criticism . . . an individual and private culture, yoga, or system of self-development which the young poet would do well to notice, but different from"—and I italicize their words—"*the public science of evaluating poems.*"

Now, "public" implies that the critic should be objective and impersonal. "Science" implies that he administers a body of universal laws, the truth of which can be demonstrated by quantitative measurements. "Of evaluating poems" implies that judgment or evaluation is the critic's essential task. Each of these implications, it seems to me, is based on a radical misconception of what the critic is able or entitled to do. Since his judgment of a work starts with his own reaction to it, he cannot, in practice, be purely impersonal. He is not entitled to speak of criticism as a science. As Paul Valéry said many years ago, "There are sciences of exact things, and arts of inexact things." The best of criticism is inexact. In these days, however, everybody wants to be a scientist and move in the air of terrified respect that surrounds the men who split the atom. Every school of the humanities wants to share in the huge endowments of the new physics laboratories and cancer-research institutes. Inevitably some of the humanists begin to speak of their work in scientific language, as if it were performed with micrometric gauges, electronic computers, and balance pans in a vacuum. But there will never be a science of taste or of belief or of the arts of language. There will only be critics who talk like scientists and some of whom end by achieving the wooden arrogance of minor critics in the eighteenth century, who also thought they were expounding the laws of universal and unchanging wisdom.

Evaluating poems and novels is not the central task of a critic. Rather than judgment that task is interpretation and definition. The first question for a critic to answer is not "How good is this poem?" but simply "What *is* this poem, in structure, in style, in meaning, and in its effect on the reader?" Judgment is the end of the critical process, but if the work has been defined and interpreted correctly, then judgment often follows as a matter of course. For example, if one defines a certain novel as "A rapid sequence of events that offers no opportunity to develop the characters in depth," one does not have to add that it is a minor work of fiction.

In deciding what a novel or poem *is*, we cannot accept the author's testimony as final, knowing as we do that authors often intend one thing and end by producing another. We think of all the authors who intended masterpieces, as compared with the small number of masterpieces, and we also think of Mark Twain, who intended a boy's book and brought forth an epic. Nevertheless, if the author has offered his testimony—in letters, in outlines, in journals, in public statements—it is probative evidence and we cannot simply throw it out of court. If we fail to consider it we may, like many recent critics, fall into the opposite or unintentional fallacy. We might substitute our own story, our own creation, our own fantasy for the book that was actually written by the author.

Some years ago Stanley Edgar Hyman, always a lively critic, wrote a long and favorable review of a book called *The Disguises of Love*, by Robie Macauley. He presented it as a novel in which "accounts of homosexual relations are disguised as accounts of heterosexual relations," since, the reviewer explained, owing to American prudishness, "our authors have no choice but to metamorphose gender." Therefore the heroine's name, Frances feminine, should be altered to Francis masculine by any discerning reader. In the following issue of *Hudson Review* the author protested against this distortion of his meaning. No homosexuality was involved or implied in the story. Frances feminine was Frances completely female.

The reviewer was not in the least disconcerted. He answered, in part, "I am sorry that Mr. Macauley, for whatever reason, prefers not to have written the interesting and complicated novel I read and tried to describe, and prefers instead to have written the poor thin novel he describes. . . . Mr. Macauley is not the first novelist to have builded better than he knows or will admit; nor will he, probably, be the last." And then this manifesto, from Mr. Hyman, of complete critical independence: "I am not prepared," he said, "to be scared out of a critical reading of a novel by the author's waspish insistence that it is not *his* reading."

Authors haven't much chance with critics who throw their evidence out of court as insubstantial, immaterial, and incompetent. What Stanley Hyman did for a single book (not without a gleam of mischief in his style), Leslie A. Fiedler has done solemnly for American fiction in general. In a work almost as long as Parrington's *Main Currents in American Thought*, he has proclaimed that all our great novelists were sexually immature, that their work represented an escape from a female-dominated world into male companionship, and that *The Last of the Mohicans, Moby Dick,* and *Huckleberry Finn* are almost identical fables of homosexual miscegenation. Mr. Fiedler's book is a final exploit of criticism cut loose from its mooring and sailing across the moon like a Halloween witch on her broomstick.

Although it seems impossibly far from Mr. Wimsatt's quasi-scientific type of criticism, still it results from the same doctrine, namely, that an author's intentions should be disregarded. The effect of the doctrine is to deprive the author of all property in his work from the moment it is printed. It becomes the property of everybody and nobody, but it doesn't long remain in that situation. Soon it will be seized upon by critics, some of whom claim the privilege of reinterpreting and in fact rewriting it into something the author cannot recognize. If the author protests, the critic feels entitled to jeer at his "waspish insistence." The critic rules supreme, and his next step—which Mr. Fiedler and others have taken—is to present the author as an immature neurotic whom the critic, disguised as a psychoanalyst, is not even attempting to cure, but is merely exposing to public shame.

I do not propose to offer still another system of criticism to set against those I have questioned. But since this started as a confession, I had better state a few of my own beliefs.

First of all I believe that a definition of criticism should be as simple and short as possible. Mightn't it be enough to say that *criticism is writing that deals with works of art?* Any narrower definition would restrict the liberty of the critic and might also restrict his usefulness.

I believe that criticism should be approached as one of the literary arts. The word "literary" implies that it should be written in the language of English literature and not—as a great deal of recent criticism has been written—in some variety of philosophical or medical or social-scientific jargon. When a critic's language is awkward, involved, and pedantic, we are entitled to question his ability to recognize good prose. As for the word "arts," it implies that criticism is not a science based on exact measurement. If it is going to be persuasive, however, it had better include a great deal of objectively verifiable information.

I do not believe that it is one of the major literary arts. The major arts are poetry, fiction, drama, and also nonfictional or documentary writing so long as this last is a field for exercise of the interpretive imagination. Without those arts, literary criticism would cease to exist for want of subject matter. Therefore a critic cannot afford to be arrogant. He is dealing in most cases with better works that he has proved his capability of writing.

I believe that the first of his functions is to select works of art worth writing about, with special emphasis on works that are new, not much discussed, or widely misunderstood. Incidentally this task has been neglected by academic critics, most of whom prefer to write about works already regarded as canonical. His second function is to describe or analyze or reinterpret the chosen works as a basis for judgments which can sometimes be merely implied. In practice his problem may be to explain why he enjoys a particular book, and perhaps to find new reasons for enjoying it, so as to deepen his readers' capacity for appreciation.

In practice, again, I always start and end with the text itself, and am willing to accept the notion of the textual or integral critics that the principal value of a work lies in the complexity and unity of its internal relations. But I also try to start with a sort of innocence, that is, with a lack of preconceptions about what I might or might not discover. To preserve the innocence, I prefer not to read the so-called secondary or critical sources until my own discoveries, if any, have been made.

What I read after the text itself are other texts by the same author. It is a mistake to approach each work as if it were an absolutely separate production, a unique artifact, the last and single relic of a buried civilization. Why not approach it as the author does? It seems to me that any author of magnitude has his eye on something larger than the individual story or poem or novel. He wants each of these to be as good as possible, and self-subsistent, but he also wants it to serve as a chapter or aspect of the larger work that is his lifetime production, his *oeuvre*. This larger work is also part of the critic's subject matter.

In this fashion the author's biography comes into the picture, and so do his notebooks and letters. They aren't part of the text to be criticized, but often they help us to find in it what we might otherwise have missed, and they serve as a warning against indulging in fantasies about the text or deforming it into a Gothic fable of love, death, and homoeroticism. We should read not to impose our meanings on a work, but to see what we can find.

Innocence is the keynote, and ignorance that tries to become knowledge by asking questions of many sorts. There are internal questions of structure and style and imagery to which the answers are vastly revealing, but there are also questions about the external relations of a work of art. Whom was it written for? Is the author a spokesman for some particular region or group or social class (as Dreiser, to give one instance, spoke for the new men of the Middle West)? Is he trying to invest some new background with the dignity of legend? What is the implied moral of his fable? If he has written several books, have they always implied the same moral? (Here I am calling to mind the simple fact that authors change, and that critics are wrong when they speak of "Hawthorne" or "Whitman" as if each name stood for a single and permanent aggregate of qualities. "Which Hawthorne?" I like to ask them, and "Whitman at what period of his career?")

One might also ask whether every book an author has written is a proper subject for certain elaborate methods of criticism, including symbolic analysis. Sometimes details from an author's life might help us to decide. We know, for example, that Melville spent about a year on *Moby Dick* and that he rewrote the book from a lost early version concerned chiefly with the whaling industry. We also know that he wrote *Pierre* in about six weeks while on the edge of a nervous breakdown. That of course is biographical knowledge, but aren't we justified in using it? Aren't critics losing their sense of proportion when they discuss both books, the masterpiece and the nightmare, in the same elaborate terms, especially if those terms make the nightmare seem more important than the masterpiece? Aren't they wrong to look for the same sort of symbols in *Pierre* that Joyce put into *Finnegans Wake*, on which we know that he slaved for almost twenty years?

Innocence is the keynote, but not innocence that refrains from learning about an author's life on the ground that such knowledge would destroy the purity of one's critical method. A truly innocent search might lead us into studies of the society in which an author lived, if they were necessary to explain his meaning. Or again, remembering as we should that a novel or a poem is not merely a structure of words but also a device for producing a certain effect on an audience, as if it were a motionless machine for creating perpetual motion—remembering this, we might try to find the nature of the particular audience for which it was written. That would be deviating into the sociological or affective fallacy, but still it might be a useful and stimulating piece of, yes, critical research.

I believe, in short, that criticism is a house with many windows.